Christmas Music from Baroque Mexico

Christmas Music from Baroque Mexico

By

ROBERT STEVENSON

UNIVERSITY OF CALIFORNIA PRESS

Berkeley Los Angeles London

University of California Press
Berkeley and Los Angeles, California
University of California Press, Ltd.
London, England
Copyright © 1974 by
The Regents of the University of California
ISBN: 0-520-02036-7
Library of Congress Catalog Card Number: 70-157826
Printed in the United States of America

A. M. D. G.

Contents

FACSIMILES

MUSIC TRANSCRIPTIONS

CONTENTS

Preface

Thanks to the initiative of the Director General of the Mexican National Institute of Fine Arts, José Luis Martínez, and to exceptional support given by the Minister of Education, Licenciado Agustín Yáñez, the date March 17, 1967, marked a milestone in Mexican music history — for on that day the Secretaría de Educación Pública purchased the Colección Sánchez Garza, a collection now hailed by informed scholars as the outstanding body of seventeenth- and eighteenth-century manuscript music by Peninsular and New World composers up to then acquired by a private Mexican citizen.

The 276 items in the collection include Christmas music by many of the best Baroque masters. To give an overview of the entire collection, Renaissance and Baroque Musical Sources in the Americas, a 1970 publication of the General Secretariat, Organization of American States, included a summary catalogue of 164 works. With the kind permission of the illustrious chief of the Technical Unit of Music and Folklore, Organization of American States, Dr. Guillermo Espinosa, the summary catalogue is duplicated below. As becomes at once apparent to any reader of the catalogue or student of the music examples from the collection published in the present volume, villancicos form the bedrock of the collection. Many of these echo folkish strains. Such works as Salazar's negro, Vaeza's negriya, and Ximeno's gallego, while not pretending to be literal transcriptions of Negro or Galician music, still embody ethnic traits that need to be sorted out by the ethnomusicologist as well as by the historical musicologist.

Twelve of the seventeen musical examples in the present volume have been transcribed from the Sánchez Garza collection, the bulk of which belonged originally (as is shown below) to a convent in Puebla. Another four examples were transcribed from manuscripts still owned in 1966 by Puebla Cathedral. A short history of the Sánchez Garza collection is therefore in order. In early December of 1964 Mrs. Adelaide Frank de Sánchez (a native of New Jersey but a permanent resident of Mexico City) telephoned the Sección de Investigaciones Musicales of the Instituto Nacional de Bellas Artes (Dolores 2, 4° piso) to offer for sale certain valuable music imprints assembled by her late husband. Miss Carmen Sordo Sodi, the distinguished successor to Jesús Bal y Gay as administrator of the Section of Music Research, thanked her for the call and, after explaining that the Section could recommend

purchases but was not empowered to buy, agreed to examine whatever was available. Taking advantage of what off-duty hours Sundays and weekday nights afforded, Miss Sordo Sodi soon learned that Mrs. Frank de Sánchez was the American widow of the Mexican historian Jesús Sánchez Garza who had devoted a lifetime to collecting documents of all sorts, but especially books and manuscripts having to do with Mexico. After visits spaced over a year, Miss Sordo Sodi was able to recommend the purchase of three hundred music imprints for the library of the National Conservatory of Music.

But greater good fortune was to follow. Late in 1965 Mrs. Frank de Sánchez confided that among her deceased husband's effects was a box of colonial manuscript music by which he had set special store. Nearly all of this manuscript treasure proved later to have been originally the property of Holy Trinity Convent in Puebla. For a wonder, the music archive had survived apparently intact during the several decades between extinction of the convent and acquisition of the manuscripts by Jesús Sánchez Garza.

Born October 14, 1891, at Ciudad Porfirio Díaz, now Piedras Negras, Coahuila (across the border from Eagle Pass, Texas), Jesús Sánchez Garza was the son of a deputy to the local congress of Coahuila, Jesús Sánchez Herrera. After elementary studies at Piedras Negras, Jesús Sánchez Garza enrolled at Draughons Business College in San Antonio, Texas. Meanwhile, his love for Mexican lore and culture did not diminish; instead, it grew as increased affluence made possible the beginnings of his various collections. The larger part of his library was assembled after his return to Mexico during patient visits to paper factories, newspaper plants, secondhand bookstores, and to old buildings being torn down — for it was in those places that he found the bulk of his treasures. What others threw away as untidy trash, he recognized as irreplaceable documentation.

Ardently devoted to the principles of the Mexican revolution, and a close friend of Mexico's leading revolutionaries, he published at Mexico City in 1932 a History of the Mexican Revolutionary Coins (translated by his wife) that brilliantly supplements Howland Wood's pioneering study published at New York eleven years earlier. Turning to another field, he edited in 1955 a 321-page account of the move for Texas independence, La rebelión de Texas: Manuscrito inédito de 1836, por un

oficial de Santa Anna. José Enrique de la Peña (1807-1841)
was the "oficial de Santa Anna" who wrote the account. If to
Jesús Sánchez Garza belongs the credit for having so pains-
takingly   gathered books and manuscripts, to his wife belongs
the credit for having been his translator during his lifetime
and for having so carefully conserved his collections after his
death. Especially is she now to be lauded for deciding in the
spring of 1967 that all her husband's manuscript musical treasure should henceforth become the property of the National
Institute of Fine Arts.

Equally to be thanked for her part in the transfer of the collection is the eminent Miss Carmen Sordo Sodi. At her ex-
ceedingly kind invitation, the present author began later that
same year transcribing a dozen villancicos for publication as
Volume II in the series, Tesoro de la música polifónica en
México, started by her predecessor. Realizations of the basso
continuo (usually unfigured) were asked for, so that the works
might be immediately performable. With the same end in view,
she arranged for the copying of these transcribed villancicos by
José Chavarría Zamora, a calligrapher of the first water. Her
colleague, Eloy Fernández Márquez, offered helpful counsel.
By the end of 1970, all the music was camera ready, along with
the literary preliminaries. In due course, when funding becomes possible, Volume II of the Tesoro will appear.

In the meantime, permission has been granted to publish the
twelve items in the present volume from the collection, but
sans realizations. To these are here added another four works
by the paramount Puebla maestro, Juan Gutiérrez de Padilla
(c. 1590-1664), each representing a different villancico type,
calenda, gallego, jácara, and negrilla. His villancico subtitled juego de cañas is his work in the Sánchez Garza collection that shows the most evident signs of long and hard use.
The manuscripts utilized as sources for his calenda, gallego,
jácara, and negrilla were very kindly xeroxed for the present
author by Professor E. Thomas Stanford of The University of
North Carolina at Greensboro during our joint visit to Puebla
Cathedral in March of 1966. Both he and his renowned collab-
orator, Professor Lincoln B. Spiess of Washington University,
St. Louis, had viewed the Sánchez Garza collection prior to its
purchase by the National Institute of Fine Arts and had borne
testimony to its unique value.

For the Hidalgo villancico without coplas transcribed in the
present volume, I availed myself of Madrid Biblioteca Nacional M. 3880, item 7. For this and many other favors I thank
the distinguished director and secretary of the Spanish National
Library, Guillermo Guastavino Gallent and José Almudévar
Lorenzo.

Among others whose help is here gratefully acknowledged, I
record my indebtedness to the archivist of Puebla Cathedral
who first began doing me favors in 1954, J. Manuel Martínez,
pbro., to Drs. Steven Barwick and Alice Ray Catalyne who
have both plowed Puebla fields with singular success, and most
especially to Cootje Franken of Lima and Montevideo who from

1958 to the present has graciously aided me in all my research
projects. Since access to archives is always the all-important
favor, I reserve my warmest thanks to the venerable Deans
and chapters of the Mexico City and Puebla Cathedrals for their
unremitting kindnesses and generosity during more than two
decades of labor in their precincts, and lastly I record my
gratitude to all those authorities in the Instituto Nacional de
Bellas Artes who have sponsored my research.

A three-paragraph postcript to the preface is due reviewers:
my bibliography stops at 1970 — in September of which year the
typescript of the present book was finished. Circumstances beyond my control or that of the Press prevented my updating the
bibliography to the eve of publication. Nor did I keep inserting
novelties into the text itself. The biography of Francisco de
Santiago has in the interim been published in Anuario Musical,
XXV-1970 (1971). In the same issue Jaime Moll Roqueta's
"Los villancicos cantados en la Capilla Real a fines del siglo
XVI y principios del siglo XVII" proved it to have been a mere
fiction that villancicos stopped being sung in the Royal Chapel
after 1596. Two publications sent me by the Brazilian Biblio-
teca Nacional would also have been used had the volumes ar-
rived in time: Rosemarie Erika Horch's Vilancicos da Coleção
Barbosa Machado (Rio de Janeiro: Ministério da Educação e
Cultura [Divisão de Publicações e Divulgação], 1969) and
Darcy Damasceno's Vilancicos Seiscentistas (same, 1970).

In the forepart of 1971 a German Fulbright grant made possible protracted firsthand study of the extensive Bayerische
Staatsbibliothek collection of early Baroque villancicos. The
results of that study, which amplifies without contradicting
certain conclusions in the present volume, will be published in
a separate monograph. Also awaiting publication by the
Fundação Calouste Gulbenkian (Lisbon) next year is a supporting study of the Baroque vilhancico = villancico in Portugal.
The music includes heretofore unpublished examples by Frei
Manuel Correa, Dom Pedro de Cristo, Gaspar Fernandes, Frei
Filipe da Madre de Deos, António Marques Lésbio, Francisco
Martins, Gonçalo Mendes Saldanha, Frei Francisco de Santiago
(also represented in the present volume), and Pedro Vaz Rego.
Six of the fourteen examples were transcribed from New World
archives (Bogotá, Cuzco, Guatemala, Oaxaca).

If any advantage is conferred by the delayed publication of
the present volume, it accrues from the recently much en-
hanced feminist interest. At pages 11, 14, and 17, I cite the
first three known New World women conductors, 1667-1754,
and at page 15 the earliest woman composer. Twelve of the
seventeen music examples concluding the present volume were
transcribed from copies originally intended for women's
voices instrumentally accompanied by women.

R. S.

Origins of Mexico's Traditional Christmas Music

For more than a half century, the charm of Mexico's tradition-al Christmas music has inspired tributes from both folk-lorists and historical musicologists.

Ralph Steele Boggs's "Bibliografía Completa, Clasificada y Comentada, de los Artículos de Mexican Folkways (MF), con Índice," published in the Boletín Bibliográfico de Antropología Americana, VI/1-3 (January-December, 1942), 221-265, still remains the indispensable guide through the maze of articles in Frances Toor's bilingual periodical that ran through 35 issues (June-July 1925 to July 1937). The most informative of these articles was her own "Christmas in Mexico" (sup-plemented with the complete text and music of ten Christmas folk songs) which appeared in Mexican Folkways, II/5 (Decem-ber-January, 1926/1927), 31-43. In her later, now widely available, book, A Treasury of Mexican Folkways (New York: Crown Publishers, 1947), she reworked her 1926/1927 article under the heading "Posadas — Christmas celebrations" (pp. 247-251) and repeated eight of the songs (pp. 389-396)—still, however, without any harmonizations.

One of the more characteristic, "En nombre del cielo os pido posada" ("In the name of Heaven I beg you for lodging") had already been published with an unmistakably Mexican har-monization to supplement her bilingual article that appeared in an earlier issue of Mexican Folkways, I/4 (December-January, 1925/1926), 16-21, with the title "Las Posadas de Vecindad en la Ciudad de México" (title translated as "Neighborhood Christmas in Mexico City"). Still another pertinent bilingual article was published in the same December-January 1925/ 1926 issue, José de J. Núñez y Domínguez's "La Nochebuena de los Totonacos" ("The Christmas Eve of the Totonacs"), pages 22-25. Not only for its regional interest but because Mexican Folkways lent its authority in the English translation to renderings of such key terms as "villancico" and "aguinal-do," Núñez y Domínguez's article deserves excerpt:

> The Totonacs, who inhabit a great part of the State of Veracruz (the former cantons of Papantla and Misantla and part of the south of Tuxpan and of the Sierra of Puebla), hurry en masse every Christ-mas Eve from their ranches, even the most distant, to the village of Papantla (now a city and seat of a bishopric). By the hundreds the Indian girls go specifically to put up the crèche in the parish churchyard. The erecting of such a crèche has been their privilege for centuries. After they have finished its decoration, they then happily donate it to the priest so that the Holy Infant

may be placed in it. Held up before the people in the priest's arms, the image is first venerated at the principal altar, then taken outside to be placed in the crèche — around which flash large candle-sticks and lamps. Meanwhile, over all the houses in the village are hung the "aguinaldos," which are lanterns of vividly colored china paper. Illumi-nated and capriciously shaped into houses or stars, these cast their rays on Christmas Eve through the streets where crowds follow in the footsteps of small errant groups of carolers. Bearing torches, these small groups wander from house to house, begging a mite for the celebration of the festival and singing their Christmas carols (villancicos).

Apart from the folkish villancicos published in Mexican Folkways, several other sources of the traditional Christmas repertory merit at least passing mention. Rubén M. Campos showed that the same piece of waltz-time Christmas music can be called a "motete" if sung to a Latin text, but a "villan-cico" when sung to a Spanish text, when in his El folklore y la música mexicana (Mexico City: Secretaría de Educación Pública, 1928) he published at pages 195 and 272 exactly the same A Major piece — first as motete, then as a villancico "from Guanajuato," the only significant musical difference being the tempo indication (moderato for the motete, alle-gretto for the villancico).

To Vicente T. Mendoza (1894-1964 [1]) belongs credit for having published one of the first studies of the villancico in Mexico carrying its history back to colonial times, "Música de Navidad en México," México en el Arte, 6 (December, 1948). This lavishly illustrated article contained "music notations of thirteen songs collected in various parts of the country by the author" and a facsimile of a music manuscript dated 1797. My "Christmas Music in Mexico" (with seven music examples) published in Etude, LXVIII/12 (December, 1950), 18-19, made available to English readers the results of Mendoza's study of 1948.

Mendoza's Panorama de la Música Tradicional de México (Mexico City: Imprenta Universitaria, 1956) distilled at pages 40-44 the findings of a lifetime in a section headed "Cantos de posadas, Navidad, pastorelas y coloquios," to which he added at pages 129-133 eighteen unharmonized ex-amples. Some of his more important conclusions are re-hearsed below.

Among our common folk, Christmas celebrations

begin almost always with las nueve jornadas o posadas ["the nine one-day marches or stopping places"] that last from December 16 to 24. At this season the ceremonies formerly taking place inside churches now customarily move out to way-side chapels, private oratories, or even open-air altars in the poorer areas. First are recited popular litanies, prayers, and praises addressed to the Holy Family en route to Bethlehem (the organists and singers of the village churches providing the music). Next come entreaties for sweets and toys, sung to the tune of a Galician dance, the muñeira. Then, lively play songs leading up to the breaking of the suspended balloon containing Christmas goodies, the piñata. After this is broken everyone shouts and joins in a dance. This dance finale, however, no longer involves traditional music.

Christmas pastorelas ("pastorals") and coloquios ("dialogues") also involve traditional Spanish music, many of the songs preserving their original regional aroma in all its freshness and simplicity whether of Galicia, Asturias, Castile, or Andalusia. Other musical influences have also seeped into the music sung during the Christmas parades and marches, for instance Italian opera choruses and arias. Occasionally the more sentimental shepherd songs bear the stamp of such well-known composed Mexican songs as Lejos de tí or La golondrina.[2] But on the other hand the lullabies all echo the most traditional Spanish strains. Among the most typical and traditional of all Christmas songs is precisely the couplet cited in his classic novelette La Navidad en las montañas ("Christmas in the Mountains") by Ignacio Manuel Altamirano (1834-1893):

> Christmas Eve comes, Christmas Eve passes,
> We will go away never more to return.[3]

Because all Mexican readers know Altamirano, Mendoza did not need to stop in midcourse for a lengthy quotation from Altamirano's novelette first published in the Album de Navidad (Mexico City, 1871), pages 199-296. But an English reader interested in Mexican traditional Christmas music will do well to consult the translation of this "beautiful rustic idyl set in a small village of southern Mexico" made by Professor Harvey L. Johnson for the Latin American Monograph Series (edited by A. Curtis Wilgus). As the translator duly notes, all three songs sung in the unnamed village of southern Mexico on Christmas Eve by the unlettered shepherds who accompany themselves on their homemade harps, rustic flutes, and hand drums were Christmas carols of provable Spanish origin (every one of the three had already been published at Madrid in an 1865 collection of Spanish folk songs).[4]

Mendoza's great services to the study of Christmas music in Mexico therefore include confirmation of the words that Altamirano put in the mouth of the Spanish-born Carmelite friar, Joseph of Saint Gregory. After hearing the local herdsmen sing "Come, oh shepherds, come to the gate of Bethlehem," "A gypsy near the Virgin's feet," and "Christmas Eve comes, Christmas Eve passes," Altamirano caused this friar to remark:

> All these old Christmas carols are of Spanish origin, and I observe that tradition preserves

them here intact as in my country. Respectable for their antiquity, and on account of being products of Christian tenderness, they perhaps originated with a mother, an unknown village poetess, a child, or unhappy blind man, but assuredly among that class of obscure troubadour who is lost in the vortex of the unfortunate. I always hear them with affection because they recall my childhood.

In her authoritative "Introducción al estudio del villancico en Latinoamérica,"[5] Revista Musical Chilena, XXIII/107 (April-June, 1969), 19-20, María Ester Grebe discerned the Spanish "filiation" of another seven Christmas songs printed in Vicente T. Mendoza's Lírica infantil de México (Mexico City: El Colegio de México, 1951).[6] Among typical traits common to all these folkish Peninsular derivatives she listed: (1) coplas of six- or eight-syllable lines, (2) strophic sectionalizing, (3) major mode, (4) stepwise or triadic melodic movements, and (5) closes on any note of the tonic triad. She also lent her authority to linking the pastorelas ("short rustic plays") still frequently performed in the Mexican countryside with the autos or Christmas mystery plays brought to Mexico during the conquest century. To strengthen a thesis already advanced by Mendoza she cited Professor Stanley Robe's Christmas folk-play study:[7] the melodies still sung by the commoners who weeks beforehand begin rehearsing, in order to be ready with these Christmas misterios, "stem from the melodies taught the natives by Spanish missionaries during long ago colonial times."

NOTES

1. For a survey of his career, see necrology in Journal of the International Folk Music Council, XVIII (1966), 79-80.

2. In Vicente T. Mendoza's La canción mexicana: ensayo de clasificación y antología (Mexico City: Instituto de Investigaciones Estéticas, 1961), pp. 616 and 618, can conveniently be found these songs by Manuel M. Ponce and Narciso Serradell Sevilla. Mendoza does not specifically mention these two songs in the passage being excerpted, but refers instead to the canción mexicana generically.

3. As musical example 65 in Mendoza's Panorama he prints the tune for the copla collected by him not in the locale chosen by Altamirano for his novelette but rather in Saltillo, Coahuila — thus showing its continued wide distribution over the Republic.

4. Christmas in the Mountains (Gainesville: University of Florida Press, 1961), p. 34.

5. Prepared for the Ethnomusicology seminar at Indiana University conducted in 1967 by Isabel Aretz, Luis Felipe Ramón y Rivera, and George List.

6. "Cantos de Navidad," pp. 53-58.

7. Coloquios de Pastores from Jalisco, Mexico (Berkeley: University of California Press, 1954), p. 32.

Bibliographical Introduction to the Baroque Villancico (Spain and Mexico)

Without further documenting the thesis of the preceding chapter, it now seems permissible to generalize: Mexico's most cherished, orally transmitted Christmas repertory grew from Peninsular roots. As far south and north as New Spain once extended, Christmas music acknowledged Spanish precedents. Even orally transmitted theater songs prove this. To cite examples, the seven included in John Donald Robb's Hispanic Folk Songs of New Mexico (Albuquerque: University of New Mexico Press, 1954), pages 24-40 (introduction pp. 8-14), denounce the Peninsular origins of all the theater music intercalated in the annual Christmas folk plays given in that once distant outpost of Spain.

But to pass from the orally transmitted repertory to the composed villancico: what literature is there for: (1) the assessment of its Peninsular precedents, (2) the study of its earliest colonial phases? Isabel Pope [Conant] brilliantly compressed the most essential data on pre-1600 Peninsular phases in her article "Villancico," Die Musik in Geschichte und Gegenwart (MGG), XIII (1966), columns 1628-1631. Of the 27 items in her appended bibliography, none more competently survey their subjects than her own "Musical and Metrical form of the Villancico: Notes on Its Development and Its Rôle in Music and Literature in the Fifteenth Century," Annales musicologiques, II (1954), 189-214, and her own synopsis of sixteenth-century development in "El Villancico Polifónico" published as a preface to the Cancionero de Upsala (Mexico City: El Colegio de México, 1944), 13-43 (each of these articles boasts a full battery of footnotes and musical examples). So far as post-1600 Peninsular innovations are concerned, her summary can be thus paraphrased and glossed (MGG, XIII, 1631):

> The seventeenth-century villancico put on pious garb and went to church. Pertinent examples of the pious type turn up in Pedro Rimonte's El Parnaso Español de Madrigales y Villancicos (Antwerp: Phalèse, 1614). Chapelmasters in all the important cathedrals composed villancicos which were interpolated into the Office and Mass at high festivals. Taking hints from the style of the Baroque cantata, these church villancicos vary in texture from accompanied solos, duets, and trios to six- and twelve-voice choirs. The accompaniment, at first organ or organ and viols, was later in the century enlarged to organ with winds or winds and strings. The ground plan — with like-named components now usually much longer than was the rule in sixteenth-century villancicos — called for a through-composed estribillo = refrain (solo, duet, or trio, followed by choral responsión = reply); next rapid-fire strophic copla[s] = verse[s] (solo) enclosed in double bar; then, back to the estribillo [or responsión] for a repeat of the cycle. Prominent villancico composers included Mateo Romero, Carlos Patiño, Juan Blas de Castro, Juan Pujol, and Juan Bautista Comes. Nearly all of this handwritten repertory surviving in Spanish cathedral archives and in Latin America remains still unexplored.

Miguel Querol Gavaldá's "La polyphonie religieuse espagnole au XVIIe siècle," published in Les Colloques de Wégimont, IV/1 — six years after delivery of his paper on the subject at Liège September 10, 1957 — (Paris: Société d'Édition "Les Belles Lettres," 1963), 91-105, includes a two-page précis of the seventeenth-century villancico largely confirming Isabel Pope. He, too, stresses the exclusively religious character of the villancico in this century. Pieces of like musical character but setting secular texts were called "tonos humanos." The musical quality of villancicos by such composers as "Mizieres, Veana, Ruiz, Galán, Cererols, and many others" rose distinctly above that of other genres cultivated in the period. "They show well-assimilated technical improvements and an entirely national feeling. Villancicos called for anything from accompanied solo to twelve-voice choir. However, polychoralism is less frequently encountered in villancicos than in Masses and Psalms taken as a whole, while accompanied solos and duos occupy a larger proportion of the output."

Querol Gavaldá continues with the suggestion that the Baroque instrumental concerto is paradoxically the foreign genre most nearly akin to the villancico in some respects. In the seventeenth-century villancico, "dialogue between soloist or soloists and choir more frequently occurs than in the Peninsular Latin repertory of the period. After an opening solo comes in all likelihood the same musical material confided to a tutti, or the whole ensemble makes the first announcement and the soloist or soloists reply. More rarely, instruments alone introduce the villancico."

Like Pope, Querol Gavaldá emphasizes the important role

of instruments in the seventeenth-century villancico. Played
by a small orchestra, certain villancicos "could today figure
agreeably in chamber music concerts." He also agrees with
Pope in stressing the enlargement of the basic ground plan inherited from the previous century of ABA (estribillo-coplas-
estribillo), in emphasizing the sharper contrast between "A"
and "B" in meter, gait, and resources that became the seventeenth-century rule (soloists sang coplas, choirs intervened
in the estribillo), and in demanding separate study of texts
and music.

"In the seventeenth century, the music of what is termed a
romance and of what is called a villancico merge; separated
from their texts, the music for romances cannot be distinguished from that for villancicos." Querol Gavaldá enlarges
on the latter point in "La forma musical del romance en el
siglo XVII," published at pages 14-17 in the literary introduction to Romances y letras a tres vozes (Siglo XVII)
(Barcelona: Instituto Español de Musicología, 1956 [Monu-
mentos de la Música Española, XVIII]). Another earlier
authority who made much the same point was Vicenç Ripollès,
who in El Villancico i la cantata del segle XVIII a València
(Barcelona: Biblioteca de Catalunya, 1935), page vii, listed
first the form of 74 villancicos by the Valencia chapelmaster
1613-1619 and 1632-1643, Juan Bautista Comes: (1) introduction for solo soprano or small vocal ensemble, (2) estribillo = responsión for large choir (from six to twelve voices),
(3) coplas for soloist or small vocal ensemble, (4) repetition
of estribillo. Mosén Urbán de Vargas, maestro at Valencia
1653-1656, "left twenty villancicos in the Valencia Cathedral
archive adhering to the same plan as Comes's — introduction,
estribillo, coplas; many of these, however, Vargas himself
called romances instead of villancicos."

In the Diccionario de la música Labor (1954), II, 2232,
Querol Gavaldá laments the poor quality of the poetry encum-
bering many Peninsular seventeenth-century villancicos — a
value judgment which if accepted justifies concentrating on
the music rather than on texts of the Peninsular repertory.
"Many cathedrals annually commissioned poets to write new
texts for the villancicos and chanzonetas, which willy-nilly
the cathedral chapelmaster was then obliged to compose for
performance at chief feasts." Nonetheless, even in Spain,
more indulgent cathedrals did allow the chapelmaster himself
to seek out suitable new poetry. Jacinto Antonio Mesa's
letter from Córdoba dated January 9, 1676 (Anuario Musical,
XX, 217) proves that chapelmasters in at least the Andalu-
sian capitals of Córdoba, Málaga, and Seville freely traded
new poetry that had proved suitable for villancicos.

At Mexico City, the cathedral authorities began as early as
1591 allowing the then chapelmaster an annual eighty free
days for the specific purpose of scouting new poetry suitable
for the Corpus Christi and Christmas celebrations and then
setting it. Such zeal shown by the Mexico City Cathedral

authorities for poetry of high quality capable of being wedded
to superior villancico music bore fruit. In the seventeenth
century, Mexico's greatest literary light — Sor Juana Inés de
la Cruz — made villancico verse one of her finest specialties.
For Mexico, Querol Gavaldá's strictures against seventeenth-
century villancico verse therefore do not always hold.

Turning now from Spanish villancico bibliography to the
available bibliography dealing with the sixteenth- and seventeenth-century villancico in specifically Mexican locales, the
reader aware of only what has been hitherto written concerning the Peninsular product will — it is true — find numerous
parallelisms but may also find himself at the same time
treated to some welcome surprises. Just as the librettos of
the earliest "operas" composed in both Spain and Mexico survive, but not the music, so also only texts of the earliest
Mexican villancicos are still extant. Librettos do matter to
the opera historian. So do texts of villancicos to the historian of Christmas and other high-festival music. For a literary history of the villancico in colonial Mexico, nothing
more authoritative happens to have been thus far published
than the section in Alfonso Méndez Plancarte's nonpareil
Obras Completas de Sor Juana Inés de la Cruz, II: Villancicos y Letras Sacras (Mexico City: Fondo de Cultura
Económica, 1952), pages xxx-xlv. To epitomize Méndez
Plancarte's sixteen-page essay:

Toribio de Motolinía (1490?-1565) mentions an
Auto de la Caída ("Auto of Adam and Eve's fall")
so well played by the Indians of Tlaxcala in their
own tongue the Wednesday after Easter of 1539[1]
that no eye remained dry while they sang a polyphonic villancico the text of which can be thus
translated: "Why did the first pair eat the for-
bidden fruit? Their doing so has brought God
down to a very humble abode." The music instruction given Indians by both the missionary
friars Pedro de Gante (1480?-1572) and Juan
Caro[2] enabled them in short space to compose
polyphonic villancicos and even Masses, according to the informed testimony of Gerónimo
de Mendieta. As early as 1543, Christmas and
Easter chanzonetas were being sung in Mexico
City cathedral by choirboys trained under Pedro
de Campoverde.[3] In a manuscript dated no later
than 1570 appears a charming Christmas Eve
villancico by Pedro de Trejo, who led a color-
ful life at various Mexican mining outposts.[4]
The earliest preserved theatrical piece by a
Mexican creole, the 1574 "Spiritual Marriage
of Her Shepherd [Archbishop Pedro Moya de
Contreras] and the Mexican Church" by Juan
Pérez Ramírez, son of a conquistador, includes some pretty little songs as does also
the Spanish-Latin dialogue printed in 1579,
"Triumph of the Saints," acts II and V of
which end with villancicos, specifically so
called.[5]

The Coloqvios espiritvales y sacramentales
y Canciones Diuinas (Mexico City: Diego
López Dávalos, 1610) by Hernán González
de Eslava (1534-1601?) abound in villancicos
and ensaladas, so called. Better still, their
literary quality matches the best Peninsular

poetry of the period according to Marcelino Menéndez y Pelayo. An anonymous 1619 Coloquio de la Conversión y Bautismo de los Cuatro Reyes de Tlaxcala, the manuscript of which is at the University of Texas, contains a delicious eucharistic villancico beginning Pedid, alma. Another early seventeenth-century Mexican manuscript, the Códice Gómez de Orozco (published by the Mexico City Imprenta Universitaria in 1945) includes numerous charming villancicos, some of them for Epiphany, Corpus Christi, Visitation, and Profession of a Nun, but most specified for Christmas. Francisco Bramón's Los Sirgveros de la Virgen (Mexico City: Juan de Alcázar, 1620), a sacred-pastoral novel dedicated to the bishop of Michoacán, contains several letras (poems to be sung) that are villancicos in all but name. The brief auto El Triunfo de la Virgen to be found therein culminates in an "Aztec dance-song" that includes this couplet: "Mexicans, dance! Let the tocotín [Aztec dance] resound on every side because Mary triumphs!"

In the Peninsula, the first to mention in a villancico the Aztec tocotín was José Pérez de Montoro (1627-1694), writer of several "sets" of Christmas villancicos sung at Cádiz Cathedral between 1688 and 1693. The earliest known "set" of villancicos printed in Spain dates from 1634. Always for Christmas, other early "sets" that have received the attention of literary scholars date from 1645 (Madrid, Royal Chapel), 1650 (Toledo Cathedral), 1661 (Huesca Cathedral), and 1689 (Madrid,Incarnation Convent).

Viewed from a literary as well as liturgical stance these "sets" are important. The most telling novelty in both the Peninsular and Mexican repertory after 1634 happens to be precisely the penchant for grouping villancicos into "suites" of nine (or eight, if the last were replaced by the Te Deum). Why nine or eight? In principal churches and convents each of the three nocturns celebrated at first-class vespers consisted of three psalms or three lessons, each of which psalms or lessons was in turn followed by a polyphonic responsory. After each of the responsories, a villancico served as entr'acte, diverting the people. Better to enliven these entr'actes all kinds of licences were allowed—comic characters, actors singing rustic, provincial, Gypsy, Indian, and Negro dialects, or even burlesque skits. In the early 1700's moralists such as the Benedictine Feijóo castigated the light opera and tomfoolery trend, but in the late 1600's both music and poetry of the villancico-suites greatly profited from their contact with the earthier aspects of Peninsular and New World social life.

The earliest villancico "suites" published in the New World were apparently those sung at matins and Mass of St. Lawrence in Puebla, 1648[6]—a copy of which passed from Francisco González de Cossio's possession to the library of Salvador Ugarte. Other villancico sets now in the same library, but not registered in J. T. Medina's bibliography of colonial Puebla imprints,[7] include a 1651 Christmas set, and a 1652 St. Lawrence set. The earliest known set published at Mexico City appeared two years later, with the title Chanzonetas de los Maytines qve se cantaron en la Santa Iglesia Cathedral de Mexico, en la fiesta del Principe de la Iglesia N. P. San Pedro, Que dotò, y fundò, el Doctor Don Antonio de Esqvibel Castañeda, Racionero de dicha S. Iglesia (Mexico: Viuda de Bernardo

Calderón, 1654). But contemporary evidence confirms uninterrupted annual publication of at least the villancico-sets sung every June 29 in Mexico City Cathedral from no later than 1638 through 1677. Under date of June 29, 1678, the Mexico City diarist Antonio de Robles wrote as follows: "Wednesday, the 29th, St. Peter's Day, the viceroy and audiencia attended ceremonies in the Cathedral, where the preacher of the day was the Dominican provincial, Fray Antonio Leal; for the first time in the more than forty years since these matins were instituted there were no printed villancicos."[8]

In 1673 the fecund poet Diego de Ribera published his St. Peter set. Beginning three years later, Sor Juana Inés de la Cruz published at Mexico City or Puebla twelve attributed and ten un-attributed sets of villancicos: Assumption of 1676, 1677, 1679, 1681, 1685, 1686, 1690, Conception of 1676 and 1689, the Apostle Peter of 1677, 1680, 1683, 1684, 1690, 1691, 1692, St. Peter Nolasco of 1677, St. Joseph of 1690, St. Catherine of 1691, and Christmas of 1678, 1680, 1689 (underlined dates designated attributed sets).

Her worthiest contemporary, so far as villancico suites are concerned, was the Mexico City Cathedral sacristán Gabriel de Santillana, who in his two sets published in 1688[9]—the first for St. Peter, the second for the Nativity of Our Lady—supplied verse that was set by the two eminent Mexico City Cathedral chapelmasters José de Loaysa y Agurto and Antonio de Salazar. Salazar's other poets, apart from Sor Juana,[10] included these seven: Francisco de Azevedo (Assumption, 1689), Luis de la Peña (Nativity of Our Lady, 1703), Alonso Ramírez de Vargas (Nativity of Our Lady, 1689), Andrés de los Reyes Villaverde (St. Peter and Assumption, 1696), Felipe de Santoyo (Our Lady of Guadalupe, 1690 and 1697; Conception, 1695), Diego de Sevilla y Espinosa (Guadalupe, 1695; Nativity of Our Lady, 1702), and Andrés de Zepeda Carvajal (Guadalupe, 1696)[11] The texts of four suites composed by Loaysa y Agurto and of eleven by Salazar refuse to disclose their poets on their title pages.[12]

Because the title pages are lengthy and repeat themselves, only the first three suites composed by Loaysa y Agurto are transcribed below, followed by the first two of suites composed by Salazar. Their other title pages can be picked up from J. T. Medina's bibliography of colonial Mexico City imprints. Although not named on the title pages, Mexico's "tenth muse," Sor Juana Inés de la Cruz (1651-1695), wrote the verse for the first two sets registered below. The music-loving patron [13] responsible for endowing the St. Peter suites was the native of Mexico City Simón Esteban Beltrán de Alzate y Esquivel (1620-1670), who was archbishop-elect of Manila at his death, and the brother of a wealthy countess. Another local Maecenas who endowed annual villancicos was the cathedral archdeacon García de Legaspi Velazco, later elevated to bishop of Nueva Viscaya (Durango) and Michoacán. To him Sor Juana dedicated her 1677 St. Peter villancico-suite. [14]

Villancicos, qve se cantaron en la santa iglesia metropolitana de Mexico. En los maitines de la Pvrissima Concepcion de Nuestra Señora. A devocion de vn afecto al Misterio. Año de 1676. Compuestos en Metro musico, por el B. r Ioseph de Agurto, y Loaysa, Maestro Compositor de dicha Santa Iglesia. Por la Viuda de Bernardo Calderon, en la calle de San Augustin.

Villancicos, qve se cantaron en la Santa Iglesia Cathedral de Mexico, à los Maytines del Gloriosissimo Principe de la Iglesia, el Señor San Pedro. Que fundò, y dotò el Doct. y M. D. Simon Estevan Beltran, de Alzate, y Esquibel (que Dios aya), Maestre-escuela, que fue, desta S. Iglesia Cathedral, y Cathedratico Jubilado de Sagrada Escriptura, en esta Real Vniversidad de Mexico. Año de 1677. Dedicalos, Al Señor Lic.^do D. Garcia de Legaspi, Velazco, Altamirano, y Albornoz, Canonigo desta Santa Iglesia Cathedral de Mexico, &c. Con licencia. En Mexico, por la Uiuda de Bernardo Calderon.

Villancicos qve se cantaron en la Santa Iglesia Metropolitana de Mexico. En honor de Maria Santissima Madre de Dios en su assumpcion triumphante. Año de 1677. Que dotò, y fundò el Doctor, y M. D. Simon Estevan Beltran de Alzate y Esquibel, Cathedratico Jubilado de Sagrada Escriptura, en esta Real Vniversidad, y dignissimo Maestre-escuela de dicha Santa Iglesia (que Dios aya) Compuestos en Metro musico, por el Br. Ioseph de Agurto, y Loaysa, Maestro Compositor de dicha Santa Iglesia. Con licencia. En Mexico, por la Viuda de Bernardo Calderon, en la calle de San Agustin.

Villancicos, que se cantaron en los Maytines de la Natividad de Nuestra Señora en la Santa Iglesia Cathedral de Mexico. Primer año de su Celebridad, por vn devoto. Escrivelos, El Br. Don Gabriel de Santillana, Sacristan de dicha Iglesia. Compuestos en Metro Musico: Por Antonio de Salazar Maestro de Capilla de dicha Santa Iglesia. En Mexico por los Herederos de la Uiuda de Bernardo Calderon, en la Calle de San Agustin. Año de 1688.

Villancicos, qve se cantaron en la Santa Iglesia Metropolitana de Mexico, En honor de Maria Santissima en sv Assvmpcion triumphante, Que instituyo, y dotò la devocion del Señor Doctor, y Maestro D. Simon Estevan Beltran de Alzate, y Esqvibel, Cathedratico de Prima de Sagrada Escriptura en esta Real Vniversidad, y dignissimo Maestre-Escuela de dicha S. Iglesia (q̃ Dios aya) Escribelos el Br. D. Francisco de Azevedo. Compuestos en metro musico por Antonio de Salazar Maestro de Capilla de dicha Santa Iglesia. Año de 1689. En Mexico por los Herederos de la Viuda de Bernardo Calderon. En la Imprenta Plantiniana.

Like opera librettos, printed villancico booklets such as those just listed often contain precious performance practice data. For instance, the third nocturn of Sor Juana's 1691 "attributed" St. Peter set (written for Mexico City cathedral) begins with a villancico listing fifteen instruments in the accompanying ensemble. She mentions them in this order: clarín, trompeta, sacabuche, corneta, órgano, bajón, violín, chirimía, marina trompa, cítara, violón, vihuela, rabelillo, bandurría, arpa (clarion,[15] trumpet, sackbut, cornett, organ, bassoon, violin, shawm, marine trumpet,[16] zither, bass viol, vihuela, small rebeck, bandore, harp). Turned into English prose, her vivacious Spanish poetry loses its luster. But at least to hint at her train of thought, the following paraphrase may prove useful.[17]

> [Estribillo]. How well the cathedral honors her shepherd [St. Peter]! Hear the peal of the bells, tan tan talan, tan tan! Listen to the clarion, tin tin tilin, tin tin! Better still the sound of the trumpet, the sackbut, the cornett, the organ, and the bassoon. Jesus, what a din they all make, so loud the violin can't even tune! Tan tan talan tan tan, tin tin tilin tin tin! [Coplas] To lend added sparkle to Peter's sacred day, one instrument joins another in sweetest harmony: the shawm accompanied by the violin. Tin tilin tin tin! Now the trumpet loudly blares, now the cornett trills, now the sackbut joins the fray of contending lines. Tan talan tan tan! Now the marine trumpet squeaks above the double bass, their pitch stabilized by the bassoon. Now echo refines the zither's trill, alternating with the violin.[18] Tin tilin tin tin! The tenor [shawm] gurgles, the vihuela runs in counterpoint, the small rebeck lends its charm, the bandore takes a part, the harp quavers: and thus they all resound. Tan talan tan tan!

Not only does she name Salazar's instrumentarium in this Peter and the Wolf villancico, but also she tells what specific consort accompanied each stanza of the coplas: trumpet, sackbut, and cornett, bassoon, and organ the first; shawm and violin the second; trumpet, cornett, and sackbut the third; marine trumpet, double bass and basson, zither and violin the fourth; tenor shawm, vihuela, small rebeck, bandore, and harp the fifth. However: fifteen different instruments did not imply fifteen different players. Throughout the Baroque period, colonial cathedral capitular acts presuppose as sine qua non for any ministril's appointment his ability to double on two, three, or even four instruments.[19] A mere eight hired ministriles could therefore have dispatched the accompaniments designated in the villancico under discussion. Such prescribed changes of tone color from stanza to stanza hark back to a century-old Sevillian precedent. As early as July 11, 1586, the Seville Cathedral chapter issued at Francisco Guerrero's request a pragmatic sanction stipulating changes of instruments from verse to verse in Salves, "because always hearing the same instrument annoys the listener."[20]

Sor Juana's rare musical prowess comes into view else-where in her villancicos. In her maiden publication (the 1676 villancicos, a product of her twenty-fifth year) she begins the second nocturn with a villancico that works out in an elaborate fundamental image many of the deepest doctrines expounded at pages 482-540, and elsewhere, in her favorite treatise El Melopeo y Maestro (1613). Mary mediates between earth's flat hexachord and heaven's sharp, because her musical sym-bol is befabemi — which unites the "unsingable" semitone b♭-b♮. As Sor Juana's authority she relies on Cerone, who wrote at page 402: "en ninguno bfa♮ mi ay mutança: por que las dos bes que ay en ellos Fa y Mi, no estan yguales: que la vna es vn Semitono incantable mas subida de la otra" ("no mutation bridges b♭-b♮, because the first b which is fa and the second which is mi differ, the second being an unsingable semitone higher than the other").[21] How deeply she delved to buttress her poetic conceits comes immediately to light in the two-page opening from her personal copy of Cerone's treatise. Here, she has annotated the margins. The sense of her signed lengthy marginal note at the bottom of Cerone's page 284 runs like this: the larger the fraction, the smaller the divisor (1/2 is larger than 1/3, but 2 is smaller than 3).[22] A facsimile of precisely this opening can be seen in Ermilo Abreu Gómez, Sor Juana Inés de la Cruz Bibliografía y Biblioteca (Mexico City: Secretaría de Relaciones Exteriores, 1934 [Monografías Bibliográficas Mexicanas, 29]), pages 448-449.

To sample the other poetic conceits in this Marian villan-cico versifying Cerone: (1) Mary's praises should be voiced not in this world's cut time (compasillo) but in heavenly ter-nary meter (compás ternario); (2) Old Testament women de-serve praise in minims, but Mary in maxima; (3) she tunes the enharmonic species perfectly, because she knows how to measure the schismas accurately; (4) her dorian mildness tempers Deity's disgust with Earth's phrygian excesses; (5) her better music than Orpheus's for a while alleviates even hell's pains;[23] (6) the Church octaves reinforce the angelic choir's bass (contrabajo); (7) at the last cadence the rise of a tritone (tritono) leads to the enjoyment of eternal consonan-ces.

Sor Juana's three published Christmas villancico-sets (1678, 1680, 1689) were all written for Puebla. The 1678 set of eight terminates with juguete-negrillo-juguete, the 1680 (composed by Salazar) closes with a negro, the 1689 (com-posed by Miguel Mateo de Dallo y Lana) after seguidillas cli-maxes in a macaronic villancico. In all, she published no less than twelve jácaras, nine negros, seven ensaladas, six ju-guetes, and three tocotines.[24] Her villancicos also include such dialectical intermezzi as a gallego, indio, portugués, puerto rico, and vizcaíno.[25] She designates as the dance measures to which others are sung, canario and folías.[26] On one occasion she calls the five-line strophes replacing coplas endechas and on another four-line stanzas romance.[27]

As a response to the poetic glorification of bravado, the seventeenth-century jácara seems always to have called for boastful, arrogant music — Francisco de Vidales's jácara in the present collection serving as a good example. Although the music of many more villancicos must be transcribed and analyzed before generalizations are safe, the seventeenth-century negro seems always to have involved certain standard musical gestures: "Vivid 6/8 with constant hemiolia shifts in 3/4 are the rule; F or C Major is the almost universal key; solo or soloists answered by chorus govern the tex-ture."[28] If Fabián Ximeno's gallego published in the present volume can be taken as typical, marching meter, ionian mode, and solo-chorus antiphony were commonplaces in Galician-dialect villancicos. Fray Gerónimo González's canario (Serenissima una noche) vaunts a perky dotted 6/8 — the main beats being stabilized by an intermittent drone bass above which the melody disports in popular thirds.

The juego de cañas, "cane contest" (not illustrated in Sor Juana's villancicos) was a horseman's mock battle during which cane spears substituted for real swords. The appro-priate music, to judge from Juan Guitiérrez de Padilla's Las estreyas se rien, sounded a typically fiery and bellicose note. Moving outside the orbit of the Sánchez Garza collec-tion to which Las estreyas se rien belongs, Professor E. Thomas Stanford distributed at the 1969 Annual Meeting of the American Musicological Society (December 28 in St. Louis) a seven-page mimeographed handout that included the first translation (with accompanying Spanish original) of any Pueb-la Cathedral villancico composed by Gutiérrez de Padilla.[29] Dated 1653, this was a Christmas jácara starting with an es-tribillo (refrain) that gave way to twelve eight-line coplas (verses). After every third copla (each line is of eight syl-lables), Padilla prescribed repetition of the opening estribillo. So clearly prescribed a return to the estribillo after every third strophe of the coplas (or after every other strophe, as in Francisco de Santiago's Christmas villancico in the Sánchez Garza collection) sets a precedent to which any pres-ent-day reviver of seventeenth-century villancicos can ap-peal who wishes to do the same — even when no written rubrics so command.

Jácara texts always emphasized bravado. Characteristic-ally, the 1653 Christmas jácara set by Padilla addresses it-self to "los valientes" ("the valiant hearted"). Although Padilla's 1653 poet made no pretense of being a prophet, all seventeenth-century villancicos nowadays recommend them-selves only to "the valiant hearted" — because only they will have the courage to cleave their way through the jungle of sources, literary and musical, and only they will have the courage to perform them wildly.

1. Not 1538. See R. Stevenson, <u>Music in Aztec & Inca Territory</u> (Berkeley and Los Angeles: University of California Press, 1968), pp. 159-160.

2. <u>Ibid</u>., pp. 156-157, 221.

3. On January 2, 1543, the Mexico City Cathedral allotted the racionero = prebendary Campoverde ten pesos annually for each choirboy whom he taught music (<u>Libro primero de Actas y Determinaciones Capitulares</u>, fol. 51^V). Although Antonio Ramos had been brought over from Spain in 1538 to serve as Mexico City Cathedral organist, Campoverde played also. On January 11, 1544, he quit organ playing "so that another could take over" (fol. 59: <u>Campoverde dexe los organos p^a que otro lo sirba</u>). Only eleven days later he was recalled to the organ bench (fol. 59^V). On July 11, 1544, he was supervising the carpenter Juan Franco's construction of a <u>façistol</u> (choirbook stand), for which Franco was being paid 40 pesos (fol. 64). Now a canon, Campoverde obtained a sixteen months' leave January 5, 1546 (fol. 74^V) to revisit Spain on business. While there he was promised continuation of his salary provided that he came back to the cathedral. He elected to remain in Spain.

4. <u>Music in Aztec & Inca Territory</u>, pp. 226-227.

5. <u>Ibid</u>., p. 203.

6. Philip II erected El Escorial to commemorate this saint (d. 258), on whose day, August 10, was won in 1557 the Battle of St. Quentin. Bishop Juan de Palafox y Mendoza (1600-1659) endowed these St. Lawrence villancicos in Puebla Cathedral (governed by him 1640-1649). During this bishop's term Juan Gutiérrez de Padilla was Puebla Cathedral chapelmaster.

7. <u>La Imprenta en la Puebla de los Angeles (1640-1821)</u> (Santiago: Imprenta Cervantes, 1908).

8. <u>Diario de sucesos notables (1665-1703)</u> (Mexico City: Editorial Porrua, 1946), I, 242-243: "Miércoles 29, día de nuestro padre San Pedro [1678] predicó en la Catedral Fr. Antonio Leal, provincial de Santo Domingo: asistió el virrey y audiencia; no hubo villancicos impresos, sin ejemplar desde que se instituyeron los maitines, que ha más de cuarenta años." Robles's memory "of forty years" served him well. On August 1, 1636 —while Antonio Rodríguez de Mata was still Mexico City Cathedral chapelmaster and Luis Coronado organist — the then <u>canónigo doctoral</u> Luis de Cifuentes had announced that henceforth 300 pesos would be budgeted annually for the June 29 matins and Mass, so that their celebration might glow "with polyphony, villancicos and chanzonetas, and with the greatest possible [musical] splendor" ("con canto de organo billansicos y chançonetas y con la mayor solemnidad que ser pueda"). See <u>Actas Capitulares</u>, IX (1633-1639), fol. 167.

9. J. T. Medina, <u>La Imprenta en México (1539-1821)</u> (Santiago: Casa del Autor, 1908), III, 41. Volume II of this set, cited below in notes 12 and 14, was issued from the same "house of the author" a year later, in 1909.

10. For Mexico City Salazar set Sor Juana's ascribed Assumption set of 1690 and her unattributed St. Peter sets of 1691 and 1692. For Puebla he composed the music of her St. Peter sets dated 1680 and 1684, her Christmas of 1680, and her Assumption of 1681. Texts of these seven sets are reprinted in <u>Obras Completas</u>, II, 148-163, 330-342, 342-353, 259-270, 291-302, 270-279, 280-290.

11. <u>La Imprenta en México</u>, III, 44-45 (Azevedo), 358 (Peña), 53 (Ramírez de Vargas), 155, 156 (Reyes Villaverde), 69, 182, 142-143 (Santoyo), 144, 346 (Sevilla y Espinosa), 158-159 (Zepeda Carvajal).

12. <u>Ibid</u>., II, 492, 553-554, III, 9, 22 (Loaysa y Agurto); III, 68, 81, 81, 82, 96, 156, 180, 218, 237, 325-326, 364 (Salazar).

13. Although he was not <u>chantre</u>, Mexico City Cathedral used Simón Esteban Beltrán de Alzate as go-between in crucial negotiations with musicians. See Mexico City Cathedral, <u>Actas Capitulares</u>, XII (1652-1655), fol. 40^V (April 21, 1654). On December 2, 1664, he proposed personally endowing Christmas Masses rather than waiting each year for a trickle of voluntary contributions (<u>Actas Capitulares</u>, XVI, fol. 112^V). In that year he was cathedral treasurer.

14. Further biographical data in <u>Diccionario Porrúa</u>, 3d ed. (1970), I, 1l67. Title page opposite 128 in her <u>Obras Completas</u>, II, continues with Sor Juana's graceful 22-line dedicatory epistle to the future bishop of Michoacán.

15. Clarions are earlier mentioned in her Kalenda (= calenda) sung at Christmas of 1680 in Puebla Cathedral. So are shawms. Salazar again composed the music.

16. Sybil Marcuse, <u>Musical Instruments: A Comprehensive Dictionary</u> (New York: Doubleday, 1964), p. 542, documents the widespread favor enjoyed by the marine trumpet as late as the late eighteenth century.

17. For the Spanish text, see her <u>Obras Completas</u>, II, 339-341.

18. Marcuse, <u>op. cit.</u>, p. 516, thus identifies the Spanish <u>tenor</u>.

19. Ample documentation from Mexico City Cathedral <u>Actas Capitulares</u> is assembled in the next chapter.

20. R. Stevenson, <u>Spanish Cathedral Music in the Golden Age</u> (Berkeley and Los Angeles: University of California Press, 1961), p. 167.

21. Cerone himself refers the reader to his pages 281-282 for a fuller exposé.

22. "Siento tambien q̃ la rraçon de llamar semitono menor el de sinco comas Y mayor el de quatro es respecto de la proporcion pues quanto Vna quantidad es mayor es menor su denominacion. Y al contrario q^{to} es menor ella su denominacion es mayor como Vn quarto es mayor en esta Raçon de Ceron su discipula juana ynes de la Cruz."

23. Méndez Plancarte's note, <u>Obras Completas</u>, II, 358-359, explains her allusion to Ildephonsus.

24. <u>Ibid</u>., pp. 10, 24, 36, 54, 107, 138, 161, 238, 266, 299, 310, 327; 15, 26, 72, 96, 143, 247, 257, 276, 315; 39, 56, 82, 94, 107, 138, 289; 109, 140, 160, 174, 256, 258; 17, 41, 289. Diminutives like <u>ensaladilla</u> are counted with the main term. Some types overlap.

25. <u>Ibid</u>., pp. 289, 142, 57, 39, 98. A Negro accompanies his singing of the puerto rico with a gourd (<u>calabazo</u>).

26. <u>Ibid</u>., pp. 247, 263.

27. <u>Ibid</u>., pp. 312-313.

28. R. Stevenson, "The Afro-American Musical Legacy to 1800," <u>Musical Quarterly</u>, LIV/4 (October, 1968), 496-497. Note that Salazar's <u>negro</u> in the present volume has been transposed down from C to G. Felipe Pedrell set the precedent for such transcription down a fourth of those numerous seventeenth-century Spanish works in chiavette ("claves transportadas"). See his <u>Diccionario técnico de la música</u>, (4th ed.; Barcelona: Isidro Torres Oriol, n. d.), p. 90a. For an example transcribed down a fourth by him facing a facsimile of the original manuscript, see José Subirá, <u>Historia de la música española e hispanoamericana</u> (Barcelona: Salvat, 1953), pp. 342-343.

29. Lines 3-6 of the second coplas properly serve as motto for the present monograph.

Mexican Archival Christmas Music (and Relevant Documentation)

As has just been shown, sources for the study of the early colonial villancico qua literature are happily very rich. Inasmuch as Sor Juana (1651-1695) remains the key Mexican poet of the century, the easy availability of her complete villancico repertory in modern reprint can be counted a stroke of fortune — more especially since her texts not only reveal so often her own musical gifts but also bear on performance practices of vital interest to the present-day musicologist.

But what of musical sources as such? In my Renaissance and Baroque Musical Sources in the Americas (Washington: General Secretariat, Organization of American States, 1970), the villancicos therein listed alphabetically by author are mixed with the Latin repertory of the same authors. Without constantly shuffling pages for dates and locations, this catalogue does not readily yield the data on the early Mexican manuscripts containing villancicos that the user of the present volume may desire. I have therefore extracted and reordered already published data in order to smooth the reader's approach to the villancicos transcribed in the musical supplement to the present volume.

A 278-folio small manuscript choirbook at Oaxaca Cathedral includes no less than 80 Christmas villancicos by Gaspar Fernandes. Dates scattered through the book range from 1609 through 1620. The happy discovery of this priceless manuscript, contents of which are itemized in Renaissance and Baroque Musical Sources in the Americas, was first announced in Excelsior: El Periódico de la vida nacional, Magazine Dominical, December 10, 1967 — two openings from the manuscript being shown in facsimile at page 3. The Christmas Guineo a 5 transcribed from the Oaxaca manuscript for publication in "The Afro-American Musical Legacy to 1800" occupies pages 490-495 of Musical Quarterly, LIV/4 (October, 1968), and was premiered July 22, 1970, at the Carmel Bach Festival, Sandor Salgo conducting.[1]

Roughly contemporary with Gaspar Fernandes (c. 1566-1629) — who after seven years at Antigua Guatemala Cathedral as organist and chapelmaster (1599-1606) transferred to Puebla Cathedral in the same capacity (1606-1629) — was the Guatemala Indian maestro Tomás Pascual (flourished 1595-1630 at San Juan Ixcoi in what is now Huehuetenango Department). Pascual's jaunty Oy es dia de placer, published as one of the three musical examples in my "European Music in 16th

Century Guatemala," Musical Quarterly, L/3 (July, 1964), 348, is but one of six Christmas villancicos in Santa Eulalia M. Md. 7 (fols. 5, 5ᵛ-7, 7ᵛ-8, 9ᵛ-10, 19ᵛ-20, 20ᵛ-21) a 36-folio manuscript formerly (1966) at San Miguel Acatán but now (1970) in the Lilly Library, Indiana University. The text in each betrays typical Indian's scribal errors, but the music breathes throughout the spirit of the ternary-meter villancicos in the mid-sixteenth-century Spanish Cancionero de Upsala.[2]

Next in chronological order come the Christmas villancicos by Gaspar Fernandes's successor at Puebla, Juan Gutiérrez de Padilla, that are still preserved in loose sheets in the Puebla Cathedral archive. El zagal que a nacido ("The Child who is born"), a villancico for soloist accompanied by instruments and for vocal trio and quintet, Oy zagales atentos ("Today, dear swains") a 3 and a 6, and Si al naçer o minino se yela ("If the Babe is born in the icy chill"), a gallego (Galician-dialect villancico) for instrumentally accompanied soloist followed by choral sections a 3 and a 4 typify Gutiérrez de Padilla's vernacular contribution to the Puebla archive. His A siolo flasiquiyo for accompanied quartet and a six-part chorus in the same archive carries a subtitle, negrilla ("black piece"), which identifies it as one of the very numerous Latin American Christmas pieces — beginning with the above-cited Guineo a 5 by Gaspar Fernandes — that cleverly exploit Negro speech patterns in the text and buoyant Negro rhythms in the music.

The next important colonial villancico collection now belongs to the Mexican Instituto Nacional de Bellas Artes, but belonged originally to Holy Trinity Convent in Puebla. Since an appreciation of the Colección Jesús Sánchez Garza presupposes an acquaintance with the history of the convent to which it originally belonged, a historical summary must here precede the listing alphabetically by author of 164 representative items in the collection.

HISTORY OF HOLY TRINITY CONVENT AT PUEBLA

According to the pioneer Puebla chronicler, Miguel Zerón Zapata, Holy Trinity Convent at its height in 1714 housed sixty Franciscan Conceptionist religiosas. The rule of this order was given by Pope Julius II. The first Puebla house of Conceptionists opened in 1593, Holy Trinity in 1619. The following synopsis is translated from Hugo Leicht's Las calles de Puebla (Puebla: A. Mijares y Hno., 1934), pages 426, 466-467:

> Alonso de Ribera Barrientos, alcalde ordinario in 1609, had two sisters in a Puebla Conceptionist convent founded in 1593, and another two married sisters. Since several girls in these three rich families were inclined toward religion, the Ribera Barrientos and another two families decided to found in Puebla a second Conceptionist convent. After obtaining royal license, they bought from Bishop Alonso de la Mota y Escobar (ruled Puebla diocese 1608-1625) his recently built episcopal residence and adjoining property, allowing him two years to move elsewhere. In 1619 the new convent was ready for occupancy by the two nuns formerly in the house that dated from 1593. Entering as abadesa and vicaria, they superintended the religious life of several nieces, whose total number rose within the next decade to fourteen. During the epoch of Bishop Diego Osorio de Escobar y Llamas (ruled 1656-1673) a sumptuous new church was built for the nuns of Holy Trinity. Because his gifts made the new church possible, he was buried in it. During 1664-1665 this bishop had temporarily served as both archbishop of Mexico and viceroy.

From approximately sixty nuns in 1714, the Holy Trinity Convent population dropped to 34 in 1852.

On February 23, 1861, the few remaining Holy Trinity nuns moved in with the Conceptionists who belonged to the older house. By blanket order, nuns were temporarily expelled from their Puebla convents Christmas night, 1862. The next year the remnant of Holy Trinity nuns moved to the Casa de Recogidas, but in December of 1864 went back to their first convent. At last on April 6, 1867, all Puebla convents were extinguished, thus ending the 248-year existence of Santísima Trinidad.

Further data bearing on the 248-year history of Santísima Trinidad convent can be gleaned from the following five works, especially the fourth:

Carrión, Antonio. Historia de la Ciudad de los Angeles. Puebla; Viuda de Dávalos e hijos, 1896-1897.

Regla, y constituciones que han de guardar las Religiosas de los conventos de Nuestra Señora de la Concepcion, y la Santisima Trinidad de la civdad de los Angeles. Puebla: Seminario Palafoxiano, 1773. Other editions, 1653, 1744, 1795.

Vetancurt, Agustín de. Teatro Mexicano, II. Madrid: José Porrua Turanzas, 1960.

Veytia, Mariano Fernández Echeverría y. Historia de la fundación de la ciudad de la Puebla de los Angeles en la Nueva España. Puebla: [Mixocoac, D. F.], Imprenta "Labor" 1931.

Zerón Zapata, Miguel. La Puebla de los Angeles en el siglo XVII. Mexico City: Editorial Patria, S. A., 1945.

CONTENTS OF SÁNCHEZ GARZA COLLECTION

The 44 items preceded by a plus sign in the following partial catalogue of the Sánchez Garza Collection celebrate Christmas. An asterisk indicates an item for which only an incomplete set of parts survives.

Abate de Rusi ("M^{ro}")

Zagales oyd las ansias mias al compas del albogue. Solo humano, Acomp^{to}. Estribillo, four coplas. A minor, 𝄵, not barlined. Subject: pangs of love.

Alva, Antonio (Dn")

Missa a 4 Con Vl.^{s} y Trompas. Ti Ti, 2 French horns, 2 violins, Ac. F Major. Concludes with Osanna. Simple broken chord string parts. An eighteenth-century work widely dispersed in Latin American archives.

Anonymous

+*Flasiquiyo q̄ mandamo lo plimiyo.

Negrilla, Duo y a 6. Usual tonic, dominant, subdominant. Coplas: (1) Y tanbe branca esa manca . . . pues q̄ hase gado . . . (2) Es glan dotor rosiquiye. C𝄵 throughout. Copied on dorse of Padilla tiple: Entre aq̄llas Crudas sombras.

+Lleguen lleguen todos a oir. This chanberga = chamberga, originally for Christmas, was later adapted for the Archangel Michael. "Responsion a la chanberga" follows the "estri^{uo} a 5." Ti Ti A seem now to be the sole surviving parts. The chamberga was an eighteenth-century fast triple-meter dance popular in Spain as well as Mexico (see my Music in Aztec & Inca Territory, pp. 235-236). "Responsion a 4" text reads thus: Tu nacimiento niño con tal belleza Cantar quiero en metro de la chanberga que lindo como del cielo mismo que alegre. To judge from this particular piece, the chamberga involved paired phrases, the first beginning on a downbeat, the next with two pickup beats.

Ardanas = Ardanaz, [Pedro de]

Ay aflijida dama. Tiples 1 & 2 (accompaniment missing). Starts imitatively, C𝄵. Frequent high a^2.

Atienza, Francisco

Como es ley y medizina. A4. Ti Ti A B. Copla answered with Resp^{ta}. Ends with the summons, "Oygan." C Major.

Missa A, 5º Vo,^{s}. Ti Ti A Te B. Marked "quinto tono" = F Major. Important music; imitations well handled. Five booklets. Ends with Osanna. Composer respectfully saluted as "Sr Ma.^{o} D.^{n}" on all parts.

Babán, [Gracián]

Alerta alerta sentinelas. A la SS^{ma} Trinidad. Although parts are marked "A 4," five are here: Ti Ti A Te B. At the end of the estribillo Babán specifies that the

invocation "Jesus" shall be repeated: <u>a media voz.</u> High
written tessiture imply performance transposed down.

Baeza, <u>See</u> Vaeza

Bazani = Bassani, Giovanni Battista

*Missa â 4 Vozes con Violines ð sin ellos. Alto, Tenor,
Tenor Bajete (present in duplicate copies, this part differs
from the Tenor only in using bass clef). Tiple missing.
This Mass ends with "dona nobis pacem." G minor (one-
flat). Alto part is inscribed: De la M. R. M. Maria
Francisca de los Dolores Campusano, Dignissima Maestra
de Capilla en el combento de Señoras Religiosas de la
SS^{ma} trinidad.

Carabantes, Francisco Manuel

+*A la reina entre el dolor. Ti A B, Ac. Villancico A4, de
Navidad.

+Mi Dios de ver que llorais. Ti Ti Contraalto Baxo. F.
Major.

Casseda, Diego de

Ay como para la flor. SS^{mo}. Ti Ti A Te, Ac.

Ola posta del Cielo. Villansico A duo. SS^{mo}.

Casseda, Joseph de

Sagrado Pajarillo que musica divina. SS^{mo} Sacramen^{to}.
Despite "A 4" on parts, there are five: Ti Ti A Te B.

Casseda, M^{ro}.

Del dorado planeta. Duo. Ti Ti, Ac. "Primero tono."
Waterstained parts.

En vna nube de niebe se ve vn hermoso Jazmin. Duo.
Ti Ti, Ac.

+Oygan la jacarilla que ha con donaire al valiente mayor de
los siglos. Ti Te Te (sung by Ines de Sta Cruz, M^e
Thomasa, Rosa Peres), Acomp^{to} de Violon a la jacara.
Dorian, no signature. Fast galloping triple meter.

*Paxarito que en el aire eleuado. Duo al Santissimo S.^{to}
Tiple, Acompañamiento. Dorian.

Coll, José

*Misa de 5° tono â 4.º Vozes. C Major. Ends with "dona
nobis pacem." Evidently this is a Mass for four sopranos,
since the one surviving part is headed Tiple Quarto.

Coradini, Francisco

El Ave al Cielo. Cantada Sola con Violines. Tiple, 2
violins, Acomp^{to}. This G Major da capo aria travels to
B minor in the middle section. To suggest the mounting
soul's panting, the accompaniment stops and starts with
many an intervening short rest.

Los Orbes admiran. Cantada à solo Ala Purisima Consep-
cion. Da capo aria for accompanied soprano (F Major,
middle section D minor), preceded by Recitado.

*Missa a 5. Tenor part. G minor (two-flat signature). Ends
with Osanna.

O Paloma remontada. Cantada à Solo Ala Asump^n de Nt^{ra}
S^a. Da capo aria in C Major (E minor middle section) for
accompanied soprano, preceded by a recitative, Nunca

puede tener pena señora.

Corchado, Juan

Ay que explendores. Villancico â Duo. Ti Ti, Ac. C
Major. Considerable vocal dexterity is presupposed
when for such a phrase as "que claridad" Corchado assigns both singers fast broken thirds. Nonetheless, the
copy looks local.

Nace la Aurora Divina. Tonada sola a la Natividad de N^{ra}
Señora. Año de 1727. Ti, Ac. Although ostensibly in
C Major, this September 8 villancico should be transposed to D Major, declares the following note on the
AComp^{to}: este se acompaña a la Me Rosa trasportado
entrando estrivillo y Coplas en dlasolre como sesto ^{tono}
con 3# ("Accompany Mother Rose by beginning on D in
both estribillo and coplas, as if playing Tone VI with
three-sharp signature"). Inasmuch as the tiple ranges
from written b^1-a^2, Mother Rose obviously sang her part
down a seventh, not up a second.

Sagaleja de perlas. Arieta sola. Only the soloist's part
(soprano clef) survives. G Major. Notated in common
meter, but the number of written sixteenths and thirty-
seconds departs from the expected in the 1720's.

Cruzealegui, P^e F. Martín de

Misa a Solo de Sexto tono. Para los dias de primera clase.
Two copies of accompaniment (basso continuo, written in
baritone clef), one beginning with breves ₵ ⫟, the
other with time-values halved and bar lines added. Different Benedictus and only one Agnus in second copy.
Also, an added voice duplicates the original solo bass in
thirds here and there. Yielding to Italianate trends,
Cruzealegui writes tunes and when they are sufficiently
catchy repeats them. The same tune serves both the
opening Kyrie and the last Agnus. The Patrem, despite
the semibreves masquerading decorously under a $\Phi\,{}^3_2$
mensuration in the older copy of the Mass, turns out to be
a blithe minuet.

Dallo, y Lana, Miguel Matheo de

Ay que se esconde. Villansico a la SS^{ma} trinidad para el
año 1689. Ti Ti A B, violon, arpa. "M^o Dallo" on all
parts.

*Credidi propter quod, a 6. Tiple 1 missing; Ti 2 A A Te
Te, AComp^{to} A 6. Marked "Tercero tono," this setting
of Psalm 115 (Vulgate) inhabits written A minor. But
the note at the bottom of AComp^{to}, "en el organo grande
por Dlasolrre," implies transposition down a fifth or up
a fourth on the large organ. Wormeaten parts.

*Dixit Dominus. Bajo de 2° Choro. G minor (one-flat).
Throughcomposed setting of Psalm 109 (Vulgate) in
common meter.

*Ego autem. Although Bajo 2° Choro A 6 ends on A,
transposition is implied by the rubric "Por Delasolrre."

Lauda Jerusalem â Duo. Psalm 147. Ti Ti, Acomp^{to}.

D Major (two-sharp signature). New sections, marked
with red capitals, begin at Quoniam, Qui posuit, Qui
emittit, Qui dat nivem, Mittit, Non fecit taliter.

*Lauda Jerusalem, Psalmo à 6. Tiple 1 missing. A Te, Ti
A Te, Acomp^to a 6. F Major and related keys. (D minor,
B♭ Major). All 4/4. Continuo lacks figures.

Quien es la que huella el primer horror ella ella y en perpetua albor es Aurora bella. Villansico A Quatro. A la
purissima Concepcion de N.^a Señora. Año de 1701. Ti A
Te, Acomp^to. C Major music. Structure: estribillo-
coplas (Al componer el orbe)-estribillo (Digalo el Agua).
The last estribillo (which does not repeat the first) is the
longest portion. The question posed by two altos moving
in thirds, at the start in canario (galloping 6/8) rhythm
evokes the response "ella ella" from tiple and tenor.

Durón, Sebastián

+Al dormir el Sol. Villancico Al Duo. Ti Ti, Ac.

Benigno favonio. Al SS^mo. Ti Ti A Te, AComp^to.
Estribillo a 4 followed by four solo coplas. After each
solo copla, the chorus replies "quedito," "passito."
Tone VIII = G Major (no signature). C₵. This same
villancico reached Cuzco, where a copy still survived
(1966) in the San Antonio Abad Seminary Library.

*Cielo de nieue. Tiple part copied at bottom of page starting
with Diego Joseph de Salazar's Ay ay q̃ me prende. Dorse
of this same sheet contains refrain and three coplas of one
anonymous villancico, Sigue mis voses; refrain and nine
coplas of another, El sol luna y estrellas.

*Con mi clarin. Although the sole extant part is headed
tiple, the clef is baritone. "Baxo" appears above third
staff. F Major, common meter.

Facco, Giacomo.

O que brillar! de Aurora (Recitado) followed by: Nacio
Luziente brillante y vella (Area). Ala Natividad de N^ra
Señora. This brilliant G Major-E minor da capo aria for
soprano (plus continuo) rises to virtuostic heights on such
words as "zenit."

Florentín, Juan

+Como se imitan los dos Ruiseñores. Villancico A Duo de
Nauidad. Ti Ti, Ac. Dorian. So outrageous did one
soloist find the nightingale runs that this precautionary
note embellishes the Tiple 1° part: Mui despassio porq̃
no sea de poder cantar por los gorgeos ("Go very slow,
because no one can manage the warbles").

Missa A 5 Vosses. Ti, Ti A Te B. G minor (one-flat),
ends with Osanna. Coro II consists of ripienists. Bajo
part serves also the continuo player.

Galán, [Cristóbal]

Oiganos celebrar un misterio. Duo al Santisimo Sacramento.
Ti Ti, B.

García, Juan

+A la mar ba mi niño. A duo y a 8. Tiple Solo, Ti Ti A A B,

Te B. F Major. Christmas.

+Hermoso amor que forxas tus flechas. Romance a 4
Nauidad. año de 1671. Para Mi S.^ra la Me Andrea del
S.^mo Sacram.^to Six coplas in G minor (one-flat), followed by estribillo, Mas ay que disparas suspiros. As
usual, the romance adheres to common, the estribillo to
triple, meter.

Kirie eleyson . . . rossa mistica. A Duo y a 6. Ti Te,
Ti A Te B, Ac. C Major music. Litany of Our Lady.

García, Vicente

*Missa Hic est vere martyr. Cantus 2° tribus choris marked
Tomasita; "et venturus est cum gloria" marked: sensillo
alphonsa (i. e., solo sung by Alfonsa). Tone VIII.
Declamatory antiphony. Duarte Lobo composed a sim-
ilarly entitled Mass, but a 4 (published in his Antwerp
Book II, 1639, at folios liv-lxxi).

González, fray Gerónimo

+Serenissima vna noche. Romance a 4°. Ti A B (one part of
the duplicate copies of the tiple is headed "belona"; she
sang the part). Estribillo following the romance is
headed:"por cruçado tañer el canario y mui volado cantarlo
mucho mucho." This Christmas dance-song begins with
ten strophes, four of which describe members of the pro-
cession to Bethlehem. Each portrait satirizes its subject — "Bartolo, who thinks gloves and a mule are enough
to make him a doctor without graduating," "Gil, the bar-
ber turned musician who is sure that he knows just what
makes a passacaglia or folia" (Yba Gil echo Barbero,
tocando vnos pasacalles, pues ellos y las folias son deste
oficio el examen). Whoever concocted the verse, González knew just how to strike the right bantering note in his
delightfully folkloric musical setting.

Gutiérrez de Padilla, Juan

*Administre sus Rayos el sol y sujete su plata la luna a 3.
Tiple 2° amd tenor. Starts with three strophes, then
estribillo (not so named), followed by two coplas. C
Major. C₵ meter throughout.

Al triunfo de aquella reyna. A 4. Romanse de la assump-
sion de n^ra s^a. Ti A Te B, plus additional instrumental
bass. Six strophes followed by estribillo: "Los espiritus
le hacen la salba y al mouer sus plumas bellas entre
coros y danças destrellas [next eight words pasted over] .

Con tal de la gala pastores. Ti Ti A Te. G minor (one-flat
signature), C 3 changing to C , then back to C 3. Estribillo continues: "volando corriendo y advertir q̃ agradese
Maria buenos deseos." After estribillo come six endechas a 4: "A Maria vella q̃ en su concepcion . . ." in
common meter. The worn parts attest heavy use of this
December 8 villancico.

De buestras glorias colijo Joseph. A 4. Ti Ti A Te. C
Major music (C 3). Text continues: "excelensias dos
que sois arbitro de dios padre del mejor hijo." After each

of the two coplas sung <u>a 4</u> Padilla specifies a repeat of
the underlined text (dal segno).

+*Dormidillos ojuelos tiene mi niño. De nabidad a 5. Ti 1 A
B. After estribillo come eight coplas a duo, sung alternately by tiple 1º and altus.

+*Entre aꝗllas Crudas sombras de aꝗl postrado edifisio.
Romanse A 4. After five strophes in common meter,
comes the estribillo: Acabose Pastores del Sielo. This
starts in common, shifts to **C** 3 in midcourse, but back
to common at close. Two coplas a duo y a 3 follow,
after which the estribillo is repeated. Like most romances in Guatemalan and Mexican archives, this is copied
longwise (villancicos are customarily copied sidewise).
Someone named Leonor played bass. On the dorse of the
only other surviving part (soprano) has been copied in
tenor clef an anonymous Negrilla Duo y a 6, beginning:
Flasiquiyo ꝗ mandamo lo plimiyo.

*La corte del cielo, a 3 y a 6. Ti Ti A, plus "Bassus a 3
con biolon" [notated in tenor clef]. After the opening
estribillo comes a responsión a 6, then three coplas a 3,
each of which is answered by the same responsión a 6.
Tone VIII. Plagally cadencing to G at closes, this villancico starts in C. Ternary meter (**C**3) throughout.
Subject matter: Company of heaven gathers to swear alle-
giance to the King of Kings. Parts copied longwise.

+Las estreyas se Rien. Juego de cañas a 3, y a 6. Three
strophes, next "estriuiyo," then three coplas, another
estribillo, and again three coplas. Ti A A Te Te B. One-
flat signature. Cadences to D and G chords (G, last ending). Performers' names appear on the heavily used,
waterstained parts: Andrea del Sacramento, Anotita,
Ysabel del SS^mo Sacra^to, Mª de St Jhoan, Mª Theresa,
Leonor.

*Mirabilia testimonia tua. Psalm 118 (Vulgate), 129-144
(= Phe and Sade). Alto 2º (clef on 2d line), common
meter, sung by Ynes de Jesu Nazareno. Page 2 (134):
mandata tua faciem; 3 (139): quia obliti sunt verba tua;
4: Gloria Patri. This same double-choir psalm (SATB,
SATB) turns up in Puebla Cathedral Libro de coro XV, at
fols. 65^V-77.

*Nada lejos de razon. Tiple 1º a 3. **C**3 . Two coplas follow estribillo, each running into a <u>Dal segno</u> repeat.
Estribillo continues thus: "ni de aquello que se cree puedo
jurar por mi fee, <u>que las tres para vno son.</u>" Coplas:
(1) Ꞇan vnido en ser esta, este ternario diuino quel sera
fin mas ladino, nada les distinguira antes de la buena
vnion, destas personas se vee con los ojos de la fee,
<u>que las tres para vno son.</u> (2) Tres subsisten y vno es, el
Dios que los rige todo y si examinas el modo, faltaras de
lo que crees la vista de la razon, as de apartar en fee
firme, y di porque se confirme, <u>que las tres para vno son.</u>
Despite the abstract text dedicated to the Trinity, the mu-

sic runs at a lilting canario rate with frequent syncopa-
tions to add zest.

*No son quatro mortales con eminencia buena cuenta blaso-
nas, y como si abonas tres personas que son vna esencia
q̄ esta en tres personas. A 3 y a 5. Only three parts
survive: Tiples 1º, 2º, "Bassus a 3 con biolon." F
Major, **C**3 . Coplas lacking in extant parts.

+O que buen año gitanas A 4. Ti Ti Altus (cover of this part
reads: "Tenores y Altos de Navidad año de 1642"), Bajon
tenor (marked at top, "Duo: Padilla"). This Christmas
piece starts with twelve coplas marked duo, in **C**3 .
The text of the Responsion a 4 (still **C**3) reads: (1)
Mientras que la peynada le bayla al niño la mantilla le
hurto para vn corpiño (2) Tañe resio maraca bayla garri-
da, mientras que le hurtamos la borriquilla. While
diverting attention with their agile dancing and their
shaking of a gourd, gypsy women steal swaddling clothes
for the Child and a small she-ass for Mary to ride on.

*Zagalejos amigos decid. Duo y A 5 con biolon. Villancico
de la SS^ma trinidad. The two nuns Maria de la Asunción
and Andrea del Sacramento sang tiple parts. Ysabel de la
Magdalena played bassus. Opens with duo. Copla a 3 and
Respuesta a 3 follow. Incomplete mixed-up parts.

Herrera, José María

*Missa a tres vozes. Ti Ti. Accompaniment missing. Ends
with "dona nobis pacem." This sentimental F Major Mass
looks like a Spanish importation — so beautiful is the
copy — but Tiple Primero is headed: Para el vso de las
R. R. M. M. Trinitarias.

Hidalgo, [Juan]

Ai de mi Dios mio en tanto fabor. Duo Al SS^mo. Ti Ti
Acomp^to. Duplicate copies of unfigured accompaniment,
the second headed "p.ª el arpa." Although in routine ternary meter, the estribillo and succeeding six coplas
cadence exceptionally on A chords. "Aqui entra por el sol
de sesto tono echo <u>re mi fa</u>" on one of the accompaniments
can perhaps be taken as meaning: "Come in here on the
note C, minor third above the finalis." Pasteovers and
indifferent penmanship identify this duo by "Mº Ydalgo"
as locally copied.

Benga a noticia de quantos en vno y otro confin. Tiple Solo.
This tonada is subtitled "Pregon" (i.e., proclamation).
Each of the first three lines of music serves for four
strophes (line one = strophes 1, 4, 7, 10; line two = 2, 5,
8, 11; line three = 3, 6, 9, 12). A last line at the bottom
(marked estriuillo) sets this text: "Volando veloz Leonido
de Assia en la nota de que fue, traidor, ardid, fixado el
cartel le espera." Leonidas, the Spartan king treacherous-
ly exposed with his defending troops 480 B.C. to the in-
vading Persians, challenges the traitor to a duel. Ternary music, one-flat signature, ending on B♭.

Disfrazado de Pastor. Tonada Sola. Tiple, Acompañamien-

to (richly figured thus: 543# $\frac{5}{4}$3#). Marked 8º tono
(= G Major, because of constantly specified F#'s), this
villancico contrasts the opening triple meter estribillo
with the ensuing common meter coplas (four of these).

Dulce amante del Alma. Duo Al Santissimo Sacram^{to}.
Tenor-clef part (marked "Por otabo tono bajo") is written
in baritone clef. Six coplas end on C.

Tortolilla que cantas en tu lenguage al sol. Solo Al Santissimo Sacram^{to}. Tiple plus Acomp^{to} Al Solo. Four coplas. Few runs, at most four notes to the syllable.
Dorian.

Labastaylla

*Missa nueba a 8 Boses. Tiple 1.º Barlined A minor
eighteenth-century Mass, ending with "dona nobis pacem."

Lasso, Joseph ("M.º D^{n}")

*Missa a 5. 5.º Tono. Two booklets of this C Major Mass
ending with "dona nobis pacem" survive, Tiple Solo de
1.º Coro a 5 and Acompañamiento. On Tiple 1º appears
this note: Para la fiesta de la SS^{ma} Trinidad en su com-
vento de Religiosas de esta Ciu^{d} de los Ang^{s} Compuso el
M.º D^{n} Joseph Lasso este Año de 1759.

*Missa A cinco con Vio^{s}. The two extant parts, Violin
Prim^{o} and Baxo, identify this as an F Major Mass ending
with Agnus.

+Octavo Kalendas Januari luna Anno a creatione mundi quando
in principio Deus creabit celum et terram. Kalenda de
N. S. Jesu Christo. Successive sections itemize the
chronology of the Flood, of Abraham, of Moses, of Daniel,
and of Augustus. Just as melisma diverts attention from
the tedious acrostic letters sung in Lamentations, so here
also elaborate runs relieve the ennui of such essentially
prosaic matter as the exact number of years since a
given event — 5690, and so on.

*Soberana Señora. Villancico a 4 con Violines Ala Purissima
Concepcion de Maria Santissima. Ti Ti A Te, Ac. F
Major. Violin parts missing. Neat copy.

Loaysa, José de Agurto y

*Vaya vaya de cantos de amores. Coplas start: Sol que
Belen iluminas. Villancico a 4. Ti Ti A Te, Ac.

Lopes [= López Capillas], Francisco

O admirabile commercium. Motete A 4 Con instrumentos.
Ti Ti A Te, Baxo. Tenor and Baxo (basso continuo)
duplicate one another. All voice parts marked "con instrumentos."

[Madre de Deos], fray Filipe da

*Retire su valentia señor rey de las tinieblas. Cantada a
Solo. Jacara a la Concepcion. Tiple.

Martínez, Simón ("Mº D^{n}")

Oygan escuchen. Solo al SS.^{mo} Sacramento. Estribillo
followed by seven coplas. Tiple, Acomp^{to} al Solo.
Eighth tone, though not so classified.

Mora

+* Al niño dios en las paxas. Navidad a 4. Las coplas a
Solas y en los fines le rresponden a 4. Tiple 2.º, Alto.
"Mariquita la baesa" sang alto (name on part).

+Baxaua del monte. Navidad A 4 para el año 1652. Ti Ti A,
Ac. Mora's name on all parts. This is also true of his
other complete pieces in the archive. Margarita,
Chonbita, and Manuela were the singers.

Por selebrar los maitines. Jacara a solas. Ti Ti Ti A,
Baxo (in duplicate). Four other parts respond "ay ay ay
que de amores se abraza" to solo tiple after strophes 5,
10, and 15 of this jacara a solas. After strophe 18 comes
the estribillo. This piece denounces itself as a local con-
fection. Singer's name on Tiple 1, Margarita [la baesa].
She also sang Mora's other pieces. Vocally he demanded
little in range or agility.

Muños, Blas ("D^{n}")

*Missa de Canto Mixto. Same music serves Kyries, Sanctus,
and Agnus. Also, Et incarnatus and Benedictus use
identical music. Although only one part is extant — a
figured bass accompaniment that specifies not a single
7th chord anywhere — that one part suffices to prevent the
shedding of tears for the loss of the others.

Navas, Francisco Marcos

Albrisias sagales q̄ ia no ayamos. Tiple solo, Acompañamiento. B♭ Major (one-flat signature), C$\frac{2}{3}$. Estribillo followed by coplas, August 15.

Misa a Sola compuesta sobre los Hymnos del Santisimo.
Starts with Kyrie quoting Tantum ergo (= more hispano
Pange lingua plainchant). Accompaniment disagrees with
the $\phi\, \frac{3}{2}$ of the solo voice, choosing instead 3/4 meter
(each half corresponds with a double whole note).

Ochando, Tomás de ("Mt^{ro} D^{n}")

*Miserere a quatro voces. Late eighteenth-century style.
Tiple segundo.

Ochoa, Miguel Thadeo de

*A los influjos. Cantada a Duo con violin. Año de 1744.
Strings and continuo; voice parts missing.

Bellos jilguerillos. Villancico a Duo a la SS^{ma} Trinidad.
Ti Ti; Ac.

Jam sol recedit. Unison chorus and accompaniment. Note
on latter part of this Saturday Vespers hymn: Para la
M. R. Me Mariana Josepha de Sta Barbara = Dignisima
Mra de Capilla En el combento de la SS.^{ma} Trinidad Año
de 1754. Ochoa's noble four-part style accords with the
local trend back to Latin and dignity after 1750.

O vos omnes. Motete a 4. 27 de enero Año de 1751. Ti A
Te Te, B.

Tota pulchra es Maria. Plainsong alternates with polyphony.
Ti Ti, Ac. December 8 antiphon. Date of copying parts,
1790.

Vengan vengan. Villancico a 3 a N^{ra} S^{ra}. Año de 1740. Ti
Ti Ti, Ac.

Rindanse los afectos. Ti Ti, Ac.

Vamo flacico en buen ola. Villancico A 4 boses A la Natibi-
dad De N,^{ro} S,^{r} Xp,^{to}. Ti A Te Te, Acomp.^{to} al 4°. The
highest voice in this <u>negro</u> is labeled "Tiple 2° a 4."

Olivera, Francisco de

*O vos omnes. A 5. Ti Ti A B. One of the few local words
in Tone IV.

Oviedo

+*El sacristan de Belem. Vill.^{co} a 4 De Nau.^{d} xocoso. 5.
tono. Ti Ti A Te, Ac. "Acomp^{to} al 4. Estriuillo,"
written in tenor clef, is marked "punto baxo." Notated in
F Major, this bell piece was evidently performed in E♭.
A sacristan, wishing to honor the Child, begins ringing
the church bells "desp^o y en dulce armonia." As they
toll he imitates their peal with a repeated onomatopoeic
formula. Four coplas, sung tutti, follow the estribillo.
Ternary meter throughout.

Patiño, Carlos

*Todo se abrase todo en incendio tan lindo sin que se esca-
pen. Text of opening estribillo changed by pasteover to:
Todo por altos es misterio. A 4. Tiple 1 (sung by
"esquibela") and AComp^{to} are the extant parts of this
ternary meter Blessed Sacrament villancico. The rubric
on the continuo: sentra aqui por otabo tono alto ("begin
here in high Tone VIII") means modern C Major.

Pereira, Manuel

Vengan vengan vevan en las aguas del Rio. Villancico A la
Sanctissima trinidad Año de 1691. Ti Ti A B, T A Te B.
C Major music.

Pérez, Andrés

Mas Ai que es esto. A 4 voses. Villan^{co} Del SS^{mo} Sa^{to}.
Ti A Te B. F Major, 1690 style.

Placeres Santos, Joseph María

+Ay señor q̄ por Amante. Area a duo para el Nazimiento de
N. S. Jesu Christ^{to}. Ti Ti, Ac. Recitative beginning:
El cielo se celebre Rey amante, precedes the da capo
<u>grave</u> duet. Keys of the da capo: A Major, F♯ minor.

Rabassa, Pedro

De amores desecho. Cantada a Solo a la SS^a Trinidad. C
Major. Like the next cantada, this lacks the usual pre-
liminary recitative.

Gosa Paloma hermosa. Cantada a Solo a la Concep^{on}
Purissima de nra Señora. Tiple, Ac. F Major. On
soprano part: "es de Maria Fran^{ca} de los Dolores."

*Silencio mudo. Cantada a Duo a la Santisima Trinidad.
More ambitious than his two other cantadas in the archive,
this involves four sections: Recitado-Duo-Recitado-Area
a Duo (allegro). Ends in C. Same name written on this
item as on preceding.

Riba = Riva Pas, Miguel de

Ay como llora. Ti, Ac. Estribillo a Solo.

Cisne no ataques. Villancico a 3 al SS^{mo}. A Te Te, Ac.

Geroglifico alado de pluma. Villancico A N^a S^{ra} a Duo.
Te Te, B.

+Para el pan bien. Villancico de Navidad a 4. Ti Ti A Te,
Ac.

+Pues Armado Cupido. Villan^o Al nacimiento de nro Señor.
1695. Ti Ti, Ac.

Que enigma tan bello. Ti Ti, Ac. Estribillo a Duo.

Rodrigues, Gregorio

El amor niño intenta con niñerias o rendirme o robarme el
alma y vida. Tono humano A 8. Ti Ti A Te, Ti A Te B.

Rodrigues, María Joachina ("D^a")

+ Musicos Ruyseñores. Cantata a Duo Al Nacimiento. Alto,
Tenor, Acompañ^{to} al Duo. Estribillo followed by coplas,
G minor (one-flat), C𝄵. Solecisms in musical grammar
betray this eighteenth-century female composer's im-
perfect schooling. Already in the opening phrase, she
presages the sentimental journey taken in the rest of the
villancico. At measure 4 she starts her first imitative
point.

Ruiz, Mathías

Muy poderoso señor el hombre. Solo A lo Divino. Blessed
Sacrament.

Varquerillo nuebo. Villancico A 4 Al ssantissimo. Ti Ti A
Te, Acomp^{to}. 𝄵 mensuration.

Salazar, [Antonio de]

+A el ver nazer entre pajas. Tiple Solo, Alto, AComp^{to} Al
Solo Y A Los Duos. F Major, 𝄵 , white notation, many
running scales. Copied in unusually neat hand. Alto
joins each of the four coplas midway through. Two alter-
native accompaniments provided for coplas.

A la estrella q̄ borda los valles A la aurora de cuia puresa.
Copla sola y a duo. Ti Ti AComp^{to}. Not credited to
"Antonio," but a New World informal copy.

Al ayre fragransias despidan las flores. Nativity of Our
Lady. Ti Ti A B, the last three parts taken by Cotita,
Belona, and Ynes de S^n Fran^{co}. G Major, without signa-
ture but with constant F♯'s.

+Angelicos coros con gozo cantad. A 8. Ti Ti A B, Ti A Te
B. Madre Mariana played "Baxo 2° A 8 Organo."
Ynesica Baeza took the textless tenor (doubtless instru-
mental also). Ti Ti Ti A A parts bear singers' names.
"M^o[= Maestro] Salazar" on all parts except recopied
Baxo 1. F Major, one-flat signature. Four coplas fol-
low estribillo.

*Atencion atencion del aire y del fuego se miran diferentes
los efectos. Villansico A 8 al SS^{mo}. Only three parts
extant: Ti Te B of 2° Coro. C Major, frequent F♯'s
and occasional G♯'s.

Ay ay de quanta fragrancia. A 6. Ti A Te Te B B. "Ma^{tro}
Salazar" on all parts. Me Andrea sang tenor 1°. G minor
(one-flat), C𝄵. Six coplas follow estribillo. Blessed
Sacrament, though not so specified.

Ciega la fe los sentidos. Asumpcion. A 8. Ti A Te B, Ti
    A Te B. C Major, occasional B♭'s. Both Baxo parts
    skip constantly in fourths or fifths. Tone VIII transposed
    up. Rough copy.

Digan digan quien vio tal. Ti Ti A Te Baxo 1⁰ Baxo 2⁰.
    F Major, **C 3** , Sacrament, four coplas. Baxos use
    tenor clef. Rosita esquibela and Jhoanica de Jho nasareno
    sang tiple parts.

+*Escuche lo nenglo que vamo a belen. One oblong sheet only
    headed: Tiple 1⁰. Solo, y a 6, picado el compas. M⁰
    ["Maestro"] Salazar."

+Guachi pelos alanbeque. [Negro] A 2 y a 6. Mᵉ Ynes de
    Sᵗ franᶜᵒ played the C Major bass part, notated mostly
    in blacks in the tenor clef.

Letania De Nuestra Señora De Loreto. Compuesta Por El
    Maestro Anttonio De Salazar = Maestro de Capilla De La
    Santa Yglecia Metropolitana De Mexico, dedicassele A La
    Madre Ysavel Del Ssantissimo Sacramentto, Religiossa
    En el Comvento Dela Santissima Trinidad; Deuocion de
    un afecto suyo Que le estima: &ᵃ = Año 1690. Although
    A minor music, one scribbler on Baxo 1⁰ A 6 has written:
    "por el Re de sesto tono" (G minor); to which another
    scribbler replied: "mᵉ ynes aunque se baje el tono no a
    de aber q̄ no puedo que no puedo" (Mother Agnes, even
    though the pitch is lowered, it shouldn't be that way; and
    I can't comply). Bajo 1⁰ marked for violones.

+*Nora buena vengais anton a alegrar a mi niño que llora con
    el tamborillo y la bos. A 3. Only part found: Tiple 2.
    C Major, **C 3** , high tessitura. On dorse: coplas 2, 4,
    6 (badly copied).

+*Oigan oigan la xacarilla. "Tiple 1⁰ Solo y, a 6" heads only
    surviving sheet of this G minor (one-flat), **C 3** jácara.

Oygan q̄ de un sirculo brebe miren salen luses tan claras.
    A 4. Ti A Te Baxo. Asumpcion. Salazar's name on all
    parts, but without identifying "Antonio." Rosita Esqui-
    vela and Andrea sang tenor. Dorian; five coplas follow
    estribillo, which closes with this exclamation: Ay Jesus
    que una forma lo causa lo causa.

+Tarara qui yo soy Anton ninglito. Negro a Duo, de Nauidad.
    Ti Ti, Ac.

+Vn ciego que contrauajo canta. Villanssico A Duo A la
    navidad del Sʳ. Oblong sheets marked "son 3 papeles."

Salazar, Diego Joseph de

A fuera Pompas humanas. Villancico Del Santissimo SS.⁰ A
    quatro Vozes. Ti Ti A Te, Acompᵗᵒ. Contrary to rule,
    four coplas precede the estribillo. Common meter. C
    Major is the terminal chord (no signature). However,
    written B♭'s occur so frequently as to force upon us the
    feeling of Tone VIII transposed up a fourth. Tessiture
    uniformly high. Figures occurring above the accompani-
    ment (tenor clef) include numerous 7's (7 7 76 7 765 7
    7 7).

*Ay ay q̄ me prende el amor en la carsel del fabor. Only

part extant: Tiple solo (estribillo followed by four cop-
    las). Lower half of same page contains Sebastián
    Durón's Cielo de nieue, copied in soprano clef (six
    coplas).

Santiago, fray Francisco de

+Ay como flecha la niña Rayos ermosos penachos del sol.
    Nauidad a 3. Ti Ti, Ac.

Sanz (= Zans), Francisco

A de la vaga campaña del M.⁰ fr.ᶜᵒ zans. Villancico a 3 de
    s.ʳ Joachin. Ti Ti Te, Bajo. An occasional high c².
    Duplicate Bajo copied in blind man's big notes. Although
    "a 3" on the cover, the respuesta to the coplas is headed
    "a 4." Coplas specify chromaticisms.

Soberanis

*Missa a 3. Alto.

Torres Martínez Bravo, José de

+A contarte vengo Gila. Villancico de Navidad a Duo. Ti Ti, Ac.
    Luz de las luces.   Tonada de Nʳᵃ Sʳᵃ de la Concep-
    cion. Printed Madrid copy.

Matizadas flores. A 4 con acompañamiento. Printed Madrid
    copy.

Libro que contiene onze partidos del Mᵒᴰⁿ Joseph de Torres.

Folio 1, Fuga (in D); 2, Obra de mano derecha de
    medio Registro de torres; 3, Grave (**C 3** , voids); 4,
    Obra de lleno de 7⁰ tono (= A minor); 4ᵛ-6, Obra de 7⁰
    tono; 6ᵛ-7ᵛ, Obra de 1⁰ tono Baxo (D minor, no flat in
    signature, many fast runs); 8-9, Partido de 1⁰ Alto
    (meter changes to 3/4 at 8ᵛ); 9ᵛ, otra de torres (dorian,
    downward arpeggios distinguish left hand part).

*Missa a 4. Ac only.

Vaeza, Juan de

A del coro seleste esuchad yo que primero canto y selebre
    el nasimiento mañana del sol. Billansico de Calenda Para
    la mᵉ M.ᵃ de la asumsion. Año de 1671. Ti Ti A B, Ti
    Ti A B. Duplicate baxo parts for 1⁰ Coro, one marked
    "biolon." Baxo 2⁰ Coro marked "Para el organo."
    Performers' names: Rosa Peres, Tomasita, Belona,
    mᵉ Ynes de Santa Theresa, Marequita La baesa ("biolon"
    part).

+*A la tierra se biene mi sol en cuerpo. Tiple Solo y a Duo.
    One extant part only.

+Ay Jesus que se mira dios en el frio. Villancico de Nauidad
    a Duo y a 4 y a 6 Año de 1668. Tiple Solo, Ti Ti A, Baxo
    1 & 2. Although notated as F Major a jotting on the alto
    part says: Por el fa de sesto tono (= B♭).

Con suauidad de boses y dulse canto. Chansoneta A 4 a la
    profesion de Theresica la chiquita. fecit Vaeza Año de
    1667. Ti Ti A Baxo. Estribillo (before pasteovers)
    started: Cuerdamente te acoxes oy a sagrado para tener
    Thereça dulce descanso. Coplas continue: Apenas
    nuestra Thereça diuiso sus quinse años quando con todo
    su alma dio su cuerpo en el claustro. C Major music.

+*Desnudo vn ynfante eterno. Romanse a 4. Ti A Baxo.
   Dorian (no flat).

Dezid alma que quereis. Billansico a duo y a 4 dela Consep-
   sion. 1669.

+En aquel pesebre. Romanze a 4 de nabidad de tres tiples de
   don Ju^o de Vaeza Saabedra del año de 1662. Ti Ti Ti Te.
   Six strophes. F Major. C?.

+Mercader q̄ en vn banco. SS^{mo} y S^n Matheo. Año de 1670.
   Ti Ti Baxo para bajon. Parte ligero. Ti Solo, Ti Ti A,
   B B. C Major. Christmas.

+Pastores velen se abraça todo son luces en el sin duda quel
   sol sesconde. R^{ce} [romance] A 4. Ti Ti A Baxo.
   Seven strophes precede estribillo. On cover: Para la m^e
   Cattalina de s.^{a} Margarita maestra de capi^a del Convento
   de la SSma trinidad año de 1667 fecit Vaeza.   G minor
   (one-flat).

+Por selebrar. Negriya a 3 y a duo en dialogo. Ti Ti B.
   Año de 1669.

Venid sagales a mirar con ese eselensia. A 4. Ti Ti A
   Baxo. Called "Romance" in alto part. Seven strophes
   precede estribillo. F Major.

Valmaña, Joseph

+En los braços de la aurora esta el sol de niño bello. Ti Ti
   A B, Ti Ti A B. "Tiple 2 Segundo Coro" changes to Tenor
   for the Responsion A 8 following coplas. Christmas vi-·
   llancico. C Major.

Vega y Torizes, ("M^{ro}")

Risueñas fuentes saltan paxarillos. Duo A el Arc^{gel} San
   Miguel y a ñra Señ^a. Frequenting high b^1♭, this D minor
   (no signature) piece abounds in Farinelli fiorituri.

Vidales, [Francisco de]

A la ensaladilla. A 4. Ti Ti A B. Three estribillos, first
   starting: Entremos zagales a ver la fiesta; second commencing: Yo quiero entrar; third: Muela el molino.
   After first and second estribillos come coplas, but not
   after third estribillo. Names of convent singers on parts.

*Al ayre que se llena de luces y claridades. A 8. Only three
   parts found: Ti 1, A 2, Te 2.

Con q̄ gala en el campo naçe la rrosa. Natiuidad de la Virgen.
   A 4. Ti Ti A Te (no bass). F Major.

Disfrasada deidad q̄ Dios de amor te veo. "Villansico a S.
   Matheo Año de 1673" on cover, but "Romance A 3" heads
   music inside. Ti A Te. G minor (one-flat), C?.
   Six strophes, homophonically set.

+Los que fueren de buen gusto. Xacara. Navidad. Ti Ti A
   B = Ac.

*Miren miren el prado que se retoca porque viene Septiembre
   con vna rosa. A 3. Tiple, Alto. Accompaniment missing. By pasteovers, someone has tried adapting the music
   to a new text honoring some other saint.

Ora es menester que flota en el puerto este amarrada. A 4.
   Ti Ti A B. Starts with introduction a 3 followed by six

coplas.

Toquen a maytines que nace el alba con mantillas de niebe
   fajas de grana toquen repiquen. A 8. Ti Ti A "Baxo 1.º
   Coro A duo y a 8," Ti A Te "Baxo 2.º A 8." G Minor
   (one-flat).

Villegas, José

Benedicamus Patrem. Responsorio septimo a 3. Ti Ti Ti,
   Ac.

Ximenes [perhaps the same as Ximénez de Cisneros]

*Missa Assumpta est Maria a 6. Año de 1755. Ti2 A Te Te
   B2. Missing: Til, Bl, Ac.

Ximénez de Cisneros, Nicolás

*Missa a Duo. Año de 1743. Tiple 2.

*Sacratisima Virgen. Villancico a Solo a la Natividad de
   Maria Santisima.

Ximeno, Fabián

Missa sobre el Beatus vir. Por el M.^{o} fauiam Ximeno.
   A 11. This is a Phrygian Mass ending with Sanctus-Osan-
   na. To Tiple 1, the sole surviving part, he assigned
   numerous melismas.

+Ay ay galeguiños a 5. Tiple Solo. Ti Ti Te B, Acompañamiento de gallego. F Major. Common meter. Copied
   exceptionally on long sheets.

Xuares, Alonso

+Venid zagales vereis a un Dios niño. Villancico Al nacimiento. Ti Ti A Te, Ac. Irregularly placed barlines.
   Ac marked "Mariana en el violon." Andrea and Maria
   dela Asuncion sang Tiples 1 and 2.

Some seventeen composers in the above alphabetized list can
be associated in one way or another with Puebla — Atienza,
Dallo y Lana, Juan García, Gutiérrez de Padilla, Lasso (=
Lazo; manuscript works by this eighteenth-century Puebla
Cathedral maestro have reached the Newberry Library,
Chicago), López Capillas, Martínez, Ochoa, Olivera,
Pereira, Riba (= Riva Pas), Rodrigues, Antonio de Salazar
Vaeza, Vidales, Ximénez de Cisneros, and Ximeno. However, because of the constant interchange between cathedrals,
three of these same composers belong more to the annals of
music at the capital — chapelmasters López Capillas, Salazar,
and Ximeno. Atienza, named Puebla cathedral maestro de
capilla in 1712, substituted for Salazar at Mexico City in 1703
and 1710; Olivera was received as a contrabajo in Mexico
City Cathedral April 29, 1614, with 200 pesos annual salary;
and Vidales (Ximeno's nephew) continued serving as second
Mexico Cathedral organist for at least a year after the death
of his uncle in April of 1654. Throughout the Baroque,
Puebla's musical ambience so closely reflected the musical
environment in the capital that the two largest cities in viceregal times must always be studied conjointly.

Although the music for villancicos composed by maestros
appointed before 1700 at Mexico City survives in smaller

quantity than for maestros at Puebla,[3] the many collections of villancico-texts published at Mexico City before 1700 (already signaled in the preceding chapter) prove that composition in this genre was no less important a part of the maestro's duties at Mexico City than at Puebla. Robert Stevenson's Music in Mexico: A Historical Survey (New York: Thomas Y. Crowell, 1952), pages 144-147, includes the music of two villancicos by Antonio de Salazar[4] appointed there in 1688, together with an aperçu of "The Villancico in New Spain." This summary remains still too easily available to require repetition here. Five villancicos in the present volume were composed by Fabián [Pérez] Ximeno (whose Mexico cathedral connections can be documented as early as 1623), José de Loaysa y Agurto (already a Mexico City singer in 1647), Salazar (maestro de capilla there from 1688 to 1715), and Vidales (second organist there in 1655).

The following brief sampling of the references to villancicos and to chanzonetas[5] (translatable as "little [vernacular] songs") in Mexico City Cathedral capitular acts, 1538 to 1756, should therefore serve the very useful purpose of placing in historical context several of the Christmas pieces included in this present volume. Interestingly, the catena begins with the earliest known New World reference to Christmas caroling. Because of his historical importance, a lengthy footnote identifies the conductor.

November 15, 1538   Canon Juan Xuárez[6] shall be paid for training and costuming the cathedral boy choristers who sing chanzonetas Christmas Eve and Day ("chançonetas dela pascua y noche santa de nauidad").

January 11, 1541   As on former occasions, the chantre[7] shall distribute 20 pesos de minas among the cathedral musicians for their special labors in preparing and performing the Christmas and Epiphany chanzonetas.

January 15, 1567   All cathedral singers must rehearse Christmas and Corpus Christi special music to the chapelmaster Lázaro del Álamo's satisfaction. Those negligent of their practice duties shall be fined.[9]

March 26, 1591   The prebendary [and maestro] Juan Hernández shall be paid two years' arrears for music paper and copying costs of the chanzonetas composed by him, 20 pesos de tepuzque for each year.[10]

November 12, 1591   At Hernández's insistence, the cathedral chapter agrees henceforth to allow him sufficient free time each year to search out good poetry to be sung each Christmas and Corpus Christi and to compose the music (eighty free days total for the music, both celebrations).[11]

May 28, 1610   Since Archbishop García Guerra [ruled Mexico see 1608-1612][12] considers excellent music absolutely vital before vespers every day of the Corpus Christi octave in order to draw crowds, he stipulates that there shall be many singers and instrumentalists present in the cathedral to sing and play villancicos and chanzonetas.[13]

February 1, 1619   Antonio Rodríguez de Mat[t]a[14] requests more than an annual 20 pesos for music paper and copying costs of his villancicos sung in this cathedral. He is granted 30 on condition that he provide free copies for the cathedral archive.[15]   On February 20 the chapter retroactively grants an additional 10 for 1618 (bringing the total to 30 for that year also).[16]

August 1, 1636   Luis de Cifuentes, now doctoral canon but a music enthusiast since choirboy days in the same cathedral,[17] decides after communicating with a like-minded prebendary named Antonio de Esquivel Castañeda, that henceforth Mexico City Cathedral shall annually budget 300 pesos for polyphonic rendition of the June 29 Mass and matins and for "villancicos and chanzonetas [performed] with the greatest possible impressiveness."[18]

December 9, 1639   Melchor de los Reyes,[19] gets permission for all the cathedral musicians, singers and ministriles, to start practicing the Christmas season villancicos and romances.[20]

December 16, 1664   The dean complains that this year's Christmas music promises to be scandalously poor. Thus far only four or five [instrumental] musicians have shown any signs of participating.   López Capillas has refused to compose the customary villancicos, even pretending that the yearly composition of new villancicos falls outside his official duties. The chapter sends him word that for eighty years [since Franco's time] composing new villancicos has indeed been a part of the maestro's regular duties. More singers as well as instrumentalists must start showing up. They have grown lax and shall be threatened with fines if they fail to brush up their lackluster Saturday Salves.[21]

January 18, 1754   Ignacio Jerusalém, a native of Lecce in the heel of Italy contracted as a theater composer for Mexico City in 1742, appointed interim cathedral chapelmaster in 1749[22] and titular maestro de capilla August 3, 1750, "must attend strictly to his cathedral choirschool duties and seek by painstaking means the boys' progress; he must allow sufficient time to practice [new] villancicos and must perform the Bugle Mass; to comply with all these demands he must move next to the cathedral because living next to St. Catherine Martyr he wastes more than half the day coming and going; he shall take charge of the cathedral loose sheet music archive which, after being delivered him under proper warranty, shall be securely guarded in a cabinet of a locked room; the endowed villancicos which it is his duty to compose for various anniversaries shall likewise be guarded in the same way."[23]

August 27, 1754   One of Jerusalém's sons being about to profess himself a Carmelite friar at nearby Puebla, Jerusalém asks a cash gift or salary advance to cover costs. "Having heard his request, discussed it, and agreed that

Jerusalém had indeed been promised a cash gift for the [Holy Week] Miserere and some new villancicos that he had composed for Assumption matins, the chapter next heard [Canon] Ximénez's proposal that the gift, to be sufficiently sizable, should be delayed until Jerusalém finishes a very special new Mass which he is just then composing in Nebra's style and which the archbishop expects to see finished before the year is out." [24]

December 23, 1756 In the future, the chantre shall search for a better poet to write the Christmas villancicos than the new 33-year contraalto (native of Segorbe) [25] recently brought over from Spain, Francisco Selma, who shall however be this one time paid 25 pesos for his villancico verses set this Christmas by Jerusalém. [26]

Despite the cathedral chapter's discontent with Selma's 1756 Christmas verse, either he [27] or some other musical expert wrote the poetry for the one Jerusalém [28] villancico thus far printed — A la milagrosa escuela de Pedro ("At [St.] Peter's miraculous school") for June 29, 1765 [28] published at pages 119-156 of Lincoln B. Spiess and E. Thomas Stanford's An Introduction to Certain Mexican Musical Archives (1969 [1970]). [29] Obviously, the two authors feel this particular villancico to be a work of great significance. A partial facsimile of the first violin part adorns the front cover of the monograph. Further facsimiles of individual parts turn up at pages 179-185. Nonetheless, the utterly charming music transgresses so many norms of indigenous Spanish and Mexican villancico composition 1600-1700, and is so patently mid-eighteenth-century Italian music, as to cast but weak light on prior native villancico traditions. [30]

NOTES

1. Program notes by Robert Stevenson at pp. 29-30 of the Thirty-Third Annual Carmel Bach Festival booklet; review by Heuwell Tircuit in the San Francisco Chronicle, Friday, July 24, 1970, p. 42.

2. Transcribed into modern notation by Jesús Bal y Gay with Rafael Mitjana's introductory notes and a prefatory study of "El Villancico Polifónico" by Isabel Pope [Conant], the Cancionero de Upsala (Mexico City: El Colegio de México, 1944) contains 54 villancicos first published in Villancicos De diuersos Autores, a dos, y a tres, y a qvatro, y a cinco bozes (Venice: Girolamo Scotto, 1556).

3. A few loose-sheet pieces in the Mexico City Cathedral archive antedating 1740 were cited in Fontes, 1955/1, pp. 10-11 (notes). Lincoln Spiess and E. Thomas Stanford, An Introduction to Certain Mexican Musical Archives (Detroit: Information Coordinators, 1969 [1970]), p. 69, limited the vernacular works still extant in Mexico City Cathedral to those found in only one legajo, but signaled Puebla Cathedral as still boasting five legajos of villancicos.

4. Belonging to the private collection of the distinguished Dr. Gabriel Saldívar Silva (Calle Diez 27, San Pedro de los Pinos, México 18, D. F.), these two villancicos, Oigan oigan un vejamen and Guarda guarda la fiera (also Manuel Zumaya's villancico a 8, Como es príncipe), first found their way into print in his indispensable Historia de la Música en México: Epocas precortesiana y colonial (Mexico City: Editorial "Cultura," 1934), pp. 109-108 (sic), 110-111.

5. Pedro Cerone, El Melopeo y Maestro (Naples: J. B. Gargano and L. Nucci, 1613), pp. 692-693, likened chanzonetas to frottole and strambotti in being set syllabically and in being "skippy" melodically. Since chanzonetas go always at fast gait, simple chordal accompaniments without suspensions best befit them. Only three singers harmonizing in open rather than close position should be enough. A deep bass beneath two sopranos, or a bass below soprano and contralto give the right timbre. Final cadences should omit the third. Their prettiest effect depends on singing them from memory, the change of text from copla to copla then always causing greatest delight.

6. Juan Xuárez (fl. 1535-1561) is listed as Mexico City Cathedral canon in the minutes of the first chapter meeting March 1, 1536, and remained continuously active as such until at least the meeting of February 14, 1561. Xuárez = Juárez had already made his mark as a musician before the first viceroy, Antonio de Mendoza, made an official entry November 14, 1535. On Wednesday August 25, 1535, the secular cabildo had "decided that to receive the viceroy properly, there should be singers and accompanying [instrumental] music; therefore sixty gold pesos shall be paid them through Canon Xuárez, who is in charge of the chanzonetas, their accompaniment, and the playlet (Terzer libro de las Actas de Cabildo del Ayuntamiento de la gran cibdad de Tenuxtitlan Mexico [October 7, 1532-December 24, 1535], transcribed by Manuel Orozco y Berra, 1859, p. 123: "Este dia dixeron que por quanto para el rescibimiento del señor bisorrey conbiene que haga cantores e musica, por ende mandaron e señalaron que se de a los dichos cantores sesenta pesos de oro de lo que corre, porque saquen sus chanzonetas e musica e ynbencion, los quales se han de dar al canonigo Xuarez . . .").
The cathedral capitular acts (Libro Primero, fols. 4^V, 10^V, 30) document Xuárez's musical activities through 1540. On February 4, 1539, the chapter appointed him maestro de capilla retroactively to February 1, allotting him an annual salary of 60 pesos de minas for that occupation. In April of 1540 the chapter decided that one-third of the absentee dean's income should be used to pay the salary due Xuárez for being chapelmaster. As a model for his musical activities the chapter asked him to look to Seville. To verify Sevillian usages, the chapter wrote a singer at Seville named Peña who was veintenero there (one of "twenty" clergy paid extra from a fund established in 1493 to sing matins in Seville cathedral).
Xuárez's choir members included Francisco Hernández and Bartolomé de Estrada, each paid 20 pesos de minas annually (Libro Primero, fol. 9), Felipe Espinosa hired at 30 on April 22, 1539, with the obligation of singing both polyphony and plainsong (fol. 15), and Juan de Morales engaged at 60 later that same year (fol. 23). A drop in tithes periled the salaries of polyphonic singers April 16, 1540 (fol. 29^V). Still a canon in 1560, Xuárez signed himself "Doctor" on March 9 of that year (Francisco del Paso y Troncoso, Epistolario de Nueva España, IX [1940], p. 50).

7. In all bulls of erection, the New World cathedral chantre was the canon to whom was entrusted general oversight of the cathedral music. He was himself seldom a practicing musician, but to him was usually delegated final authority on all administrative and financial details relating to the cathedral music.

8. Libro Primero, fol. 35: "xx pesos de oro de minas por el trabajo delas chançonetas y cantos de esta Pascua de nauidad y Reyes."

9. Ibid., fol. 208: "todos los cantores vayan a probeer las nauidades o corpus christi con el maeso de capilla donde se ubiese de prober sopena q̄ el que asi no lo hiziese sea

puntado. "

10. Actas Capitulares, IV (1588-1605), fol. 46: "que se paguen al R⁰ [racionero] Ju⁰ Her^Z dos años de salario de puntar las chançonetas xx pesos de tepuzque cada año."

11. Ibid., fol. 62^V: "para buscar letras y componer la musica de Navidad y Corpus Christi."

12. Concerning this prelate's services to Mexico City Cathedral music see Robert Stevenson, "La música en la Catedral de México: 1600-1750," Revista Musical Chilena, XIX/92 (April-June 1965), 12-17 (especially 14).

13. Actas Capitulares, V (1606-1616), fol. 189^V. The archbishop "propuso de quanta ymportancia era para la devocion y frequencia del puebla Xpiano ultra del solemnidad referida para las horas canonicas que en las extraordinarias despues de medio dia antes de entrar en visperas vbiese mucho concurso de cantores e ynstrumentos que tañesen y cantasen los villansicos y chançonetas que pudiessen = y ansimesmo acabadas las visperas hasta entrar en maytines."

14. Stevenson, "La música en la Catedral de Mexico," pp. 17-18. He lasted from 1614 to his death in 1643, but during the first eleven years "shared" the title of maestro with the valetudinarian Juan Hernández.

15. Actas Capitulares (A.C.), VI (1617-1620), fol. 85.

16. Ibid., fol. 90^V.

17. A.C., V (1606-1616), fol. 436^V. On August 5, 1616, the cathedral chapter raised his salary. He was then tiple.

18. A.C., IX (1633-1639), fol. 167: "maytines y missa con canto de organo billancicos y chançonetas y con la mayor solemnidad que ser pueda."

19. In 1647 he was "Sustituto de M⁰" (deputy maestro de capilla), a post that he had probably been holding for a decade. See Isabel Pope, "Documentos Relacionados con la Historia de la Música en México," Nuestra Música, VI/21 (1er Trimestre, 1951), 23. On May 14, 1632, he stood fourth in the list of cathedral singers (A.C., VIII, fol. 374^V).

20. A.C., IX, fol. 405^V.

21. A.C., XVI (1664-1667), fol. 122^V. So far as music quality was concerned, the dean "nunca lo hauia reconocido tan indecente por no hauer concurrido mas que quatro o cinco Muzicos . . . que hauiendo llamado al Maestro de Capilla [Francisco López Capillas] para sauer por que se hauian escusado los Villancicos y demas solemnidad q̄ se acostumbra, Respondio no ser de su cargo, Cossa que le hiço mucha nouedad a Su Señoria y assi hacia esta propuesta . . . = Determinose se notifique al Maestro de Capilla acuda segun ha sido costumbre de ochenta años a este partte a Componer los Villancicos, segun que le toca por su obligacion, y de no hacerlo assi se proueer el remedio que combenga. . . ."

22. Stevenson, "La música en la Catedral de Mexico," p. 31.

23. A.C., XLII (3 Agosto 1753 á 3 Agosto 1756), fol. 63: "y que al Maestro de Capilla, se le notifique, que asista con puntualidad y exactitud a la escoleta, solicitando con el maior esmero el aprouechamiento delos Niños, repasandoles con tiempo los Villancicos; que haga la Missa de clarines; y que para todo esto se le mande que viua immediato a esta santa Iglesia, por Viuir aora adelante de Santa Chatarina Martir, y perder lo mas del dia en ir, y venir a su Casa; que se le haga Cargo de los Papeles de Musica que estaban en el Archiuo de esta santa Iglesia, solicitandosse el que los entriegue y que para su correspondiente seguro, se pongan y guarden en vn estante en la Chaueria; y que los Villancicos que tiene Obligacion de hazer, para varios Aniuersarios, y en los que para esso tiene asignacion, que tambien los entriegue y se

guarden. . . ."

24. Ibid., fol. 108^V: "Que hauiendosse oido, y tratadosse de materia, y expressadosse, que era cierto el que al Suplicante se le hauia ofrecido alguna gratificacion quando hizo, el Miserere, y para quando hiciesse algunos Villancicos nuebos, lo que hauia hecho para los Maitines de la Assumpcion, y dicho el Señor Ximenez, que dha gratificacion, para que fuesse de mas consideracion, se podia guardar para quando el dho Hyerusalem acauasse de hazer vna missa nueua que estaba trabajando con mucha especialidad, al modo de la de Nebra, y que su señoria assegurava que la acauaria en todo este año. . . ."

25. A.C., XLII, fol. 116^V (September 26, 1754). He could reach high C and had been a chief court singer at Madrid.

26. A.C., XLIII (1756-1759), fol. 57.

27. Apart from Jerusalém himself, Selma remained the highest paid member of the cathedral capilla in 1768, in which year both received 600 pesos. See A.C., XLIX (1768-1769), fol. 147^V (October 1, 1768).

28. Jerusalém died in late December of 1769. See A.C., L (1769-1770), fols. 126^V-127. Here appears the act of January 10, 1770; if not at the close of 1769, he died before this date, on which the chapter argued lengthily whether to issue edictos (notice of a competition to fill his place left vacant by death).

29. See footnote 3 to this chapter. At page 120 of the transcription, third note in continuo is a third too high and first three bars of alto voice part are transcribed a step too low; at 123, text beneath measures 3 and 4 of tiple should read "sol, sol"; 142, measure 4 of alto part should be transcribed a whole step higher; several other minor matters require attention.

30. If transcribed correctly, Jerusalém's music for the copla (measures 155-235) does not repeat. Also, the copla begins in a different key from that in which both it and the estribillo end. Jerusalém's estribillo text contains an internal refrain, but his estribillo music is throughcomposed. A series of five imitative points precede the three bars in 3/2 (p. 129 [measures 65-67]); another five follow. The three 3/2 bars are the "heart piece" of a large chiastic structure.

Performance Practice Problems
Posed by the Seventeenth-Century Villancico Repertory

No present-day continuo player need be told the chords suitable for Jerusalém's just-discussed 1765 villancico A la milagrosa escuela de Pedro. Despite being unfigured,[1] the continuo constantly joins company with paired violins, the figuration of which, plus the vocal movements, never leaves the slightest room for doubt. For instance, the player must choose inverted seventh chords at measures 36, 48, 52, 61-64, 79^3, 80^2, 84^3, 112^1, 119-120, and 124, to go no further than the so-called "estribillo." Even if only voice-parts survived, any continuo player would still know the progress of the harmony. This is so because Jerusalém — himself an Italian of the Italians — makes only those harmonic gestures already thrice familiar to any connoisseur of the late Italian Baroque.

But how different and more perplexing the situation, as it relates to the distinctively Peninsular seventeenth-century villancico repertory, comes to light in discussion of even carefully preserved collections, such as the late seventeenth-century Spanish Codices 133/199 now at the Munich Staatsbibliothek. As J. J. Maier's 1879 catalogue of the Munich musical manuscripts correctly states, ten codices in this group still include individual parts for instruments other than harp and organ. Codices 134-136, 149-150, 153, 169, 174, 185, and 193 = Music Mss. 2873-2875, 2889, 2891, 2894, 2906, 2912, 2923, and 2932 of this lengthy set include, for instance, extant parts for clarín (2874-2875, 2906, 2923), violín (2873, 2923), violón = bass viol (2873, 2891, 2894, 2889), corneta = cornett (2912), bajoncillo = soprano bassoon (2891, 2932), and bajón = bassoon (2932). All lost, however, are the 103 villancicos that included parts for noncontinuo instruments (the usual number of instruments in a villancico is specified as not less than three) catalogued in the Primeira Parte do Index da Livraria de Mvsica do Mvyto Alto, e Poderoso Rey Dom Ioão o IV (Lisbon: Paulo Craesbeek, 1649). Because noncontinuo instruments and the running lines to be played by them raise problems even more severe than those posed by the mostly unfigured, single-line seventeenth-century continuo parts, our wisest course here is first to assemble a body of opinion on how the continuo parts should be realized — leaving for later discussion in this chapter the role of noncontinuo instruments.

Albert Geiger's remarks on continuo accompaniments come at pages 486-488 of his essay "Die spanishchen Ccs. 133/199 der Muenchner Staatsbibliothek," Zeitschrift für Musikwissenschaft, V/9-10 (June-July, 1923). Somewhat abbreviated and paraphrased, his comments read thus:

> The accompanying instrumental bass parts for villancicos in our Spanish codices are headed acompañamiento, guion general, or ac[to] continuo. In polychoral works, each coro is provided with its own continuo. As a rule any given continuo part consists of an unfigured line that merely duplicates the lowest sounding voice of its coro (tenor for coro 1, bass for coro 2). Since during tutti passages the tenor of coro 1 and bass of coro 2 tend to move in parallel octaves (or unisons), the continuos accompanying the several coros in a tutti turn out to be identical or nearly so.[2] The continuo part for vocal solos usually looks like just another voice part.[3] In such examples as fray Dionisio Romero's solo villancico honoring Our Lady, Mas valeis vos señora (Codex 172), and Mathías Ruiz's solo Lady villancico Atencion al candor (Codex 179) the continuo makes an imitative point with the vocal solo part. Any bass idiomatically conceived for a particular instrument cannot be found until well into the eighteenth century, when the continuo for the "Musica del Bayle con violines" included in the printed score of Joaquín Martínez de la Roca's Los Desagravios de Troya (Madrid: En la Imprenta de Música, 1712) does contain some fleet runs and skips suitable more for a gamba than a vocal bass.[4] But again let it be said that this type of instrumentally conceived continuo is a stranger to the Spanish seventeenth-century Codices 133/199 at the Munich Staatsbibliothek.

> Although figured basses are to be found in villancicos for five or more voices at Munich, pieces for four or less voices usually lack any numerals whatsoever.[5] When used, numerals go above the continuo to tell which consonance or dissonance to play. Intervals higher than ninths are not specified. Should the harmony require accidentalizing, the numerals are then prefixed or followed by the appropriate sharps or flats (flats serve as naturals in sharp-signature pieces). If, as often happens, a sharp or a flat appears alone without any numeral, it serves to specify a major or minor chord. To confirm our assertion that in seventeenth-century Spain the figuring of basses never be-

Musical de Olot," Anuario Musical, XVIII (1963), at page 58 of which he writes thus: "The music of those cancioneros[30] always included accompaniments; but the accompaniments were as a rule written in separate books kept by the accompanist or the chapelmaster and have gone astray, perhaps never more to be found."

Complete "fidelity" to the written notes, and nought else, betrays Lope de Vega's Mañanicas floridas = Soberana María. Such "fidelity" betrays no less surely Juan Hidalgo's mere written notes for the last chorus (Quedito pasito) in Pedro Calderón de la Barca's Ni Amor se libra de amor ("Not even Cupid can free himself from love"). Felipe Pedrell published the four voice parts with the unfigured single-line continuo part in Cancionero Musical Popular Español (Valls: Eduardo Castells, 1922), IV, 22-28.[31] In Calderón's play, Psyche summons offstage musicians to lull Cupid asleep. This they do with the just-mentioned lullaby "Softly, be still, my lord is sleeping." John Reeves White conducted the New York Pro Musica recording of this excerpt (band six of side one) in the album Music of the Spanish Theater in the Golden Age (Decca 79436). The harmony of four voices somewhat atones for the unrealized continuo throughout this one short excerpt. But any accompaniment for a full opera such as Hidalgo's setting of the Calderón libretto Celos aun del aire matan (premiered December 5, 1660)[32] that wore no more clothing than a fig leaf unfigured bass[33] would flout every known decency statute of the period. Kastner made this exact point when he wrote the Juan Hidalgo article for Die Musik in Geschichte und Gegenwart, VI (1957), columns 374-375.

> The surviving source material for [his] music includes only voice parts and the unfigured instrumental bass. It is therefore clearly impossible to paint anything like an even approximate picture of Hidalgo's accompaniment and his handling of the orchestra.[34] The tremendous difficulty of any plausible reconstruction militates against early Spanish opera revivals. Nonetheless, the orchestral components of the Royal Chapel involved in addition to strings and woodwinds also harps (at least four!), harpsichord, guitar, and drums, thus implying not only a full-bodied but also a very colorful accompaniment. It would certainly be a praiseworthy task to try reconstructing his style on the basis of some smaller extant fragments,[35] and on their foundation to try restoring the orchestral score of Celos aun del aire matan.

Nor was Hidalgo's stage music uniquely unfortunate, in so far as loss of instrumental parts is concerned. A turn of the century manuscript twice described by Subirá (see note 31 below at p. 32) reaches 370 numbered pages of theater music. But as Subirá himself summed up the situation: "Except for the continuo, instrumental parts of any kind fail to appear anywhere in this bulky album (three items call for violins [pp. 238, 262, and 314 of the manuscript])."[36] Plays by Calderón that specifically mention stage instruments account for the verse set in items 14, 15, 17, 19, 20, 21, 28, 29, 30, 33, 34, 40, 42, 44, 50, and 54 of this particular manuscript.

When noncontinuo instrumental parts for even the costliest court spectacles fail to survive (the individual instrumental parts belonged to the player, the vocal parts and director's continuo guide to the management), small wonder that cathedral and convent archives still retain instrumental parts in but rare instances. The minute inventory of manuscript music at the Las Palmas Cathedral, Gran Canaria, published 1964-1965 by Lola de la Torre de Trujillo,[37] registers among numerous surviving works by Diego Durón,[38] maestro de capilla there 1676-1731, the following 23 Christmas villancicos, each with separate parts for noncontinuo instruments (only such instruments are here extracted; see her catalogue for voice parts, violón, continuo[39]).

> Criaturas que devéis todo el ser, C/I-13, dated 1679, "instruments" (which ones are not specified)
> A de este portal, C/I-23, 1681, "instruments," flutes
> Del amor que nace, C/II-1, 1682, flutes (and harp)
> Al arma, C/II-4, 1682, shawms (and harp)
> Silencio, C/II-10, 1685, flutes (and harp)
> Al arma, C/II-13, 1686, shawms, sacabuche [sackbut]
> Oygan atiendan, C/III-3, 1689, "instruments" (and harp)
> Ya rompen sus velos, C/III-6, 1690, shawms, sackbuts (and harp)
> Dorado bajel del sol, C/III-9, 1691, shawm and sackbut
> Contra la noche, C/III-15, 1692, shawms and sackbuts
> Navidad, B/IV-3, 1692; set of three chirimías [shawms], soprano, alto, tenor
> Deliciosas auras, C/III-19, 1694, shawms
> Qué sacra eterna palabra, C/IV-1, 1700, shawms and sackbut
> Al monte, C/IV-10, 1702, shawms
> Alegre Gileta, C/IV-12, 1702, cornetas [cornetts]
> Del común horror, C/IV-14, 1703, shawms (and harp)
> Oir parar, C/V-4, 1705, "instruments" (and harp)
> Altas montañas, C/V-14, 1713, "instruments" (and harp)
> Teme asustada, C/V-19, 1716, shawms (plus bass viol and harp)
> Ha de esa voz luciente, C/V-21, 1717, shawms (plus bass viol and harp)
> Con nueva armonía, C/VI-2, 1721, shawms (and harp)
> Qué tempestad amenaza, C/VI-16, 1729, shawms, sackbut (plus bass viol and harp)
> Abramos las puertas, C/VI-24, undated, shawms

Just because there do survive in an undisturbed Spanish island outpost the instrumental parts of these particular Christmas villancicos by an otherwise rather obscure Spanish composer of the period (certainly he was "obscure" in comparison with his half-brother Sebastián discussed on pp. 39-44 in this volume), or for some other reason, the eighth villancico in the above list enjoyed the distinction of being the first Spanish Baroque villancico recorded (January 1967) by Deutsche Grammophon Gesellschaft in their influential Archiv Produktion series (Meister der Barock, "Hispaniae Musica," 198 453 Stereo). The well-known authority Lothar Siemens Hernández supervised the musicological aspect and wrote the jacket notes, which describe at some length the proper setting for a seventeenth-century villancico performance.

His prescient analysis deserves extracting:

During the seventeenth century, the Latin motets and psalms sung in Spanish cathedrals by professional choirs of singers and instrumentalists were designed to invest the divine office with greater solemnity on specified days of the church year. The resulting office was indeed magnificent, but the common folk's participation could be no more than that of bystanders. On the other hand, the Baroque church carol (villancico), with its text in the vernacular, was the one part of the solemn office with a distinctly popular tinge.

At Christmas, Easter, and Corpus Christi, the public flocked to the great churches as on no other days of the year to hear these carols — which were doubtless livelier and worldlier than the Latin music. They also went to see them, for not infrequently the carols were sung and performed with some degree of stage art by the choirboys. The walls of the churches were decked with sumptuous hangings, and the floor was covered with sweet-smelling leaves or pine branches on which the public could sit.

Cristóbal Pérez Pastor in La Imprenta en Toledo (Madrid: Manuel Tello, 1887) registered 121 sets of Christmas villancicos published in Toledo alone between 1662 and 1820 and at page 294a called attention to a custom that prevailed during all these years. Before the performances began, the choirboys richly attired and with silver salvers in their hands, passed out to the assembled crowd printed texts of the carols to be sung at the hours of nocturns, so that the public could follow the music and better appreciate the details of the often involved poetic texts. At times, these printed libretti for the villancico-cycles were even dropped from the dome in some churches, along with flower petals and colored paper birds.

The carol Ya rompen sus velos was composed by Diego Durón (ca. 1658-1731) for Christmas, 1690. It is for two choirs and general accompaniment; the first choir is for voices and the second for wind instruments — chirimías and sacabuches. The instrumental choir aloft represents heavenly music, while the voice choir does the same for human. In the carol Ya rompen sus velos the heavens open and the angels join with men to sing of the birth of God here on earth.

In his soulful Adiuva nos for Good Friday, [40] two oboes, a soprano bassoon, [bajoncillo], a violin, and harp (continuo) support the contralto soloist. This is Durón's masterly reworking of a similarly entitled Latin work a 4 (with continuo) [41] by his immediate predecessor at Las Palmas Cathedral, the Portuguese João de Figuereido Borges (maestro de capilla 1668-1674 [42]).

Siemens Hernández's allusion to the "Portuguese" maestro Figuereido Borges at once recalls to mind the one other Peninsular seventeenth-century work thus far recorded with anything like its proper full instrumental complement — Dom Pedro da Esperança's "Four Responses for Christmas Matins, for Choir, Tenor, and Four Instruments." Recorded in the Wren Church of St. Vedast, Fetter Lane, London, June, 1966, by Oryx (EXP 37), with Denys Darlow conducting The Tilford Bach Festival Choir, the album to which Esperança's Responses belong bears for its title Portuguese Baroque (Oryx Exploring The World of Music series). At the Biblioteca Geral, Coimbra University, M. M. -18 preserves at folios 40^V-48 and 65^V-74, eight compositions by Dom Pedro da Esperança, the insignis pulsator organorum (Códice 1741, Coimbra University Library) who died a canon of Santa Cruz in Coimbra June

24, 1660. To the first gathering of his works in M. M. -18 belong the four Christmas responsories that each include a "Verso Para instrumentos" in which four a broken consort accompanies the texted Superius 1. Untexted Superius 2 and 3 are in the manuscript respectively designated fagotillo and violim. The two lower instruments are in the first "Versso" (Hodie illuxit) designated bayxão and guyão. "Equivalent" instruments replace these in the Oryx recording: oboe, violin, bassoon, gamba. In the Coimbra manuscript, the fagotillo (a Spanish, not Portuguese, term) plays from Middle C to f^2 an eleventh above. The guiam or guyão = Spanish guión runs from plainsong gamma G to Middle C. Like the other parts, the guyão specifies F♯, C♯, G♯ in addition to "white-key" notes. As with guión parts generally, the "written" guyão implies an unwritten chordal realization for a keyboard instrument.

Another Coimbra manuscript — M. M. -52 — dating from the same Babylonian captivity period when the entire Peninsula acknowledged one and the same sovereign carries for its title "Contrapontos concertados." Originally belonging to São Vicente de Fóra monastery at Lisbon [43] this manuscript contains also nine anonymous tentos = tientos (items 20-28); but the first nineteen pieces are all concertados a 3 above a given bass by the Frei Teotónio da Cruz who was presumably the member of São Vicente de Fóra community dropped in 1617 [44] but readmitted before March 23, 1638 (this is the date above the top voice on fol. 2).

Cerone explains "Contrapunto concertado" at length in El Maestro y Melopeo, bk. IX, ch. 29. His examples (ch. 30) fit a "Tiple que sirue de Cantollano." But this "Cantollano" is no uniform-tread cantus firmus of the kind favored in species counterpoint. Instead, it is florid "fifth-species" melody. The present easy availability of Cerone's explanations and examples at pages 592-594 in the first volume of the facsimile published at Bologna in 1969 (Forni Editore) make required reading for anyone interested in adding upper instrumental parts to the basses of the villancicos by Loaysa y Agurto, Salazar, Vaeza, Vidales, and Ximeno in the present volume. It was precisely Spain's continuing obsession with Cerone and Lorente's rules of counterpoint (contrapunto concertado being counterpoint's ultima thule) that drove Antonio Eximeno y Pujades (1729-1808) into spasms of ridicule. In turn, Eximeno's two-volume 1800-1806 novel Don Lazarillo Vizcardi [45] became Felipe Pedrell's favorite big gun. [46] Even today, the war waged against the Spanish Baroque by Eximeno, and his echo Pedrell, still causes much that was most typical in Spanish Baroque musical practice — especially its contrapuntal "excesses" — to remain hidden by the smoke of gun battle. [47]

As Eximeno knew full well, the heart of Baroque Spanish church music pulsed in its maestro de capilla system. Throughout his 1800-1806 satirical novel, Eximeno allows Don Cándido Raponso to epitomize the flaws induced by that system.

To prepare for one of the regularly announced public competitions leading to a church maestro's post, Raponso "had perverted his native genius in working contrapuntal puzzles." Even the best musician deputed to be an examiner at the competition entered by Raponso — Padre Diego Quiñones, suffered equally from the contrapuntal disease. The organist of the church where the competition was staged "blindly worshiped all the twaddle of the ancient authorities on counterpoint."[48]

Everywhere evident in colonial American cathedrals was this same "sick" idolizing of counterpoint that so annoyed Eximeno. The "blind worship" in the New World mirrored, in particular, Sevillian use. The Sevillian influence took such heavy toll because all primitive Spanish American sees started as Sevillian suffragans — Santo Domingo (1513), Santiago de Cuba (1522), Mexico (1530), Nicaragua (1531), Panama (1534), Cartagena (1534), Cuzco (1538), to name no others. What is more, every emigrating clergyman destined before 1700 for the Indies had to pass an examination given by ecclesiastical authorities at Seville.[49] The last rule takes on added significance when it is remembered that Hernando Franco, Guitierre Fernández Hidalgo, Cristóbal Belsayaga, Juan Gutiérrez de Padilla, Fabián Ximeno, Francisco López Capillas, and most other early immigrant New World composers whose status can now be determined were clergy. The Mexican church historian Mariano Cuevas sums up the case for Seville thus: "From the beginning of the sixteenth to the eighteenth century Seville continued being the 'heart' of America, and it was Seville that dictated not only the norms of culture but even of ecclesiastical discipline to New World diocesan clergy."[50]

What, then, were the specific Seville Cathedral statues governing examination of postulant maestros de capilla? As long ago as 1904 Simón de la Rosa y López published in extenso the statutes enforced at Seville Cathedral throughout the colonial period.[51] Ten of a total of fourteen statutes specifically tested the candidate's contrapuntal skills. Inasmuch as Seville's rules were aped at Mexico City, Puebla, Lima, and Bogotá, they can be profitably translated here.

> (1) Add a counterpoint above a bass and below a treble cantus firmus in **C** and in **₵** meters[52] (2) Do the same, using circle mensuration (3) Same, bisected circle mensuration (4) Same, hemiolia.
>
> (5) Add a counterpoint below a florid treble in **C** and in **₵** mensurations (6) Same, circle mensuration (7) Add a third voice to a duo, then sing the third voice while simultaneously pointing to the notes in the [Guidonian] hand that will make a suitable fourth voice (8) Add a fourth voice to a given trio (9) While the candidate conducts at the choirbook stand two or three voice parts that increase to four or five — one of the said parts being sung in proportion, some of the singers are to miss their designated moment of entry to see whether he immediately catches and rectifies the mistake (10) All but two voices are to stop singing for an interval to see whether he can follow the silent parts mentally and bring in anew the interrupted voices.
>
> (11) He is to make up a four-note canon that will work

above a given cantus firmus, singing the dux, pointing to the comes with his hand; he is next to make up a cantus of minims and a cantus of semibreves that will fit a given florid melody (12) One singer is to skip a staff, whereupon he is to show the other singers how to cover the first singer's mistake by making compensating skips without stopping the performance (13) One singer in the ensemble is to drop pitch a step, whereupon the candidate is to bring the other singers down to the first singer's lower pitch level without changing the mode (14) To given texts, he is to compose within twenty-four hours a motet based on a particular musical passage, and also a chanzoneta.

These were the tests required at Seville. What were the tests elsewhere in Spain?

Antonio Lozano González, <u>La Música Popular, Religiosa y Dramática en Zaragoza Desde el Siglo XVI hasta nuestros días</u> (Saragossa: Julián Sanz y Navarro, 1895), pages 45-47, printed in full the tests required of competitors for the post of maestro de capilla at the Saragossa Cathedral (La Seo) in 1636. The competition began Monday, November 17, and ran six days. After answering four theory questions, each candidate was asked on Monday for two counterpoints above a bass in cut time, two in common, one each in 3/4, 3/2, 6/4, 3/8, and for three notes in the added melody against two notes in the cantus firmus. On Wednesday, he was asked for all the same counterpoints above another given plainsong, plus canons at the unison, second, third, fourth, and fifth. Thursday the ordeal continued with a given fifth species voice part to which each aspirant was required to add a voice-part proceeding in uniform breves, in semibreves beginning on beat 1, in semibreves (tied) beginning on beat 3, in minims beginning on beats 2 and 4; a running counterpoint of three semibreves against two semibreves of the fifth species, three minims against one semibreve of the given fifth species, six to a semibreve, nine to a breve; canons at the unison, second, and fourth. Against the given fifth species the candidate was next asked to sing one counterpoint while he signaled another by pointing to the appropriate knuckles in the Guidonian hand. On the fourth day, counterpoints against a given duo and trio were required; also a counterpoint signaled by the Guidonian hand while the postulant sang a different added melody.

On the fifth day the candidate was required to conduct common and ternary, correcting errors deliberately intruded by the singers, moving the singers up or down a step without starting over again, moving them forward when the bass skipped over rests, and bringing them in at a precise spot after conducting in silence. On the last day a local poet handed the candidate a text to be set as a six-part villancico in forty-eight hours. Also at the same time a choirboy picked out at random a plainchant from a choirbook picked up at random. This chant became the required soprano cantus firmus for a motet <u>a 5</u> due forty-eight hours later at the same time as the the villancico.

The seventeenth-century Saragossa Cathedral chapelmasters included: Bernardo Peralta Escudero (December 9, 1611-March 10, 1612), Francisco de Silos (July 4, 1614-August 21, 1632), Sebastián Cueto (December 17, 1632-September 22, 1636), Sebastián Romeo (November 26, 1636; died middle of 1649), Diego Pontac (September 7, 1649-July 8, 1650), fray Manuel Correa (August 5, 1650; died July 31, 1653), Juan de Torres (November 7, 1653- end of 1654), Sebastián Alfonso (February 19, 1656-April 24, 1687), Andrés de Sola (April 24, 1687-October 8, 1691), Tomás Micieres=Mizieres II (June 1, 1692-October 22, 1694), and José = Joseph de Casseda (appointed April 22, 1695).

These Saragossa maestros, no less than those at Seville, counted among the leading lights of the Spanish Baroque. Since the tests that each had to pass against come-one, come-all competition have now been specified, no present-day Baroque specialist can continue doubting how supremely important was fluency in written and improvised counterpoint. It was the ability to add unpremeditated counterpoints to a given cantus, florid or plain, that made or broke the candidate. The same drastic emphasis on what would now be called pyrotechnical contrapuntal display continued in vogue until at least the latter part of the eighteenth century in all Spanish dominion cathedrals. José Artero's "Oposiciones al Magisterio de Capilla en España durante el siglo XVIII," Anuario Musical, II (1947), pages 191-202, clinches the case. However much the Italians imported in droves by the eighteenth-century Spanish Bourbons might ridicule the system, they succeeded in intruding themselves only into appointive court posts, never into competitive cathedral posts. The wall over which they could not leap was the antiquated tests in counterpoint required of all cathedral postulants.[53]

From the sixteenth century onward, instrumentalists in all the better Spanish cathedrals improvised added parts.[54] One of the most basic differences between Spanish and French cathedral music throughout the sixteenth and seventeenth centuries touched precisely on the matter of noncontinuo instruments — supremely important in Spain, scarcely used in France.[55] Moreover the Spanish cathedral ministril had to play many different instruments. At the typical 1718 "Examen de los Ministriles" in Seville Cathedral (always the best example because Sevillian usage was looked to as a model everywhere in the Indies), the pretender to the titular cathedral post of bajonista (bassoonist) had to prove his simultaneous competency on five other instruments as well — violin, French horn, shawm, oboe, and recorder.[56] Even more importantly, he had to prove his ability as a composer. The organist candidate under scrutiny in the same November of 1718 had to evince "excellent keyboard technique, play all the same instruments as the bassoonist except bassoon, and show himself a knowledgeable composer of melody."[57] The winners of this particular competition for bajonista and organista each emerged

on December 2, 1718, with a 300-ducat annual salary and an added 100 ducats for expenses.[58]

Cerone epitomizes his rules in the ninth and tenth books of El Melopeo y Maestro. Whether Cerone's precepts are dismissed as pedantic and precious — witness Eximeno — or whether they are lauded as "free of mathematical and philosophical pedantry to an astonishing degree, essentially human, broad, scholarly, clear and sincere"— as Ruth Hannas rated them[59] — depends in no small measure on taste. In like manner, taste will decide to a degree one's reaction to contrapuntal accompaniments for villancicos such as those in the present volume. But whatever one's taste, no one can rightly dispute the enormity of Cerone's influence in both the Peninsula and the Americas with which this present anthology is concerned. He reserved his crucial discussion of "Conciertos, y conueniencia de los Instrumentos musicales; y de su temple" for his twenty-first book. Even the censorious Pedrell could not escape praising this book which according to him is the best in El Melopeo.[60]

Andrés Lorente, whose El Porqve de la Mvsica (1672), Libro Tercero ("Arte de Contrapunto") expands on Cerone's books 9 and 10, quotes the bergamoto at length, but in addition tries always to answer the question, "why?" Why the prohibition against consecutive perfect fifths and octaves (bk. 3, ch. 9),[61] why the cavil against diminished fifths, root position (ch. 10), are but the beginning of the "whys" that Lorente seeks to satisfy. Among welcome distinctions made by him are his contrasting rules for "contrapunto suelto" (two voices), "contrapunto de concierto" (three voices), and counterpoint involving four or more voices. No conscientious reader of Lorente's El Porqve can deny him the distinction of having published the finest and fullest treatment of counterpoint in Baroque Spain (pp. 233-440). Janus-like, he willingly accepted futurisms that were native and not imposed from abroad; while at the same time he glanced back with unfeigned pride in all that was truly national in the classic Peninsular polyphonic heritage — showing especially keen knowledge of Alonso Lobo's key works. Lorente's willingness to allow "circumstances" their due in determining the validity of any rule, to cite authorities who contravene what he himself considers good rules,[62] and to recognize and explain other theorists' terms and teachings even when opposed to his, help make him an authority still worthy of all encomium.

For him, "nothing is so splendid as a good dissonant suspension" (p. 282); indeed, "dissonances are the very life of music" (p. 275). Taking him at his word, any editor today adding contrapuntal lines to the Spanish seventeenth-century repertory ought constantly to favor dissonant suspensions, made and resolved according to his doctrines. His voice resounds over the centuries in favor of adding contrapuntal lines, not thin "Italian homophony." Through no less than 207 pages he plays variations above this ostinato: "Counterpoint is the

basis, the root, the foundation of all composition, the giver of
its general rules and the source of music's best beauties. "[63]
His rules for "Contrapunto de Concierto" at pages 353-408
alone supply any would-be restorer of Spanish Baroque glories
with the needed "thesaurus of devices. "

So much for brief documentation on chapelmasters' examina-
tions, ministriles' tests, and the hegemony of counterpoint in
Baroque Spain. Apart from Sebastián Durón, fray Gerónimo
González, Francisco de Santiago, and Alonso Xuares — the
four composers in the present volume who enjoyed connections
with the "mother cathedral of the Indies"— another four were
similarly connected with seventeenth-century Mexico City
Cathedral: Fabián Ximeno, Francisco de Vidales, José de
Loaysa y Agurto, and Antonio de Salazar. Our next documentation therefore comes from the colonial Mexico City Cathedral capitular acts and bears on ministriles — which topic takes
a close second to the "worship of counterpoint" as the most
sui generis aspect of Spanish Baroque church music.

May 1, 1543   Bishop Zumárraga and the chapter formally
   engage Indian instrumentalists to play regularly in the cathedral, each to be paid an annual 24 gold pesos. [64]

January 11, 1575   Effective retroactively to January 1, Archbishop Pedro Moya de Contreras and the chapter engage four
   instrumentalists at 1, 000 gold pesos annually (to be divided
   among the four)— Francisco de Covarrubias, Bartolomé de
   Luna, Miguel de los Reyes, and Rodrigo de Saavedra. [65]

May 13, 1575   Retroactively to May 1, Pedro de Ribas is
   hired as cathedral sackbut at a yearly 250 pesos. [66]

January 13, 1576   Each cathedral shawmer (number of shawmers not specified) receives 50 gold pesos for this one year
   only as a special living expense grant. [67]

March 15, 1580   At the archbishop's suggestion, each of the
   five cathedral instrumentalists is raised from 200 gold pesos
   annually to 300, care being taken to ensure that no one instrumentalist earns more than another on the cathedral
   roll. [68]

April 14, 1581   The ministril Miguel de los Reyes is readmitted. [69]

July 6, 1582   Anticipated critical losses in cathedral revenues
   oblige the chapter to reduce all musicians' salaries, the instrumentalists affected being Julián Hurtado de Mendoza,
   Miguel de los Reyes, Francisco de Cobarruvias and his son
   Álvaro, and Bernardino Rodríguez. The first two ministriles accept the cuts, but Francisco de Cobarruvias demurs
   saying that neither he nor his son can live on any mere 200
   gold pesos annually and moreover that he had left a chapelmaster's post paying 500 annually to accept Mexico City's
   offer. Rodríguez quits also. [70]

August 22, 1582   In the interim since July 6, Archbishop
   Moya de Contreras has called to his palace Doctor Pedro
   Garcés, cathedral treasurer. Without saying whether the
   chapter did well or ill, he has assured the treasurer that

new funds are imminently expected in the fleet due from
Spain, and that there will assuredly be enough money to pay
musicians' salaries. The chapter therefore now makes
overtures to all the musicians out on salary strike. [71]

August 16, 1588   At 100 pesos de tepuzque Luis de Montes de
   Oca is received with the double duty of playing the bassoon
   on principal days and singing on lesser days. [72]

June 7, 1591   A special allotment for trumpets and shawms is
   budgeted "en Razon de la Presidencia. " [73]

January 17, 1595   The chapter votes to pay 900 pesos de
   tepuzque for a set of twelve flutes with case and key. These
   flutes are for choir service. Dr. Dionisio de Ribera
   Flores[74] offers to guard them. [75]

February 25, 1595   The two ministriles Juan Maldonado and
   Andrés de Molina continue to disobey the cathedral chapelmaster Juan Hernández. Like all the rest of the ministriles
   they must submit without question to his orders, and must
   play the Magnificat, psalm, offertory, communion, and
   whatever else he requires. Should their malice not abate,
   the chapter promises severe punishment. [76]

April, 1595   Gaspar Maldonado (son of the rebellious Juan[77])
   may continue to play although still an apprentice. One instrumentalist having recently absconded rather than submit
   to discipline, the others must be tolerated. [78]

May, 1595   No instrumentalist or singer whatsoever may be
   excused during the Corpus Christi octave. [79]

January 19, 1596   Numerous fines assessed against ministriles
   because of their laxness are now remitted and several
   instrumentalists get their pay raised.

January 12, 1607   Lorenzo Martínez, a bassoonist who has
   been a cathedral ministril at least a decade, [80] gets a salary
   raise of 150 gold pesos over the 50 pesos de minas already
   being paid him, the reason being that during Advent and Lent
   he alone of the instrumentalists (apart from organist) plays
   with the singers weekdays. He plays also at offices of the
   dead. [81]

1609, undated act just before October   The maecenas who is
   now archbishop, fray García Guerra (1608-1612), orders
   special payments to the seven musicians who in concert with
   one another had played and sung during "special hours" of
   the previous Corpus Christi octave. Three had played harps,
   two had played portable organs, one had played guitar. [82]

May 28, 1610   Archbishop Guerra deems it absolutely necessary to have excellent music every day before vespers
   throughout the entire Corpus Christi octave if people are to
   come. This "excellent music" should consist of villancicos
   and chanzonetas played and sung by ministriles and cantores. [83]

March 16, 1611   Alonso Baptista, son of the deceased ministril Juan Baptista, shall replace him at 200 Castile ducats
   annually, this being the same amount paid the other ministriles. [84]

August 5, 1611   At this identical annual salary, Francisco de

Medina presbítero is named Músico bajón to replace the recently deceased bassoonist Lorenzo Martínez. Simultaneously, the chapter raises both Alexo García ministril corneta chirimía y bajón (cornettist, shawmer, and bassoonist) and Alonso Arias ministril sacabuche (sackbut) from 150 to a yearly 250 Castile ducats. Archbishop Guerra, now Viceroy of Mexico, has himself suggested these two latter salary sweeteners.[85]

August 30, 1611   Antonio Baptista, a youthful ministril sacabuche (scion of the same Bautista clan to which Juan and Alonso belonged), brings before the chapter a recommendation from the Archbishop-Viceroy, who prefers this youth to the elderly priest Francisco de Medina for the post formerly held by Lorenzo Martínez. Since the chapter only three weeks earlier has awarded the veteran priest the post, two canons now vote against this youthful protégé of the Archbishop-Viceroy.[86]

February 14, 1612   Miffed by the favors shown this clan of virtuoso instrumentalists, the chapter votes to dismiss Alonso Baptista ministril for having used a sick leave to visit nearby Puebla. Only Juan Hernández, the now aged chapelmaster (appointed January 17, 1586[87]), counsels delay until the Archbishop-Viceroy can offer his opinion.[88]

November 26, 1613   Having recently returned from Castile, Gerónimo del Río ministril sacabuche wants the same salary being paid Juan Maldonado ministril corneta — 250 pesos annually.[89]

March 11, 1614   At an annual 100 pesos de oro común, the chapter hires Joseph Xuárez to be ministril corneta y chirimía tiple (cornettist and soprano shawmer).[90]

May 27, 1614   Chapelmaster Juan Hernández confides the special music during Corpus Christi octave this year to "keyboard instruments, harps, guitars, and other such [string] instruments."[91]

May 12, 1620   The chapter allows Francisco Rodríguez sufficient leave and a salary advance so that he can return to Spain to pick up his wife.[92]

December 1, 1623   On this date, the Mexico City cathedral musical staff consists of 28 professionals,[93] of which number two are organists,[94] one is a músico de la capilla,[95] another maestro de los infantes,[96] and eight are ministriles: Juan Maldonado (350 pesos annual salary paid from fábrica [cathedral foundation] funds), Juan Baptista (350), Alonso Arias (250), Alexo García (300), Joseph Xuárez (150), Pablo de Escobedo (300), Lázaro Rodrigues (200), Francisco de Herrera (200).

March 22, 1639   The ministril Juan Muños earns his annual 200 pesos from ouenciones de capilla alone (offerings for burials and other special ceremonies) — being assigned no other stated salary.[97]

September 12, 1639   The two new ministriles, Alonso de Rivas baxón and Diego Antonio baxon y chirimía shall not be confirmed in their 100-pesos annual salaries until they each promise in writing to remain with the cathedral at least four years.[98]

April 8, 1642   "Jusepe Suares" [= Joseph Xuárez, hired as cornettist and soprano shawmer March 11, 1614] wishes his son to play during this Easter season, and asks chapelmaster Rodríguez Mata (died 1643) to certify the son's readiness."[99]

May 26, 1651   Several instrumentalists formerly employed by Puebla Cathedral apply for entry. Ordinarily a gentleman's agreement keeps one cathedral from competing with the other for personnel. However, in this instance Mexico City feels free to negotiate, Puebla's declining budget having forced dismissal of many first-class players shortly before.[100]

February 9, 1652   Nicolás Grinón, ten years earlier a Mexico City músico,[101] returns from Puebla. The chapter again hires him for harpist at 100 pesos.[102] But the next September 3, Puebla (home of his parents) lures him back.[103]

April 14, 1654   Because of his extraordinary skill, the Mexico City chapter offers Antonio de Mora ministril del choro the high sum of 200 pesos' annual salary, plus a guarantee of a like take from obençiones.[104]

December 7, 1654   Hernando López [Calderón], another harpist who vacillates between the two cathedrals petitions December 4 to be received. To avoid offending Puebla or because "we are so poor," Mexico City chapter now offers him 60 pesos for his part in the coming Christmas special music, and agrees to call him thereafter "when needed."[105]

February 18, 1656   Hernando López Calderón wins a raise from 60 to 150 pesos annually.[106]

January 17, 1681   Nicolás Bernal is admitted as bajón.[107]

December 10, 1688   The chapter denies Balmaña's request to be named corneta, because all instrumentalists' posts are filled.[108]

May 17, 1695   When asked of what use is the proposed stop called punto alto on the new cathedral organ, the principal Mexico City organist Joseph (de) Ydiáquez (appointed 1673[109]) replies: none except to accompany bassoon, shawm, or cornett when they ascend to the organ loft to play verses — at which time it saves the organist the effort of transposing. He then explains that punto alto is a mixture sounding one step higher than the rest of the organ. However, it is a stop that is quite needless when the organist plays tientos. The organist who can transpose needs no such crutch as a punto alto stop anyway.[110] To Ydiáquez's lengthy explanation, a pair of assistant organists add that these three woodwinds in Spain play in E and A, whereas here at Mexico City they play in F and B♭, "in other words half a step higher here than there."[111]

May 14, 1700   A talented prospect for corneta, Domingo de Castañeda, comes from a poor family. He needs clothing. The chapter proposes letting the archbishop, who recommended him, clothe the youth until such time as the chief corneturo (cornettist) Miguel Ordoñes and Chapelmaster Salazar certify that the youth applies himself and progresses. [112]

October 1, 1700 The postulant having impressed Salazar, he is certified for financial aid and studies with Francisco Astasio. [113]

July 20, 1734 Pedro Rodríguez having shown talent and industry during his previous year's study of violin and vajon-sillo (soprano bassoon [114]) is certified by Chapelmaster Manuel de Zumaya for cathedral employment at 200 pesos annually. [115]

April 24, 1736 Three new ministriles are admitted. Between them they play violins, violas, [116] bass viols, bugles, French horns, and small bassoons [= vajonsillos]. [117]

October 9, 1745 The standard reinforcing (colla parte) instruments for a vocal trio or quartet [118] are on this date listed as Biolon de quatro, Vajon y Vajoncillo (four-string double bass, bassoon, and soprano bassoon).

November 15, 1748 Antonio Zerezo, a player whose social rank entitles him to the prefix "don" wishes to play only violin or bass viol. Despite his social pretensions he must play vajoncillo o corneta when requested. [119]

August 8, 1754 The three cathedral vajoneros each earn a sizable 600 pesos annually. In addition, the Guaxaqueño Velasco ("native of Oaxaca, [Juan de] Velasco") earns 500 as organist and another 200 as vajonero (bassoonist). Nonetheless, the cathedral chantre considers all four so inept at improvising counterpoints above a given plainsong that he wishes the chapter to hire Antonio Zerezo for this duty. [120]

January 7, 1755 Not only Zerezo but several other cathedral ministriles must henceforth renew the former custom of adding counterpoints to the antiphons of the Magnificat de la O. [121]

January 9, 1756 The bassoonist Nicolás Gil has shown up loud-mouthed, drunk, and with a bleeding hand. The 'cellist Juan Rodríguez follows his example. More of this and they will both be properly punished. [122]

February 13, 1756 Antonio Zerezo claims 24 years' service as violinist and supply bassist. Since bowed strings never play at funerals, and since he has a wife, mother, and children to support, he requests a 100-peso raise to make up for the lost obenciones ("tips") for funerals. Everyone at chapter meeting agrees that he deserves the total of 300 now requested, because he is "apt, industrious, and prompt. " [123]

March 4, 1756 Dn Matheo Tollis de la Roca Maestro de Claue, Organo, y Compositor applies for a regular appointment. His opponents claim that el Instrumento de Claue, solo seruia en al choro en el Miserere ("harpsichord only accompanies the choir during the Miserere" [of Holy Week]). [124]

September 19, 1758 Both cathedral harpists Joseph Pardo de Lago and Jacinto Zapata are in a dire way. The first claims

to have syphilis, and if so must commit himself to the Hospital de el Amor de Dios. The second claims to be at death's door without even money to assure himself a decent burial. [125]

1759 (undated entry) The chapter deputes Antonio Palomino, a cathedral musician given two years leave, to buy the following instruments for Mexico City Cathedral while in Spain. They are each to be of prime quality bought as quickly as possible, and sent immediately to a designated warehouse in Cádiz for dispatch securely packed in the next sailing. The widow of Joseph Díaz de Guitián, who has been the cathedral's business agent at Cádiz, is to supply Palomino with any needed letters of credit.

6 violins made by Gagliano of Naples [126] or by any other better maker

2 short oboes, 2 long

2 cross flutes with interchangeable middle sections to raise or lower the pitch

2 recorders and two piccolos

2 large bassoons built in B♭

2 Neapolitan portative organs, or from a good maker elsewhere, each of eight or nine stops, but sending here only the pipework and the chest so that the organs can be assembled here

2 small clarions in F

1 pair of tympani, constructed with all possible care so that they are perfect, in D

2 French horns, but not in the same keys that the cathedral already owns. [127]

NOTES

1. See facsimile of this part at page 179 of Lincoln Spiess and E. Thomas Stanford, An Introduction to Certain Mexican Musical Archives (Detroit: Information Coordinators, 1969).

2. Andrés Lorente, El Porqve de la Mvsica (Alcalá de Henares: Nicolás de Xamares, 1672), p. 560, says the same: "In writing for two or more coros some composers allow the basses to contend with each other, but this is a defect to be avoided. In polychoral writing the basses should duplicate each other at the unison or octave, unless an imitative point demands otherwise. "

3. Pedro Cerone, El Melopeo y Maestro (Naples: J. B. Gargano and L. Nucci, 1613), p. 1069, urged that the instrumental parts should always be singable no matter what instruments entered any given ensemble. Because of his authority, Cerone's demand that instruments attempt only what can be done by the noblest of all instruments — the voice — stymied for a long time any attempts at idiomatic writing for such instruments (mentioned by him at pages 1038-1039) as "Sacabuches, Fagotes ò Baxones, Doblados, Flautas, Dulçaynas, Cornetas, Cornamusas, Cornamudas . . . Vihuelas de arco, Violones, Rabeles, Rabequinas. "

4. Details concerning the score are given in Higinio Anglés and José Subirá, Catálogo Musical de la Biblioteca Nacional de Madrid (Barcelona: Instituto Español de Musicología, 1951), III, 62-64.

5. Anyone who still cherishes the fancy that seventeenth-century Spanish maestros figured their basses should glance at the facsimiles of Juan Hidalgo's Celos aun del aire matan in José Subirá's La musica en la Casa de Alba: Estudios históricos y biográficos (Madrid: Hauser y Menet, 1927), opposite p. 6, and his edition of Celos aun del aire matan (Barcelona: Institut d'Estudis Catalans [Biblioteca de Catalunya, 1933]), p. vii. Not a single numeral appears anywhere in these long stretches.

6. Nota xxvii Que enseña, y declara lo que significan los Numeros, que algunos Maestros ponen sobre los Acompañamientos, en los Baxos de las Composiciones Musicas. Algunos Maestros acostumbrauan en sus Composiciones . . . poner sobre algunos puntos en los Acompañamientos (esto es, en los Baxos que se hazē para el Organo, ò el Arpa) algunos Numeros 4, 7, 9, 6, 6♯, 3♭, 5♯, 5♭, 3♯.
Muchas vezes se halla lo sobredicho en las Composiciones que se sacan de Tono, Poniendo dichos numeros, para que las vozes se pongan bien colocadas en la consonancia accidental, que por algun espacio de tiempo se canta la Obra de Musica, hasta que se buelve al Tono natural en que está hecha.

7. Jul. Jos. Maier, Die musikalischen Handschriften der K. Hof- und Staatsbibliothek in Muenchen (Munich: Palm'schen Hofbuchhandlung, 1879), pp. 101 (156-161) and 102 (165-166) specifies Hidalgo's six Lady villancicos a 3 and a 4 and Navas's two responsiones a 8. Navas, royal harpist 1702-1709, cooperated with Sebastián Durón in writing the three-act zarzuela held by the Madrid National Library, Apolo y Dafne (Catálogo Musical de la Biblioteca Nacional, I, 260-265).

8. After careful review of the entire colonial music archive, Andrés Sas wrote thus in "La vida musical en la Catedral de Lima durante la colonia," Revista Musical Chilena, XVI/81-82 (July-December, 1962), 29: "Desgraciadamente no he encontrado en los archivos religiosos consultados ninguna parte 'realizada' de arpa ni de órgano; en cuanto a los cronistas, hablan a veces de las ejecuciones brillantes de los arpistas, pero se quedan mudos respecto a lo que ejecutaban esos virtuosos." (Translation: "Unfortunately, I have found no 'realized' harp or organ part in any of the church archives consulted; so far as annalists are concerned, they speak at times of the 'brilliant performances' of the harpists but remain silent as to what [notes] those virtuosos actually played.")

9. Santiago Kastner echoes the same sentiment when he laments: "Leider sind die Harfen-Continuostimmen fast niemals vollständig ausgesetzt, meistens ist nur der Bass mit oder ohne Bezifferung überliefert geblieben, so dass man sich eigentlich keine vollkommene Vorstellung von dem machen kann, was die Harfner tatsächlich auf ihrem Instrument realisierten" ("Harfe und Harfner in der Iberischen Musik des 17. Jahrhunderts," Natalicia Musicologica Knud Jeppesen septuagenario collegis oblata [Copenhagen: Wilhelm Hansen, 1962], p. 168.

10. Facsimile three-volume edition of Marin Mersenne's Harmonie universelle (Paris, 1636), published by Éditions du Centre national de la Recherche scientifique, 1963.

11. Cf. Rosalyn Rensch, The Harp (New York: Philosophical Library, 1960), for a typical example; unfortunately none of her bibliography (pp. 183-185) does any better by Spain.

12. Santiago Kastner, "Le 'clavecin parfait' de Bartolomeo Jobernardi," Anuario Musical, VIII (1953), 193, describes this as a 45-folio bilingual miscellany containing mostly mathematical treatises (Spanish text on versos, Italian on rectos).

13. José Subirá, "Dos músicos del Rey Felipe IV: B. Jovernardi y E. Butler," Anuario Musical, XIX (1964), 216. According to Subirá, whose article gives numerous other biographical data, Giobernardi's treatise, dedicated to Philip IV October 15, 1634, comes in a densely packed 41-folio manuscript. Subirá epitomizes Giobernardi's Tratado de la Mussica at pp. 218-220.

14. Ibid., p. 203.

15. Anthony Baines, European and American Musical Instruments (London: B. T. Batsford Ltd., 1966), includes a photo of the same cross-strung harp [404]. He credits it to the Victoria and Albert Museum, 830-1884, calls it presumably French, and dates it c. 1800. Two other cross-strung harps are pictured on the same page [items 405, 407], each dated c. 1895. At page 68 of his text Baines thus defines the cross-strung harp: "Cross-strung harps are double-strung harps in which two sets of strings are arranged in planes which cross one another at some point, so that every string is directly available to either hand, whether above or below the point where the strings cross." Unaware of Spanish usage, he dates his first specimen "in the eighteenth century." Describing the model pictured by Cametti and by himself [404], he writes: "A later example [404] has two divergent necks supported by two posts crossed in an X."

16. "Harfe und Harfner," p. 167.

17. Francisco Perrenot de Granvela (born c. 1558), the putative prototype of don Bela, was already "described in 1583 as muy entendida en las letras y música e instrumentos de tañer [very well informed in literature, music, and musical instruments]). See Alan S. Trueblood, "Substance and Form in La Dorotea: A Study in Lope's Artistic Use of Personal Experience," Harvard University Ph.D. dissertation, 1951, p. 29.

18. Stevenson, Juan Bermudo (The Hague: Martinus Nijhoff, 1960), p. 59. The reference to "el nōbrado Ludouico" comes at fol. 110ᵛ, col. 2, of Bermudo's 1555 Declaración.

19. Failing to keep abreast of even the one authority whom he quotes, Edwin S. Morby (see note 124 on page 180 of his "segunda edición revisada," Lope's La Dorotea [Berkeley and Los Angeles:University of California Press, 1968]) still harks back to H. J. Zingel's out-of-date doctoral dissertation, Harfe und Harfenspiel (Halle: Eduard Klinz, 1931)—page 19 of which he continues quoting verbatim. But in his doctoral dissertation, Zingel labored under the erroneous impression that the cross-strung harp (zwei reihig gekreuzt) was "invented" at Paris c. 1845. Morby has apparently never seen Zingel's own correction of his doctoral dissertation. When not even critical editors keep abreast, encyclopedists such as Alfred Einstein can be forgiven for the gross errors in the eleventh edition of Riemann's Music-Lexikon (p. 706).

20. Revista Musical Chilena, XVI/81-82 (July-December, 1962), 29.

21. Spanish text reprinted in Monumentos de la Música Española, XXVII (1966), p. 28, col. 1, lines 3-4.

22. See the presto gigue transcribed by Kastner, "Harfe und Harfner," p. 172, and attributed by him to Jordi Rodríguez (appointed Valencia Cathedral harpist February 15, 1703: ibid., p. 170).

23. Contents listed, Catálogo Musical de la Biblioteca Nacional, I, 260-265.

24. Ramón Adolfo Pelinski, "Die weltliche Musik Spaniens am Anfang des 17. Jhs. Der Cancionero Claudio de la Sablonara," Ph.D. dissertation, Ludwig-Maxmilian-Universität, Munich, 1969, p. 11, considers this the earliest seventeenth-century secular collection ("die vermutlich die früheste ist").

25. Felipe Pedrell, Diccionario técnico, 4th ed., p. 124, states that this finger position yields a different standard guitar chord, "according to system of ciphering adopted." The chord would be a 6/4 minor in the system illustrated in 1693 by José García Hidalgo (see Frederick V. Grunfeld, The Art and Times of the Guitar [New York: The Macmillan Company, 1969], p. 76, upper left box).

26. "Respecto al acompañamiento instrumental de este repertorio, solamente hay un simple indicio en la página 76 de la tercera voz, donde en el margen superior se lee: 'Bassus a 3. I⁰ Tono, por cruzado remisso.' No obstante, es de suponer que todas estas piezas se cantarían con acompañamiento de tecla, arpa o guitarra, según el uso de la época."

27. So classified in Obras de Lope de Vega, Real Academia Española edition (Madrid: Sucesores de Rivadeneyra, 1894), p. lxxix. The song is printed in the same volume at p. 181.

28. Monumentos de la Música Española, XVIII, 29 (literary introduction).

29. Compare F. T. Arnold's strictures against omitting the continuo from even so full-throated a work as the opening chorus of Bach's St. Matthew (The Art of Accompaniment from a Thorough-Bass as Practised in the XVIIth and XVIIIth Centuries [London: Oxford University Press, 1931], p. viii).

30. On the preceding page he lists six hitherto unpublished choirbook-form, early seventeenth-century sources of profane polyphony: (1) Tonos Humanos, M. 1262 at the Biblioteca Nacional, Madrid, with 226 compositions; (2) Cancionero de Claudio de la Sablonara, Cod. hisp. 2, Cim. 383, at the Bayerische Staatsbibliothek, Munich, with 75 pieces; (3) Cancionero de Olot, MS I-VIII at the Biblioteca pública de Olot, 74 pieces; (4) Tonos Castellanos, formerly MS 13231 in the Biblioteca de los Duques de Medinaceli, Madrid, now Biblioteca Bartolomé March, Madrid, with 70 pieces; (5) Cancionero Musical español, at the Biblioteca Nazionale Università di Torino, 50 pieces; (6) Cancionero de la Biblioteca Casanatense, MS 5437 in the Casanatense Library, Rome, 20 pieces.

31. For a facsimile of the original manuscript fronting Pedrell's transcription, see José Subirá, Historia de la música española e hispanoamericana (Barcelona: Salvat Editores, 1953), pp. 342-343. Note that Pedrell pitches everything a fourth lower than written. Rafael Mitjana republished an excerpt from this same Hidalgo Quedito pasito lullaby in Encyclopédie de la musique, 1ʳᵉ partie, IV, 2062-2063. In Anuario Musical, IV (1949), 187 (item 44), and again twenty years later in the same annual, XXII (1967[1969]), 201 (item 44), Subirá identified the same Quedito pasito as an "anonymous" item at page 220 in a 370-page (many pages gone) album guarded at the Archivo de la Congregación de Nuestra Señora de la Novena, Madrid ["Archivo de la plurisecular Congregación Española de Actores, de Madrid" (Anuario Musical, XXII, 200)].

32. José Subirá, editor, Celos aun del aire matan: Ópera del siglo XVII Texto de Calderón y música de Juan Hidalgo (Barcelona: Biblioteca de Catalunya, 1933), p. xv.

33. Facsimiles of the original score in the just-mentioned edition, p. vii, and in José Subirá, La música en la Casa de Alba, opposite p. 61.

34. Subirá, Celos aun del aire matan, pp. xiii-xiv, lists the components of the Royal Chapel in 1633: two bassoons, a soprano bassoon, three harpists, two vihuelists, two bass viol players, shawms, cornetts; to which group were added a biennium later seven violins.

35. In Subirá's Historia, p. 342, he credits the manuscript containing fragments of Hidalgo's incidental music for Ni Amor se libra de amor to the "Archivo de la Congregación de Actores. See n. 31 above.

36. Subirá, "Un manuscrito musical de principios del siglo XVIII," Anuario Musical, IV (1949), 191.

37. Heartiest thanks are here recorded for her kindness in sending the two offprints, "El Archivo de música de la Catedral de Las Palmas, I" and "II," 1964, 1965. The Las Palmas periodical El Museo Carnario, numbers 89-92 (1964 [1965])

and 93-96 (1965[1966]) carried the two instalments of her catalogue at pp. 181-242 and 147-203.

38. Half-brother of the much more famous Sebastián Durón whose biography comes first in the Biographical Data section of this present volume.

39. "El Archivo de Música de la Catedral de Las Palmas," El Museo Canario, XXV/89-92 (1964[1965]), 197, 203-208.

40. Ibid., p. 197 (B/IV-4).

41. Ibid., p. 196 (B/III-3).

42. Ibid., p. 193. Mazza, Vasconcellos, and Vieira ignore this Portuguese composer.

43. At fol. 32ᵛ, after an anonymous Tento do 4.⁰ Tom (a 4): "Este liuro he do Mosteiro de S. V̄ᵗᵉ de fora Lx. ᵃ"

44. Expelled December 13, 1616, for rebellion and disobedience and deprived of the habit January 5, 1617, if this is the same Frei Teotónio da Cruz of this community mentioned in Códice 632, "Crónica da fundação e catálogo dos Priores de Mosteiro de S. Vicente de Fóra da cidade de Lisboa, por D. Marcos da Cruz," a Coimbra University manuscript extracted by Joaquim Martins Teixeira de Carvalho.

45. Published by the Sociedad de Bibliófilos Españoles (Madrid: Imp. de M. Rivadeneyra, 1872), with a 61-page preface by Francisco Asenjo Barbieri.

46. See the excerpts in Pedrell's P. Antonio Eximeno (Madrid: Unión Musical Española, 1920), pp. 168-198 (Barbieri's preface, pp. 161-167).

47. Claude Palisca not once mentions Spain anywhere in his standard text Baroque Music (Englewood Cliffs: Prentice-Hall, 1968). Manfred Bukofzer's Music in the Baroque Era (New York: W. W. Norton, 1947) gave "Music in the Iberian Peninsula, New Spain, and Colonial America" six pages (174-179), but allowed Eximeno's prejudices to become his own when he wrote: "Spanish church music reflected in its hyperconservative attitude the spirit of severe orthodoxy that prevailed in Spain; the innovations of the baroque style were shunned."

48. Pedrell, P. Antonio Eximeno, pp. 165-166.

49. Gobernación espiritual y temporal de las Indias, edited by Ángel de Altolaguirre y Duvale (Madrid: Tip. de la "Rev. de Archivos Bibliotecas y Museos,"1927 [Colección de documentos inéditos relativos al descubrimiento, conquista y organización de las antiguas posesiones españolas de ultramar, XX]), p. 25.

50. Historia de la Iglesia en México, quinta edición (Mexico City: Editorial Patria, 1946), I, 124-125: "En Sevilla estaba ya, desde entonces, y siguió estando hasta el siglo XVIII, el corazón de América, y Sevilla era la norma de la cultura y aun disciplina eclesiástica para el clero secular."

51. Los seises de la catedral de Sevilla (Seville: Francisco de P. Díaz, 1904), p. 151.

52. According to Lorente (1672; see footnote 2 of this chapter), p. 154, 𝘊 = "compasillo" (two minims to the bar); at p. 164 he defines 𝄵 = 𝈾 = "compas mayor" (four minims to the bar). At his p. 166 he explains "proporcion menor en el tiempo menor" = 𝘊3 or 𝘊$\frac{3}{2}$ or 𝄵3 or 𝘊3. The last two are the common signatures for "Villancicos y Musicas de alegria" ("happy music"). In these "happy" mensurations "es el Semibreve perfecto, por vso, no por razon" (the semibreve is perfect, not for any good reason but merely as the result of custom"). His explanation of seventeenth-century "tiempos que oy se vsan en Canto de Organo" extending from his pp. 148-179 can scarcely be overpraised.

53. Nicolás A. Solar-Quintes, "El compositor Francisco Courcelle," Anuario Musical, VI (1951), 203. Compare the objections to appointing Ignacio Jerusalém titular maestro at Mexico City (Stevenson, "La música en la Catedral de México: 1600-1750," Revista Musical Chilena, XIX/92 [1965], 31). In 1761, long after the deed, the Queen Mother's having forced the appointment of a second Royal Chapel maestro at Madrid in the person of the nonentity Italian, Filippo Falconi, was still recalled in faraway Mexico as a national scandal (Mexico City Cathedral, Actas Capitulares, XLIV [1759-1761, fol. 298^V]). During 1734—four years before José de Torres's death—Falconi was earning the same salary as he (2,000 ducats annually [Anuario Musical, VI (1951), 180]). Subirá (Historia de la música española, p. 544) voices Spanish sentiment when citing Falconi as "infamous and insignificant." Nonetheless, Torres had to retire to make room for him, because the Queen Mother would have it so.

54. For contemporary documentation from Seville Cathedral dated July 11, 1586, see Stevenson, Spanish Cathedral Music in the Golden Age (Berkeley and Los Angeles: University of California Press, 1961), pp. 166-167.

55. Denise Launay, "À propos d'une messe de Charles d'Helfer," Les Colloques de Wégimont, IV-1957 (Paris, 1963), pp. 191-193.

56. Seville Cathedral, Actas Capitulares, XCIV, fol. 144 (November 18, 1718). On the preceding October 17 Gaspar de Úbeda (Sevillian chapelmaster 1710-1724 [Rosa y López, op. cit., p. 328]) received two months leave to compose the 1718 Cathedral Christmas villancicos. (Such leave was by then standard custom in the Indies also.) The act at folio 144 reads: "Examen de los Ministriles que pretenden serlo desta Sta Yg^{la} . . . Bajonista muy diestro y sientifico en la melodia, y q^{ue} juntam^{te} tenia la auillidad de tañer todos instrumentos como eran Violin, Trompa de Caza, Chirimia, Obuè, flauta dulze, y compositor . . ."[underlining mine].

57. Ibid.: "y que el otro tañia Organo excelentemente de buenas manos, y acompañamiento y los mesmos instrumentos que el antecedente excepto Bajon, y en todo lo dho mui diestro, y sientifico y compositor de dha melodia."

58. Ibid., fol. 148. Juan Espiquerman and Arnaldo Esper were the winners. Their contracts forbade their playing in the private houses of anyone except cathedral officials.

59. "Cerone, Philosopher and Teacher," Musical Quarterly, XXI/4 (October, 1935), 421: see also her "Cerone's Approach to the Teaching of Counterpoint," Papers Read by Members of the American Musicological Society . . . 1937, pp. 75-80.

60. P. Antonio Eximeno, pp. 123-147.

61. He shows fine historical acumen when he observes, El Porqve, p. 541: "Some musical authorities of the last century forbade successive strong beat octaves or fifths, even if other consonances intervene between said strong beats. But modern composers tolerate them, even if the intervening consonance is so fleeting as a semicorchea [semiquaver] between fifths. I accept modern usage."

62. Ibid., p. 260.

63. Ibid., p. 274: "el Contrapunto es principio de la Composicion, raiz, y fundamento de ella; y en èl se toman noticias, y se aprenden Reglas generales, para hazer despues primores conocidos en la Musica."

64. Actas Capitulares, I (1536-1559), fol. 58: "Recibieron por su s^a y mds los menestriles yndios con partido cada vn año de xxiiij p^{o}s de oro comun."

65. A.C., II (1559-1576), fol. 303^V: "Reçibieron por musicos de esta s^{ta} igla y ministriles a fran^{co} de couarrubias y Bar^e de Luna y Miguel de los Reyes y R^o de Sayabedra con mill

pesos de oro comun de salario en cada vn año."

66. Ibid., fol. 308: "se rreçibio por musico de esta Sta yglesia de sacabuche a p^o de rribas con dozientos y çincuenta p^{o}s de salario por vn año como los demas ministriles gana desde primero de mayo."

67. Ibid., fol. 318: "se dio por ayuda de costa a los chirimias cinquenta pesos de oro comun a cada vno y esto se entiende por solo este año."

68. A.C., III (1576-1609), fol. 92^V.

69. Ibid., fol. 115.

70. Ibid., fol. 151 and 151^V.

71. Ibid., fol. 154. The archbishop had assured Garcés that "en la flota se aguardaba que bendria la m^d de los dos nobenos de que estaua suplicado a su mag^d fuese seruido hazer limosna a esta s^{ta} iglesia y que viniendo esta m^d auria con que los poder pagar sus salarios."

72. A.C., IV (1588-1605), fol. 5^V: "con cargo de tañer el bajon los dias principales. . . ."

73. Ibid., fol. 49^V.

74. According to Joaquín García Icazbalceta's Bibliografía Mexicana del Siglo XVI, revised by Agustín Millares Carlo (Mexico City: Fondo de Cultura Económica, 1954), p. 443, Ribera Flórez studied at Salamanca University, arrived at Mexico City in 1560, took a doctor of canon laws degree at the University of Mexico in 1584, became a Mexico City cathedral canon January 31, 1591, and published at the viceregal capital in 1600 a bulky but extremely informative Relacion historiada de las exeqvias fvnerales de la Magestad del Rey D. Philippo II (described and excerpted, ibid., pp. 442-451).

75. A.C., IV, fol. 111: "un terno de doze flautas con su caja y llave para el seruicio del coro. . . ."

76. Ibid., fol. 113.

77. Ibid., fol. 112^V.

78. Ibid., fol. 116^V.

79. Ibid., fol. 120.

80. Ibid., fol. 184; in 1597 the chapter loaned him 50 pesos de oro común.

81. A.C., V (1606-1616), fol. 21^V.

82. Ibid., fol. 157.

83. Ibid., fol. 189^V. See footnote 13 of the immediately preceding chapter for the Spanish text.

84. Ibid., fol. 227.

85. Ibid., fol. 242^V.

86. Ibid., fol. 245 and 245^V.

87. A.C., III (1576-1609), fol. 219^V.

88. A.C., V, fol. 264.

89. Ibid., fol. 343.

90. Ibid., fol. 352.

91. Ibid., fol. 356^V: "instrumentos assi de tecla, como harpas, guitarras, y ministriles. . . ."

92. A.C., VII (1620-1625), fol. 42^V.

93. The complete list, solicited from Mexico City cathedral authorities, occupies folios 149-151 of the Guatemala Cathedral Libro de el IIIᵉ Cabildo de sanctiago de Guatemala delos aquerdos . . . que se acen desde el Año de 1599: en adelante [A. C., 1599-1650].

94. Juan Ximénez earned an annual 300 pesos de salario but by some anomaly Fabián Ximeno, "segundo organista scriptura," more than twice that (700). At least this is what he was earning, according to the figure on fol. 149ᵛ of the Guatemala source.

95. Antonio Rodríguez Mata, a contestant for the title of Mexico City Cathedral maestro de capilla so early as September 23, 1614 (Mexico City Cathedral, A. C., V, fol. 366ᵛ), had to await 1625 before exercising complete control (Stevenson, "La música en la Catedral de México: 1600-1750," Revista Musical Chilena, XIX/92, 18).

96. Juan López de la Garda arrived in fray García Guerra's personal retinue (A. C., V. fol. 101ᵛ [October 7, 1608]). Further details in Stevenson, Revista Musical Chilena, XIX/92, 13.

97. A. C., IX (1633-1639), fol. 364.

98. Ibid., fol. 384ᵛ.

99. A. C., X (1640-1650), fol. 159ᵛ. This act but duplicates dozens of others in colonial capitular documents proving that instruments became family specialties. Concerning dynasties of instrumentalists, see further Stevenson, Revista Musical Chilena, XVI/81-82, 23, 26-27, and XIX/92, 15; also Stevenson, The Music of Peru: Aboriginal and Viceroyal Epochs (Washington: Pan American Union, 1960), pp. 96-97.

100. A. C., XI (1650-1653), fol. 43: "Mando despachar Cedula para si se han de rescibir o no Los musicos menestriles que vinieron de la Puebla."

101. A. C., X, fols. 176 (July 8, 1642; given ten days to take his parents to Puebla); 198 (November 21, 1642, Grinón decides to stay in Puebla).

102. A. C., XI, fol. 138ᵛ.

103. Ibid., fol. 199ᵛ.

104. A. C., XII (1652-1655), fol. 37 and 37ᵛ.

105. Ibid., fol. 139.

106. A. C., XIII (1656-1660), fol. 21ᵛ.

107. A. C., XXI (1680-1683), fol. 111.

108. A. C., XXII (1682-1690), fol. 336: "No ha lugar." This was probably a polite way of telling Belmaña that he was not good enough a player. Antonio de Salazar, who had just been named Mexico City cathedral chapelmaster August 25 (1688), had decided to raise standards.

109. Stevenson, Revista Musical Chilena, XIX/92, p. 25.

110. A. C., XXIV (1695-1697), fol. 29. In reply to the prebendary don Juan de Narbáez's query, why punto alto? "Idiaquez dixo, que solo sirue para acompanar Vn ministril quando sube a el Organo a tocar Vajon, Chirimia, o Corneta y . . . que son Vnas mixturas que estan Vn punto mas alto que el tono del Organo, y que nunca se pueden tañer /fol. 29ᵛ/Tientos Con el, y que lo que se toca con el, que es acompañando los ministriles quando suben al Organo a cantar Versos, que eso se hace, y puede hacer muy bien el Organo sin dho punto alto, por que este se toca solo en el Organo ="

111. Ibid., fol. 29: "Y dixo El Bʳ [Francisco de] Orsuchi y Diego de Leon, que no sirue dho punto alto, respecto de tocarle los Ministriles de España por A la Mi Re, y Ela mi, y los de aca tocar, por fefaut, y Befami, que viene a ser medio punto mas alto aca que alla."

112. A. C., XXV (1698-1701), fol. 187ᵛ. Presumab ly Juan de Ortega y Montañés was already acting archbishop. See Pius B. Gams, Series Episcoporum (Regensburg: Josef Manz, 1873), p. 156.

113. A. C., XXV, fol. 234.

114. Concerning the baxoncillo = bajoncillo = vajoncillo, see Lyndesay G. Langwill, The Bassoon and Contrabassoon (London: Ernst Benn, 1965), pp. 6, 31-32.

115. A. C., XXXIII (1735-1736), fol. 36.

116. Andrés Sas failed to find any mention of the "viola" in Lima Cathedral documents. See Revista Musical Chilena, XVI/81-82, p. 30. Perhaps the "viola" mentioned in the Mexico City act was a viola da gamba.

117. A. C., XXXIII, fol. 174ᵛ. Instruments are listed in this order: "Violines, Trompas, Clarines, Violones, Violas, y Vajonsillos, y otros instrumentos de viento."

118. Vocal quartet or trio consisting of "tenor, contralto, primeros o segundos tiples."

119. A. C., XXXIX (1747-1749), fol. 324.

120. A. C., XLII (1753-1756), fol. 104ᵛ.

121. Ibid., fol. 136ᵛ. These antiphons shall be sung "como antes y como se debe, con la Musica, Vajones, y de Contrapuntto." The new Italian Ignacio Jerusalém (appointed titular maestro de capilla August 3, 1750) saw no point in continuing with this antiquated Spanish custom. He also agitated for discarding choirbooks with notes "que llaman de Vanderilla, o de Canoa, las que mui pocos de los Musicos las entienden" (A. C., XLIII [1756-1759], fol. 92 [April 19, 1757]).

122. A. C., XLII, fol. 230.

123. Ibid., fol. 245ᵛ.

124. Ibid., fol. 252ᵛ.

125. A. C., XLIII (1756-1759), fol. 256ᵛ. Syphilis = "Galico." The chapter considered Pardo de Lago to be an inveterate troublemaker (January 9, 1759 [fol. 285ᵛ]).

126. Gennaro Gagliano (1690-1771) was the acknowledged chief of the clan. See Walter Hamma, Meister italienischer Geigenbaukunst (Stuttgart: Verlagsgesellschaft MBH, 1964), pp. 242-243.

127. A. C., XLIII, fol. 298 (extra leaf). "6 Violines de Gallani el Napolitano, o de otro mejor fabricante si lo hubiere 2 Obues Cortos, y 2 Largos / 2 Flautas Trabisieras con sus piezas de Alzar y Vajar / 2 Flautas Dulzes con 2 Octauinas / 2 Fagotes largos por Be. Fa. Be. mi. / 2 Organos Portatiles Napolitanos o de otra parte donde se fabriquen bien, de ocho ö nuebe rexistros, traiendo no mas que la Cañuteria y su Secretto para que aqui se armen / 2 Clarines Octauinos de Fe. Fa. Vt. / Vn Par de timbales, en que pondra todo el esmero posible para que se logren de la maior perfeccion, por De. La. Sol. Re. / 2 Trompas, teniendo presente las que la Iglesia tiene, para que estas y que de nueuo se piden, puedan seruir de mas.

Editorial Procedures

Lauro Ayestarán's "El Barroco Musical Hispanoamericano" Yearbook of the Inter-American Institute for Musical Research, I (1965), page 66-78, explains the notation system in vogue throughout the Peninsula and Spanish America, 1625-1750. Readers deficient in Spanish will at least find instructive the facing pages 76-77, at which he opposes his transcription of the "Tenor 3º coro" in Juan de Araujo's Oigan escuchen atiendan, a villancico a duo y a 10 with a facsimile of the original manuscript. Now in the Museo Histórico Nacional, Montevideo, Uruguay, the original manuscript came from St. Philip Neri Church, Sucre, Bolivia. The composer Araujo served as Sucre Cathedral maestro de capilla from 1680 till death in 1712 and the notation system in the manuscript differs in no essential from the system prevalent in the items of the Sánchez Garza collection transcribed in the present album. Ayestarán's remarks on "Realización del 'bajo continuo'" run thus:

> The realizer was left entirely to his own devices and taste. It was as if the composer went begging for performances by being so deliberately nonspecific. "Realize me as you please but at least perform me somehow," each piece seems to cry out. "Use whatever instruments you can muster."

Carlos Vega anticipated Ayestarán's explanation of the Spanish Baroque notational system in his "Un códice peruano colonial del sigo XVII," Revista Musical Chilena, XVI/81-82 (July-December, 1962), 55-58. At page 72 he transcribed a four-voice chanzoneta Dime Pedro por tu vida by fray Manuel de Correa (died 1653 at Saragossa, while chapelmaster of La Seo). Immediately above his correct transcription Vega included a facsimile of the original Cuzco, Peru, manuscript dated c. 1690. On the other hand, he erred at measures 4-5[1], 6[1] in his transcription of Correa's Por que firme os adoro published at page 88 (facsimile on p. 87). The facing pages 342-343 in José Subirá Historia de la música española e hispanoamericana (1953) contain the facsimile of a Juan Hidalgo manuscript and Pedrell's unrealized transcription; pages 346, 497, and 501 of this same history show other useful facsimiles.

Half of the ten facsimiles in the present anthology match transcriptions. In the first, the folded dorse (lower half) of the accompaniment for Juan García's R.ce [= romance] a 4. de Nauidad. año de 1671 has been photographed side by side with the upper half of the long sheet for Tiple 1º. Juan

Gutiérrez de Padilla's Juego de cañas (facsimile II) and Fabián Ximeno's gallego (facsimile V) have also been copied longwise. The other Sánchez Garza items transcribed in the present anthology survive in sidewise copy. The name "Andrea" above the top music line (Tiple 1º) of García's romance designates the Holy Trinity nun who was the singer. Her full name in religion appears on the dorse of the accompaniment, where the dedication reads: "Para Mi S.a la M.e [madre] Andrea del S.mo [Santísimo] Sacram.to" Just as abbreviations are rife in dedications, so the composer's name at the upper right of Tiple 1º in this romance is abbreviated: "Juo Gª". The abbreviation at the end of the second music staff " ∿ estriuo" stands, of course, for estribillo = refrain, which comes next. According to Miguel Querol Gavaldá, "El romance polifónico en el siglo XVII," Anuario Musical, X (1955), 113, 119, the most usual mid-seventeenth-century romance type (his Type II) matches exactly the scheme chosen in García's present example: several initial strophes in common meter, followed by a refrain in triple. The refrain can be variously sung—after every strophe of the romance, every other strophe, or every third strophe. The copyist of García's romance groups three strophes, leaves space, then adds the other three. This spacing suggests that the estribillo should be sung after strophes 3 and 6.

Describing the music of the estribillo, Querol Gavaldá writes thus (p. 113): "It is rhythmically more diversified, looser, and more playful." Text repetition regularly occurs in the estribillo. García complies with this rule by repeating the last seven words of his refrain. But according to Querol Gavaldá, the strophes in staid common meter very rarely allow for text repetition. As the facsimile shows, García seems to break this latter rule by repeating the final word or two, at the close of each second line of his strophe quatrains. This textual repetition is to be seen only in Tiple 1º, not in any other of the original voice parts. Did García intend an echo effect in the top voice? Possibly. If so, the facsimile can serve as the conductor's authority for reintroducing the text-repetition suppressed in our transcription.

As comparison of the facsimile with the transcription at once reveals, both strophes and refrain of the García have been transcribed in 4:1 reduction ratio (minim in the manuscript equals eighth-note in the transcription). Although Querol

Gavaldá chose a 2:1 reduction ratio in Romances y Letras (1956), two decades earlier Jesus Bal y Gay chose a 4:1 for much the same repertory. Whether one prefers the quarter-note motion of item 21 in Querol Gavaldá (p. 36) or pre-dominantly eighth-note motion for exactly the same music transcribed from the same manuscript source in Bal y Gay's Treinta Canciones de Lope de Vega (Madrid: Residencia de Estudiantes, 1935), pages 39-40, depends somewhat on taste. By having elected 4:1 reduction ratios, I run the risk of pub-lishing music that looks too "modern." Bal y Gay's having reduced by 4:1 so famous a piece as Antonio de Cabezón's Diferencias sobre el canto llano del Cavallero (pp. 59-62 of the same album) gives two or three pages a curiously recent appearance. The same piece in the Davison-Apel Historical Anthology of Music, I, 145-146, or in Monumentos de la Música Española, XXIX, 60-62, looks far older.

Throughout the transcription down a minor third, I avoid the necessity of constantly naturalizing c's to correspond with García's e♭'s by the simple expedient of omitting c♯ from the "key signature." Above the unnamed highest part of fray Gerónimo González's guitar-accompanied Serenissima una noche (next in our anthology) appears the rubric baile un punto mas alto ("dance, whole-step higher"). Despite my having resisted the invitation to transpose this delightful carol to G, any brave conductor obviously enjoys the composer's authori-zation for doing so.

In the second facsimile, six separate sheets lie atop one another, the tiple part being fully visible but only the top half-inch of each of the other five parts. The inscription heading the tiple part identifies the singer as having been the same nun Andrea del Santísimo Sacramento to whom García dedi-cated his just discussed romance. Anotita, Ysabel del SS^{mo} sacra^{to}, M^a [María] de S^t jhoan, m^a Theresa, are the names on the next four parts. The latter nun sang the tenor. How-ever, the untexted bajo suggests that the lowest part was played on an instrument. Whether in cathedral or convent, colla parte instruments doubtless doubled the other parts in any actual seventeenth-century Puebla performance of this "cane game." Formally, this juego de cañas recalls two ensaladas each en-titled Las Cañas, one a 4 by Mateo Flecha the Elder (1481-1553), the other a 5 by Mateo Flecha the Younger (1530-1604). The ensaladas of both elder and younger Flechas are long, sec-tionalized pieces with internal repetitions and numerous meter changes. Transcribed from the Prague editio princeps of 1581, six ensaladas by the elder Flecha are easily available for con-sultation in the Barcelona Biblioteca Central series, Publica-ciones de la Sección de Música, XVI (1954 [1955]).

Padilla's third copla ends at measure 67 of my transcription. Next he inserts .S· calling for a repeat of the tutti at measures 43-61. Four:one is again the reduction ratio for the 𝄴 sec-tions of this juego de cañas. However, the 𝄴 sections are transcribed 2:1 so that, metronomically, an eighth in tran-

scribed measures 1-9 will equal an eighth in 10-39.

Like García's romance, Loaysa y Agurto's villancico Vaya vaya de cantos de amores has been transposed down — but in this instance a perfect fourth. Numerous Pedrell transcrip-tions set a precedent. An example already cited (because facsimile and transcription are printed on facing pages) is found in José Subirá's Historia de la música española e his-panoamericana, pages 342-343. The reduction ratio in the estribillo is 4:1, in the coplas 2:1. If this villancico shows an effervescence not to be expected from the composer whose staid canonic tribute to his patron saint was copied in Mexico City Cathedral Choirbook IV, fols. 45^V-47, and transcribed in the Spiess-Stanford An Introduction to Certain Mexican Musi-cal Archives, pages 99-104, one can but reply by pointing to similar stylistic conflicts between the Latin hymns and vernac-ular villancicos of Loaysa's two immediate Mexico City suc-cessors, Salazar and Zumaya. Or for that matter, to the con-trast between Padilla's always dignified Latin style and his untrussed vernacular vein.

In the third facsimile (Salazar's Negro a Duo, de Nauidad), the cover of the instrumental Baxo and the front side of Tiple 1° lie side by side. The barlines in the Tiple 1° part are a later addition to the original manuscript. Attention need only be called here to the following procedures: (1) transcription down a fourth; (2) reduction throughout in 4:1 ratio. So long ago as 1952 I published two unrealized Antonio de Salazar vi-llancicos, the ternary-meter sections being reduced only 2:1 (Stevenson, Music in Mexico: A Historical Survey [New York: Thomas Y. Crowell, 1952], pp. 144-147). The manuscripts of both carry their date of original performance, 1691, and belonged in 1952 to Dr. Gabriel Saldívar Silva's private col-lection. Both escape a too tedious thinness by including sec-tions a 5 or a 4, a relief not available to performers of the two Salazar unrealized duos in the present anthology.

More recently, Guillermo Orta Velázquez's Breve historia de la música en México (México: Manuel Porrúa, 1970) in-cluded at pages 202-207 Salazar's 1710 villancico a 4, Si el agravio Pedro, realized and "arranged" by J. Jesús Estrada, Mercaderes 45, Mexico City. At the risk of criticism such as Leo Schrade voiced against Hans Redlich in Musical Quar-terly, XL/1 (January, 1954), 138-145, The Music of Peru: Aboriginal and Viceroyal Epochs (Washington: General Secretariat, Organization of American States, 1960) included realizations of a negro and a hymn by Juan de Araujo, of a cantata by José se Orejón y Aparicio, and of a 1701 loa and excerpts from a 1701 representación música by Tomás de Torrejón y Velasco. Schrade, it will be remem-bered, berated Redlich for "a version over-romantic, with little musical taste and understanding of style, but with serious changes in the original text." True, the last charge cannot justly be leveled against the villancicos published in The Music of Peru. But some may feel that the second full paragraph on page 144 of Schrade's review applies. Some authorities may also question Cerone or Lorente's counterpoint rules, just as Schrade "could never convince himself that [Michael] Praetorius's version" represents Monteverdi's intentions. In a lecture largely devoted to Monteverdi realizations May 29, 1967, at the Auditorium Gulbenkian, Lisbon, Santiago Kastner took like exception to Denis Stevens's "dissonant and audacious" realizations of Orfeo (published by Novello, 1967). Bruno Maderna's of the same he utterly discounted. But Kurtz Myers and Richard S. Hill's Record Ratings (New York: Crown Publishers, 1956), page 177, classed Schrade's review of the performance using the Redlich edition of Vespro della Beata Vergine as the only negative review among nine. Differing from Kastner, Robert Donington called Denis Stevens's "continuo realizations beautifully within the style," filled with "many happy touches of inventiveness," and even thinner than need be (Musical Times, 108/1492 [June, 1967], 539).

Although the fourth facsimile shows principally the Tiple for Francisco de Vidales's jácara [= xacara] a 4, Los que fueren de buen gusto, the top inch or so of Alto and "Baxo" (= acompañamiento) parts can also be seen in the same facsimile (baxo part lacks a text). The temptation to adjust text to the baxo was resisted because at measures 38-40 the texted tiples and alto sing, "cantemos a las tres; tres a tres" ("let us sing a trio, a trio for three"). To have texted the baxo would at this point in the jácara have saddled us with four parts. As can be surmised from the facsimile, Vidales's original manuscript parts survive in extremely poor condition. The nun "esquibela" sang tiple. The abbreviation "M.º" before "Vidales" at the top of the baxo part stands of course for the courtesy title of "maestro"—used in addressing either principal cathedral organist or chapelmaster.

In the introduction to Monumentos de la Música Española, XVIII (1956), page 15, Querol Gavaldá disposed of sung jácaras thus: "'Jácaras,' as is well known, were nothing but romances on a picaresque subject." Because of his editorial responsibilities, the article in Diccionario de la Música Labor (1954) II, 1298, may also be attributed to him. Somewhat paraphrased it reads:

> The stage jácara began as a picaresque interlude designed to provoke laughter among the poorer spectators with its gay descriptions of a ruffian's exploits. Juan de Esquivel Navarro's Discvrsos sobre el arte Del Dançado (Seville: Juan Gómez de Blas, 1642), folio 30^v, decrees that the Rastro, Iacara [= jácara], Zarauanda [sarabande], y Tarraga, estas quatro pieças son vna mesma cosa, which is to say that the lively dance steps in all four were identical. Old Spanish instrumental anthologies for guitar, organ, and keyboard instrument include purely instrumental jácaras. Joan Cabánilles's Xacara 1º tono labeled "un prodigio" in one manuscript source [see Biblioteca de Catalunya, Publicacions del Departament de Música, VIII (1933), pp. xxvi and 146-152], affords an example of the purely instrumental jácara, Cabanilles's being constructed over a recurrent bass pattern. Sacred sung jácaras frequently turn up in the seventeenth- and eighteenth-century villancico repertory. Felipe Pedrell published an enchanting example for three sopranos and chorus in his Cancionero musical popular español, IV, no. 101.

In his Diccionario crítico etimólogico de la lengua castellana (Madrid: Editorial Gredos, 1954), II, 1023, Joan Corominas derived "jácara = xacara" from "xaque." English "check" comes from the same Arabic root as does "xaque." Already in Alfonso X's 1283 Libro de Ajedrez "dar xaque" signified "to threaten the king" we are reminded by Corominas (II, 1034). Cervantes used the word "xacara" in El Rvfian Dichoso to mean a "disordered, licentious life" (II, 1022). In the Iornada segvnda of Cervantes's just mentioned play, "to sing in the manner of a xacara" meant to sing in a rowdy, roistering way: "La musica no es diuina / porque, segun voy notando / al modo vienen cantando / rufo y de xacarandina."[1] In La Ilustre fregona ("The Illustrious Washerwoman") Cervantes used "xacara" to mean a "big racket."[2] Quite apart from musical usage, the term can be copiously documented from other early seventeenth-century sources to mean simply "boastfulness" or a "quarrelsome attitude." Matching this general sense, the music of the seventeenth-century sacred jácara frequently called for widely leaping basses, more than usually heavy accents (many displaced), and risoluto rather than piacevole or scorrevole movement.

The fifth facsimile again shows individual parts laid atop one other. Like Padilla's, Ximeno's parts are copied longwise. The Acompañamiento identifies this as a "gallego." That the opening refrain must be sung after Copla 1ª comes clearly to light at the bottom of the "Tiple a Solo" first page. Alonso Xuares's Venid venid zagales forces D♭ into the accompaniment of measure 8^4, C♯ in 17^6, E♭ in 29^1, A♭ in 37^4 and 38^1, because (for once) liberal figures appear above the instrumental Acompañamiento part. Although the accidentals can nearly always be surmised from flats or sharps written in the voice parts, their presence in the continuo foretells the next century, when figures at last became standard operating procedure in some Peninsular accompaniments.

Facsimiles VI through X illustrate other types of music in the Sánchez Garza archive. Like the gallego, the viscaino = viscaíno (Facsimile VI) echoes Peninsular regional strains. Highly characteristic of viscaino texts are these refrain words: "Borrico Juancho." The copyist clearly specifies Dal segno repeats after coplas 2, 4, and 5. Although C Major cannot be at once deduced from only Tiple 1º of this four-part anonymous 1679 Christmas viscaino, the accompaniment leaves no room for doubt. In the photograph, the first five notes of the tenor-clef accompaniment for the coplas peer through beneath the title (copied on the dorse of the accompaniment). They read: c f e e d c. Above the title, notes 4 through 9 of the estribillo accompaniment show through: C C F E E A.

As in Vidales's jácara, the copyist of the chanberga=chamberga (Facsimile VII) chose $\}$ instead of the more usual $c\}$ for mensuration sign. The convent singers' names visible at the top of Tiples 1, 2, and Alto parts read: .S. miguel, ysabel, and ynes. Only these three of the original five parts seem to survive. Even so, they tell us that the chanberga, like the other folkloric types heretofore mentioned (negro, negriya, gallego, viscaino) inhabited major. The bottom line in this facsimile sets this text: "Tu nacimiento niño, con tal belleza / Cantar quiero en metro de la chanberga que lindo." ("Your birth, Child, with such beauty, I wish to sing in the meter of the chanberga so pretty.") Even if from other sources[3] the chanberga were not known to have been a Baroque dance type, the just-cited text of the "R. on [= Responsión] ala chanberga" would forbid our confounding "chanberga" with the name of the composer.[4] Does the scrawl before each singer's name clue the composer's name? The numerals 1, 2, and the plus signs above the Alto notes are a later addition. Without the missing vocal parts, one dare not risk the presumption that guitar chords equaling tonic, subdominant, and dominant chords are thereby indicated (obviously the 17th alto note forbids the tonic).

Facsimile VIII shows all of Tiple 1º and the top rims of the only other three surviving parts of a Good Friday Tone IV "Motete de fran[co] de olibera." Transcribed, these four texted parts make a perfectly full whole. Indeed, in the successive imitative points a fifth voice part would clutter the scene.[5] Francisco de Olivera, later a Puebla Cathedral succentor, was a Mexico City Cathedral contrabajo in 1616[6] (no longer so on December 1, 1623).

Facsimile IX combines the left two-thirds of "Tiple Primero Solo, y a Seis" with the right dorse of the accompaniment. The calligraphy is more than usually handsome. Facsimile X carries us into the next century, Francisco de Atienza y Pineda succeeding to the Puebla chapelmastership in 1712. Although his is a Mass postdating 1712, Puebla villancico prints dating from 1715, 1716, 1717, 1719, 1720, 1721, and 1722 confirm his continuing vivid interest in the vernacular. Our facsimile of his parody Missa A, 5º Vo, s shows the cover of the Tiple 1º booklet alongside the first page of the Tiple 2º part. The Pfundnoten in the Christe eleyson give this particular page an archaic, constricted look not in keeping with the easy F Major flow of the harmonies throughout this amiable and gratefully concise movement.

NOTES

1. Obras Completas: Comedias y Entremeses (Madrid: Bernardo Rodríguez, 1916), II, 70. Original spellings.

2. Obras Completas: Novelas exemplares (Madrid: Gráficas Reunidas, s.a., 1923), II, 324: "donde se exercita todo genero de rumbo y xacara y de extraordinarios juramentos y boatos" ("where they make a big show and roister and curse loudly and brag").

3. Stevenson, Music in Aztec & Inca Territory (Berkeley and Los Angeles:University of California Press, 1968), pp. 235-236.

4. An Introduction to Certain Mexican Musical Archives (Detroit Studies in Music Bibliography, 15), pp. 65, 80.

5. Possibly the "fifth" part was merely a now-lost basso seguente.

6. Actas Capitulares, V (1606-1616), fol. 436^V (August 5, 1616).

Biographical Data

The distinguished Jesuit José López Calo called the strangely neglected and misunderstood Spanish seventeenth century a century of enigmas ("El Archivo de Música de la Capilla Real de Granada," Anuario Musical, XIII [1958], 125). José Subirá labeled it an epoch when contrapuntal wizardry was enthroned, while at the same time the concertante style reigned supreme (Historia de la música española e hispanoamericana) (Barcelona: Salvat Editores, 1953), p. 394 — so much so that no religious festival could attract a sizable public without promising the merry jingle of shawms, cornetts, sackbuts, bassoons, harps, joined by assorted stringed instruments. This was the century at the middle of which so staid a monastery as El Escorial paid for new two- and three-manual organs with stops imitating every known instrument, and with pedals that controlled drums and 59 bells — 32 of them chromatically tuned (p. 401 [Francisco de los Santos, Descripcion breve de San Lorenzo el Real, 1657]). This was also the century when every provincial cathedral boasted a maestro de capilla adept in puzzle canons, no fewer than 94 of which maestros attained sufficient stature to be remembered by name in Subirá's chapter on "La música religiosa en el siglo XVII."

Yet in contrast with Subirá's cornucopia of names, so standard a vademecum as Gilbert Chase's The Music of Spain (New York: W. W. Norton, 1941; Dover Publications, 1959) mentions no Baroque Spanish composer whatsoever, except those few who contributed to the lyric stage. Why not? The seventeenth century saw publication of the supreme monuments of Spanish literature. This was also the century of Velázquez and Murillo. Why have the literature and painting of the period enjoyed such esteem but the music suffered oblivion abroad? Failure to appreciate the paradoxes of Spanish seventeenth-century style may be one basic reason. But this failure surely stems from other problems as well, among them inaccessibility of the music itself.

Huge quantities of vernacular as well as Latin music flowed from the pens of Peninsular and New World composers during the reigns of Philip III, Philip IV, and Charles II. But it was rarely published, and its composers did not travel outside the Spanish orbit. In the preceding century Encina, Peñalosa, Morales, Escobedo, the two Guerreros, Las Infantas, Soto, and Victoria had all spent lengthy periods abroad, usually in Italy. What is more, the Latin works of Morales, Francisco Guerrero and Victoria reached print in Italy, France, and Germany during their own lifetimes. Not the impotence of seventeenth-century Spanish and New World composers, but their failure to circulate, and their failure to publish and to propagandize their works abroad may account for the obscurity that prevents even their names from entering standard histories and encyclopedias.

By the very nature of convent musical life, it is not to be expected that the most taxing and ambitious Baroque masterpieces should have been frequently performed in the Holy Trinity Convent at Puebla, to which all the music in the Sánchez Garza Collection originally belonged. Nonetheless, many of the composers rated among the best that Spanish dominions had to offer and their biographies are therefore correspondingly significant.

Of course it is not to be expected that the mere quantity of biographical data here assembled concerning any one composer in the Sánchez Garza Collection infallibly indexes the given composer's musical importance. Still, it is gratifying to realize how extensive are the biographies that can now be written of Sebastián Durón, Juan Gutiérrez de Padilla, and Francisco de Santiago — to mention only three composers whose biographies are presented below. Since practically none of the biographical data here offered is to be found in any standard reference work, the following twelve biographies should prove extremely welcome to lexicographers, while at the same time supplying the background needed for an appreciation of the twelve composers whose Christmas pieces are included in the present volume.

SEBASTIÁN DURÓN (Baptized April 19, 1660, at Brihuega; died August 3, 1716, at Bayonne or nearby Cambo)

Although no Spanish composer of his era enjoyed wider notoriety, Sebastián Durón has been confounded in every dictionary to date with his elder half-brother Diego Durón — a maestro de capilla of Las Palmas Cathedral in the Canary Islands 1676-1731,[1] whose fame in his lifetime never transcended the merely local. Sebastián's music can be found scattered through all the important archives of the Americas, from Mexico City to Sucre, Bolivia.[2] But his half-brother's has been inventoried almost nowhere except in Las Palmas, and only lucky accident accounts for a 1967 recording (Archiv 198 453, Meister der

Barock, "Hispaniae Musica").

As if the geographic spread of his works were not enough, Sebastián Durón cuts a fine figure in early eighteenth-century books published as far afield as Peru. For instance, Pedro Joseph de Peralta Barnuevo's Lima trivmphante, glorias de la America (Lima: Joseph de Contreras y Alvarado, 1708), fol. M3, compliments the Marqués de Castelldosrius (Manuel de Oms y Santa Pau, viceroy of Peru from May 24, 1707, until his death on April 24, 1710) for having brought from Europe his private band of nine musicians who excel in tonadas and villancicos of Sebastián Durón as well as in instrumental music by Corelli. Among the nine musicians brought to Peru by this viceroy, Roque Ceruti thirty years later earned the supreme accolade of being declared now equal to Andrés Lorente and Sebastián Durón. So wrote Pedro Joseph Bermúdez de la Torre in Trivnfos del Santo Oficio Pervano (Lima: Imprenta Real, 1737, fol. 53).

In Portugal, the name of Sebastián Durón shone no less brightly than in Peru. Only five years after Durón's death the retired chapelmaster of Évora Cathedral, Pedro Vaz Rego (1670-1736), called him the wonder of his times. Six quatrains from Rego's 36-page Armonico Lazo, con que se une una metrica correspondencia de Portugal a Castilla (Évora: 1731 [copy in Biblioteca de Ajuda, 55-II-13] can be thus paraphrased. [3]

> While matters still remained up in the air, along came the more diplomatic Durón to whom was confided the task of harmonizing everything. In Madrid he worked wonders and became the chief composer. Why he left for France passes understanding. A lengthy correspondence passed between us and I have saved his letters. Feijóo [1676-1764] condemned him unjustly. Durón wrote dignified church music and only in comedy gave way to the vogues that delight the public. He should not be blamed for this. But the double sharpened sword of Feijóo, who readily believed mere conjectures, spares nothing. God pardon all of those who dogmatically legislate on matters that are neither their business nor their area of competence.

In a marginal note Rego cites Feijóo's Theatro Crítico, tom. 1, discurs. 14, § 8 (fol. 303 of the 1726 edition). Frequently reprinted, Feijóo's attack has now become a classic of Spanish invective. According to the puritanical Benedictine monk, the third thing wrong with church music in his time was "the liberty taken by composers who modulate when and where fancy dictates, without holding fast to any one subject treated imitatively." [4] Contemporary taste had been subverted by the horde of foreign executants flooding Spain who lacked the science necessary to compose contrapuntally. "Because they are unable to write this class of music, they try to cover their defect by proclaiming to everyone within earshot that imitative writing is old-fashioned." [5]

> This "up-to-date" Italian musical style was foisted on us by their admirer Maestro Durón, for it was who corrupted Spanish music with foreign admixtures. True, some of these foreignisms have

been so purified in the meantime that if Durón were now brought back to life he would not recognize them. Still, however, he must bear the blame for all these novelties, because he first opened the gate to them, allowing Italian airs to rush in upon us like the winds of which Virgil wrote in the Aeneid [I, 83]: "Winds rushed forth where the opening was made, and swept over the land in a tornado." Under the illusion that musical progress was at stake, Spain bowed before the Italians as obsequiously as Italians were in the habit of bowing to Greeks long ago when Pliny the Elder moaned: "Art changes every day, being furbished up again and again, and we are swept along on the puffs of the clever brains of Greece" (Natural History, Book 29, 5, 11). [6]

Not content with calling up the shades of Virgil and Pliny to testify against Durón, Feijóo lays other charges at Durón's door. Some composers try to vary the music for every single word in a text like Mors festina luctuosa, writing fast runs for festina but slow music for mors and luctuosa.

> More than anybody, the famous Durón fell into this trap — so much so that at times he changed the musical expression six or eight times within the same verse, in order to express the sense of each individual word in a line. To make such frequent shifts requires great dexterity, which of course he possessed. Still, he turned his skill to very bad ends. [7]

Without specifically naming Durón, Feijóo also seems to blame him for "the shrieking violins that cannot help sounding shrill, even when in tune, and that inspire childlike transports far distant from the sober attention due the sacred mysteries." [8] Violinsts even ascend nowadays to the bridge, says Feijóo. But on the other hand he is willing to tolerate the bass viol, harp, spinet, and organ — although "of course organists, when they so desire, make their instrument sound like a hurdygurdy or a drum (which all too often is just what they want it to sound like)." [9]

Right or wrong in his criticisms, at least Feijóo's frontal attack proves how capital was the role played in the epoch by one sole individual. Even if in a negative way, he thus substantiates Durón's primacy in the period. Thanks to the researches of Nicolás A. Solar-Quintes embodied in "Nuevos documentos para la biografía del compositor Sebastián Durón," of José Subirá in "La música en la Real Capilla madrileña y en el Colegio de Niños Cantorcicos," and especially of Lothar G. Siemens Hernández in "Nuevos documentos sobre el músico Sebastián Durón: once años de vida profesional anteriores a su llegada a la corte del rey Carlos II" and "Nuevas aportaciones para la biografía de Sebastián Durón"—all four of which articles appeared in issues of Anuario Musical, X (1955), 137-162, XIV (1959), 207-230, XVI (1961), 177-199, and XVIII (1963 [1965]),137-159, the biography of this remarkable innovator

and musical genius can now be traced with admirable accuracy and wealth of detail.

Born fifty miles northeast of Madrid and twenty northeast of Guadalajara at the town of Brihuega, Durón was baptized April 19, 1660. His father, a church sacristan in Brihuega, was born in 1626. Bearer of the same name, Sebastián Durón, the father was a native of the town. So were the composer's paternal grandparents, Juan Durón and Ana de San Martín. It was a child of Sebastián Durón [de San Martín]'s first marriage with Francisca de Ortega who emigrated to the Canary Islands, there serving as chapelmaster of Las Palmas Cathedral 55 years. Margarita Picazo, the second wife, married the widower Sebastián Durón [de San Martín] August 12, 1659. She was a native of the nearby village of Romancos. Before November 3, 1662, two younger brothers were born, Francisco and Alonso. The composer's father died October 6, 1668, at the age of 42, leaving besides the four boys by first and second marriages three girls, Ana, Jerónima, and Baltasara Pascuala.[10] At least two of the girls, Ana and Baltasara Pascuala, outlived the composer and at his death were nuns in the convent of San Ildefonso in Brihuega.[11] The composer's mother (born 1634) was still alive in 1685.

The composer's first known organ teacher was Andrés de Sola, who on January 12, 1672, succeeded Joseph Ximénez (Sola's uncle) as first organist of La Seo, the cathedral at Saragossa. On June 19, 1679, Sola's recommendation that "his pupil Sebastián Durón be accepted as his paid assistant" was read and approved at a chapter meeting (La Seo, Actas Capitulares, 1676-1680 [1679, p. 41].[12] However, Durón continued as Sola's paid assistant no longer than nine months. So brilliant were his already demonstrated gifts that on March 18, 1680, the Seville Cathedral chapter appointed him second organist there with the munificent annual salary of 600 ducats.[13] For introducing him at Seville, emporium of the Indies and mistress of Spanish wealth, Durón had the then cathedral chapelmaster to thank, Alonso Xuares (held the post 1675-1684).

On April 26, 1679, the dean of Seville Cathedral announced to the assembled chapter the death of the previous second organist. At once, steps were taken to advertise the vacancy far and wide. No sufficient candidate having presented himself before the end of the year, the chapter sent Xuares on a trip scouting for not only a new second organist but also for other needed musicians. Xuares fell ill at Guadalajara, twenty miles from Durón's hometown, and in his letter to the Seville Cathedral dated January 8, 1680, asked leave to remain at Guadalajara until recovered. The Seville chapter acceded with six weeks' sick leave. On February 28, 1680, was read a letter from Xuares to the chapter announcing his imminent arrival with an organist candidate. The said organist was of course Durón. How brilliantly he performed at the competitive examination held Thursday night March 14, before three judges — Xuares, Francisco de Medina (first organist of Seville Cathedral[14]), and fray Juan de San Francisco (Jeronymite in San

Isidro de el Campo monastery) — can be inferred from the vote of the chapter members present, 43 for Sebastián Durón,[15] 5 for Esteban Lloz, 1 for Juan de Torres.

Durón remained in Seville until September 24, 1685.[16] His earliest surviving villancicos date from 1683. After Alonso Xuares quit Seville and returned home to Cuenca in May, 1684, Sevillian cathedral music lacked a director until Diego Joseph de Salazar was appointed November 26, 1685 (died June 25, 1709). During the intervening months several singers died, among them the chief sopranist Francisco Navarro (February 15, 1685), who had served as interim conductor of the cathedral choir until August 18, 1684. Thus decimated, the choir could not sing old repertory. New was needed, tailored to the survivors. Although Durón had been negotiating with Burgo de Osma Cathedral for a new organistship since October 11, 1684,[17] the Seville Cathedral chapter on March 22, 1685, requested that he delay moving[18] until he had composed a Compline Service for use during Lent that year, a Miserere and Lamentations for Holy Week, and some other Holy Week music. On Monday April 30, 1685, he received 250 reales for these works.[19] He probably composed the Ascension, San Fernando, and Corpus Christi music performed later that same year by the still undermanned Sevillian cathedral choir.[20]

Durón took at least minor ecclesiastical orders before December 22, 1683, on which date the Sevillian chapter sent word for him to wear his proper ecclesiastical garb whenever he played, and to stop allowing a pupil to substitute for him at mattins (maitines).[21] However, he still remained only a deacon four years later (February 22, 1687[22]), by which time he should certainly have been ordained priest if that was his goal. As a deacon he was eligible to hold a prebend, with the attendant prestige that a tenurable cathedral post offered. The post of second organist paid well at Seville. But only the first carried a prebend. Burgo de Osma, a less opulent cathedral, could compensate for Sevillian wealth with a prebend. At the outset of negotiations, Burgo de Osma also held out the hope of hiring simultaneously as maestro de capilla Sebastián's half-brother Diego Durón (who had been recently called to Teruel on the strength of his reputation).[23] To save the expense of a formal tryout, the Burgo de Osma chapter solicited a written testimonial from Sebastián Durón's great protector and stimulus, the former chapelmaster of Seville Alonso Xuares. On October 31, 1684, Xuares's letter of recommendation reached the Burgo de Osma chapter. In it he vouched under oath for Sebastián Durón's habilidad y suficiencia. Also he called Diego Durón "a very worthy and knowledgeable"[24] choice for maestro de capilla.

All the evidence thus far assembled goes to prove how right was Juan de Loaysa (1633-1709), the Colombina librarian who knew both, in claiming that Xuares not only reared him but also obtained for Sebastián Durón his organ prebends.[25]

Certainly it was Xuares who gave him his start at Seville and then kept interest in him at Burgo de Osma alive while Durón slowly disengaged himself from Seville. On February 21, 1685, the Burgo de Osma chapter wrote Durón a warning letter "that if he is not here by Palm Sunday, he need not come at all because he will not be accepted."[26] He did not arrive. On May 2, the Burgo de Osma chapter told the secretary to write him that "if he is not here by Saturday Vespers of Pentecost, he will be considered dismissed."[27] Still he delayed. Only Xuares saved the post for him with excuses read at the Burgo de Osma chapter meeting of August 29, 1685, and the promise that Durón would without fail be there on October 18. This time Durón did arrive.[28] On October 22 the chapter fixed his salary for organ playing at 150 ducats annually, a paltry sum which must have been considerably augmented by the perquisites of the prebend. To meet moving expense costs the Burgo de Osma chapter gave him 200 reales on November 14, and to pay the expenses of the character and genealogy investigation (limpieza de sangre) prerequisite to any formal installation in a prebend loaned him another 512 reales (= 17, 408 maravedís) in December. This latter debt, equal to almost a third of his annual organist's salary, remained still largely unpaid 24 years later.[29] However, the Burgo de Osma chapter could not have incurred a better "bad debt." Nearly all the primary sources for Durón's family history were destroyed in the war of 1936-1939 and only the copies at Burgo de Osma Cathedral now survive to establish Durón's origins.[30]

The Burgo de Osma chapter paid an organ repairman named Ventura de Chabarri 150 reales for fixing and tuning the cathedral organs during a stopover in the town that lasted from April 27 to May 31, 1686.[31] On July 17 (1686) Durón asked permission to transfer elsewhere because he could not live on the Burgo de Osma salary.[32] The canons immediately responded with the offer of another annual 50 ducats and 12 additional fanegas of wheat, beginning August 1. But Durón already knew where next he intended to move, the cathedral at Palencia ninety miles west.[33] Written agreements with the Palencia chapter dated July 27 and October 7, 1686[34] led to his formal induction in the Palencia organ prebend December 1. On October 29 he attended his last chapter meeting at Burgo de Osma.

During his five years at Palencia, he won various financial benefits,[35] suggested various new musical appointments,[36] taught at least two budding organists,[37] and continued building his own reputation as an outstanding virtuoso. Francisco Zubieta was cathedral chapelmaster there in 1689-1690.[38] Seven months after the retirement of the royal organist Joseph Sanz,[39] Durón succeeded him at Madrid September 23, 1691. Starting with 500 ducats plus rations and other benefits for two persons, he was also allowed September 23 (1691) 200 ducats to cover basic expenses for moving furniture and family ("su Cassa y Familia"). On January 25, 1696. his organist's

salary rose by 300 ducats annually.[40] In 1702, two years after Charles II's death, he served as Royal Chapelmaster and Rector of the Royal Choirschool[41] at an aggregate salary of 1,500 ducats annually.[42] At the close of 1703 he petitioned for even more money, but Philip V refused him his request. Disgruntled with the new king's economies or for some other unknown reason, he sided with the Austrian party during the War of the Spanish Succession, and on July 23, 1706, was seized on the Bridge of Viveros[43] where in the company of several high ecclesiastics he fruitlessly awaited the entry into Madrid of the Archduke Charles (= Charles VI of Austria, 1685-1740, proclaimed Charles III of Spain at Vienna in 1703). Shipped off to Bayonne, he lived the rest of his life in exile just across the border from San Sebastián. Mariana of Neuburg assuaged the sorrows of exile with a band of nine or ten musicians,[44] most of whom to judge from their names were French.[45] On October 25, 1715, she appointed Durón her chief almoner ("primer limosnero").[46] However, he lived less than a year to enjoy the £4,000 paid by the position. On August 1, 1716, he added at Cambo a codicil to his will (originally drawn up and signed at Bayonne February 6, 1715[47]) and died two days later.[48] Tended in his later years by a clergyman in minor orders named Juan de Peralonso, Durón made him an executor and heir. Two years later Peralonso still busied himself at Madrid and elsewhere settling Durón's complex business affairs. After lifetime bequests to his sisters Ana and Baltasara Pascuala, Jeronymite nuns in San Ildefonso convent, Brihuega,[49] he directed that the whole income from his estate should endow the chapel of Our Lady of the Reed (Nuestra Señora de la Zarza) in the Brihuega church where he had been baptized, San Felipe.[50] Long before decease, Durón had already started accumulating expensive tapestries, paintings, and ornaments.[51] His testator Peralonso paid almost 880 reales in November of 1717, to two shawmers and a bass player, a painter, sculptor, three carpenters, an ironmonger, a tailor, and others[52] whose combined efforts made it possible to open the chapel endowed by Durón. In Madrid during the preceding September and October Peralonso paid the architect, goldsmith, silversmith, and merchants who had been responsible for the retable.[53]

Durón's six or seven extant zarzuelas and his importance in the history of this musico-dramatic type[54] justify his peculiar devotion to Nuestra Señora de la Zarza. His Salir el Amor del mundo and La Guerra de los Gigantes prompted an extended musical analysis by Ambrosio Pérez (first published in Baltasar Saldoni's Diccionario biográfico-bibliográfico de efemérides de músicos españoles, III, 139[55]). In 1932 Cotarelo y Mori added his detailed analysis of Veneno es de amor la embidia[56] (text by Antonio de Zamora). Five Durón theatrical works entirely his and one written with Juan Navas enter the Anglés-Subirá Madrid catalogue.[57]

At Cuzco, Peru — ancient capital of the Incas — the San

Antonio Abad Seminary still owns four vernacular works by Durón, one of which was still being sung as late as 1753 (five-voice jácara in honor of the Blessed Sacrament, Elaba la jacarilla). Like his latest, so also his earliest piece at Cuzco, Benigno favonio, is a Blessed Sacrament villancico. Two other villancicos a 4 pay homage to the Blessed Virgin (August 15), Delicadas aves and Hombres luses). A fifth work at Cuzco calls for harp accompaniment — Laudate pueri a 4 (dated 1694). At Guatemala Cathedral are found ten of his vernacular works,[58] one of which is the Madrid imprint using Negro-dialect text, Negliya que quela, a 4, for Christmas. The sole Latin work at Guatemala, a Lamentation a 8, Quomodo sedet, illustrates the common custom in his time of writing polychorally to Latin texts (three choirs in this instance). The same Maundy Thursday Lamentation turns up at Mexico City Cathedral in a 25-page score (violins 1 and 2 at the top, continuo at the bottom, voices between [Microfilm 66 at the Mexico City National Institute of Anthropology and History Library]). Sucre Cathedral in Bolivia owns duplicate copies of his 1683 Bolcanes de amor and six other precious villancicos.[59]

NOTES

1. Lola de la Torre de Trujillo, "El Archivo de Música de la Catedral de Las Palmas," El Museo Canario, XXV/89-92 (January-December 1964), 193. Diego Durón's surviving repertory at Las Palmas includes 422 villancicos indexed at pp. 203-216, and 40 Latin works, pp. 197-202.

2. Stevenson, The Music of Peru: Aboriginal and Viceroyal Epochs (Washington: Pan American Union, 1960), p. 190. Bolcanes de amor in Tone V composed by Sebastián Durón in 1683 continued still popular at Sucre in 1741. Composed at Seville, this same villancico is in the Las Palmas archive (El Museo Canario, XXV/89-92, 192). Sucre owns another Sebastián Durón 1683 villancico, Por que penas fatiga.

3. Reprinted with errors in Joaquim de Vasconcellos's El-Rey D. João o 4.to (Oporto: Typographia Universal, 1905), p. 154, and also in Felipe Pedrell's Catàlech de la Biblioteca Musical (Barcelona: Palau de la Diputació, 1909), II, 328, the six quatrains correctly read thus in the 1731 original: "Vino mas blando Duron / y mientras que no se ajustan / las cosas, fuè midiendo / la harmonia por industrias. // En Madrid hizo prodigios, / y era la mayor altura / de su Polo: no sè como / dexò por Francia su cuna. // Mucha atencion le debi / en cartas, que guardo suyas, ni hallo razon à Feyjoò, / porque en falso le mormura. // El compuso para el Templo, con decorosa cordura, / y à lo Comico diò libres / las modas, que el Pueblo gusta. // En esto no hay que culparle, / mas la espada bis acuta / de Feyjoò, nada perdona, / y aun cree por conjeturas. // Perdonenos Dios a todos, / que haciendo en el orbe bulla, / cada cual à su negocio / aficiona lo que estudia."

4. Teatro Crítico Universal (Madrid: Joachin Ibarra, 1773), I, 299: "La tercera distincion está en la libertad que hoy se toman los Compositores para ir metiendo en la Música todas aquellas modulaciones que les ván ocurriendo á la fantasía, sin ligarse á imitacion, ó thema."

5. Ibid., I, 299-300: "Los Estrangeros que vienen á España, por lo comun son unos meros executores, y así no pueden form r este género de Música, porque pide mas ciencia de la que tienen; pero para encubrir su defecto, procuran persuadir

acá á todos, que eso de seguir pasos no es de la moda."

6. Ibid., I, 300: "Esta es la Música de estos tiempos, con que nos han regalado los Italianos, por mano de su aficionado el Maestro Durón, que fue el que introduxo en la Música de España las modas estrangeras. Es verdad que despues acá se han apurado tanto estas, que si Durón resucitára, yá no las conociera; pero siempre se le podrá echar á él la culpa de todas estas novedades, por haber sido el primero que les abrió la puerta, pudiendo aplicarse á los ayres de la Música Italiana lo que cantò Virgilio de los vientos. Qua data porta, ruunt et terras turbine perflant. Y en quanto á la Música se verifica ahora en los Españoles, respecto de los Italianos, aquella facil condescendencia á admitir novedades, que Plinio lamentaba en los mismos Italianos, respecto de los Griegos: Mutatur ars cottidie totiens interpolis, et ingeniorum Graeciae flatu inpellimur."

7. Ibid., I, 303: "En este defecto cayó, mas que todos, el célebre Durón, en tanto grado, que á veces, dentro de una misma copla variaba seis, ú ocho veces los afectos del canto, segun se iban variando los que significaban por sí solas las dicciones del verso. Y aunque era menester para esto grande habilidad, como de hecho la tenia, era muy mal aplicada."

8. Ibid., I, 305: "Sus chillidos, aunque harmoniosos, son chillidos, y excitan una viveza como pueril en nuestros espíritus, muy distante de aquella atencion decorosa que se debe á la magestad de los Mysterios; especialmente en esta tiempo, que los que componen para Violines, ponen estudio en hacer las composiciones tan subidas, que el executor vaya á dár en el puente con los dedos."

9. Ibid., I, 306: "Es verdad que los Organistas hacen de él, quando quieren Gayta, y Tamboril; y quieren muchas veces."

10. All the aforesaid data in this paragraph is documented from the composer's Información de linpieza de linaxe in Legajo 4.º, número 7, 1685 (belonging to a bundle running from 1653 to 1699), found by Lothar G. Siemens Hernández at Burgo de Osma Cathedral (capitular archive). See Anuario Musical, XVIII, 138-141.

11. Anuario Musical, X, 143.

12. Ibid., XVIII, 147: "Leyose un memorial de don Andrés de Sola, organista del Santo Templo del Saluador, en que pide se le dé aiudante a Sebastián Durón, su discípulo, y se le dé lo que se daba a Gerónimo la Torre, el que antes era su aiudante. Hízosele la gracia y como tenía Gerónimo la Torre, su antecedente substitución."

13. Ibid., XVI, 180. Concerning the date, see also Anuario Musical, XVIII, 150, n. 15. Unlike other Spanish cathedrals, Seville demanded much of the second organist and ranked him not much lower than the first organist (ibid., XVI, 179). Even so, "600" ducats may be a lapsus calami.

14. Entered the first organist's prebend February 3, 1671; died June 20, 1694. Preceded by Juan Sanz (March 10, 1653-April 23, 1661) and José Sanz (May 5, 1661-August 27, 1670); followed by Joseph Muñoz de Monserrate (appointed December 6, 1694).

15. The Seville chapter secretary recorded him as a native of Saragossa ("natural de Zaragoça"), a mistake easily understandable after Durón's term there as assistant to Andrés Sola.

16. Anuario Musical, XVIII, 153.

17. Ibid., XVI, 183.

18. Ibid., XVIII, 152.

19. Ibid., XVI, 184-185.

20. Ibid., XVIII, 153.

21. Ibid., XVI, 182.

22. Ibid., p. 192.

23. Ibid., p. 183.

24. Ibid.:"sugeto muy a propósito y científico."

25. Simón de la Rosa y López, Los seises de la Catedral de Sevilla (Seville: Imp. de Francisco de P. Díaz, 1904), p. 156.

26. Anuario Musical, XVI, 184:"que si no estubiere en esta Santa Yglesia para el Domingo de Ramos no se mueua porque no se le admitirá."

27. Ibid., p. 185:"si quisiere uenir esté en esta Santa Yglesia el sáuado víspera de Pascua de Espíritu Santo, y si este día no estubiere se dé por despedido."

28. Ibid., p. 186.

29. Ibid., XVIII, 155-157.

30. Ibid., p. 138.

31. Ibid., p. 154.

32. Ibid., XVI, 188:"no se allaba con medios ni renta para poder pasar."

33. Alonso Xuares was again the intermediary who helped him move (ibid., p. 189).

34. Ibid.

35. Ibid., pp. 192-193 (February 22, 1687, 50 reales for Masses although not priested; March 6, 1687, other salary sweeteners of the kind granted his predecessor Gerónimo García; September 28, 1687, 100-ducat loan to help his sister defray certain costs attendant upon her becoming a nun).

36. Ibid., pp. 193-197 (September 1, 1687, tenor from Seville Cathedral; December 5, 1687, virtuoso instrumental bassist from Seville; November 23, 1688, bassist from Madrid certified by   fray Domingo Ortiz de Zárate; March 12, 1689, tenor "from a distance" named Román Ballestero; February 4, 1690, tenor named Francisco Mançano).

37. Ibid., pp. 191, 198 (January 24. 1687, Antonio Martínez de Ollora, choirboy;   March 3, 1691, Joseph de Peralta, choirboy).

38. Ibid., pp. 196-198.

39. Nicolás A. Solar-Quintes, "Nuevos documentos para la biografía del compositor Sebastián Durón," Anuario Musical, X (1955), 137: "por su cortedad de vista y achaques, Su Magd. le dió lizencia de separarle . . . 13 de febº de 1691."

40. Ibid., p. 138.

41. Ibid., p. 140:"Don Sebastian Durón, Maestro de la Real Capilla y Rector del Colegio de Su Magd."

42. Ibid., p. 141.

43. Emilio Cotarelo y Mori, "Ensayo histórico sobre la zarzuela, o sea el drama lírico español," Boletín de la Academia Española, XXI/105 (December, 1934), 912: "Fue preso en el Puente de Viveros y conducido a Bayona con otros eclesiásticos en 23 de julio de 1706. Creyó que el Archiduque entraría en Madrid y se acercaron a recibirle él, el Patriarca Benavides, fray Benito Salas, Obispo de Barcelona y otros muchos que cayeron en manos de los filipinos, pues el Puente de Viveros estaba guardado por soldados franceses."

44. Second wife of Charles II, Mariana de Neuburgo (1667-1740 [Neuburg lies just west of Ingolstadt in Bavaria]) greatly favored music and musicians all her life. See Nicolás A. Solar-Quintes, "Músicos de Mariana de Neoburgo y de la Real Capilla de Nápoles," Anuario Musical, XI (1956), 167.

45. While Charles II still lived, she favored an Italian castrato named Mateucci (ibid., p. 173).

46. Ibid., p. 172; entire document printed in Anuario Musical, X (1955), 142.

47. Cotarelo y Mori, op. cit., p. 911: "En 6 de febrero de 1715, en Bayona, don Sebastián Durón, sacerdote, natural de Brihuega, en España, en plena salud, de pie, hace su testamento en esta forma. Se le enterrará en el lugar de Francia, donde fallezca; pero sus honras fúnebres se harán en Brihuega."

48. Isaac Albéniz died also at Cambo in 1909.

49. Anuario Musical, X, 143. They were to enjoy half the income of his property in Brihuega, Juan de Peralonso the other half. The same applied to income due Durón at death from a simple benefice in Torija and from a 100-ducat pension ceded by Cuenca diocese.

50. Ibid., p. 144: "sea para dha. Iglesia del Señor Sn. Phelipe, que es donde tuve la fortuna y grazia de rezibir la del Bauptismo (aunque indigno)."

51. Ibid., pp. 148-149.

52. Ibid., p. 153.

53. Ibid., p. 152.

54. Ibid., p. 158. At pp. 156-158 Solar-Quintes lists Durón's surviving repertory at Madrid and Barcelona. See also, Boletín de la Academia Española, XXI/105 (December, 1934), 912-913. Nearly every Spanish cathedral from north to south owns something or other by him. As one typical example, Cuenca boasts a Salve Regina, the surviving accompaniment of which is dated 1721, a compline service a 8 (Cum invocarem, Qui habitat, Nunc dimittis, Te lucis, Regina coeli), and a villancico a 4 (A la rosa mas bella) dedicated to Our Lady of the Rosary (2 tiples, alto, violin 1, accompaniment). See Restituto Navarro Gonzalo, Catálogo Musical del Archivo de la Santa Iglesia Catedral Basílica de Cuenca (Cuenca: Instituto de Música Religiosa, 1965), pp. 107, 219, 123.

55. Boletín de la Academia Española, XIX/95 (December, 1932), 766. Ambrosio Pérez, the tenor whose Apuntes biográficos served Saldoni, died November 13, 1873.

56. Ibid., pp. 767-771.

57. Catálogo Musical de la Biblioteca Nacional de Madrid, I (Barcelona: Instituto Español de Musicología, 1946), pp. 358-362. Other works listed at pp. 292-293, 347.

58. Atended sonoras aves mis ecos suaves (Tonada al SSmo Sacramto) for accompanied solo voice; Ayresillos suaves, Christmas solo with harp accompaniment; Donde vas amor, Sacrament accompanied solo: El blando susurro, Christmas quartet; Ha de el Olvido, Christmas villancico a 4, accompanied; Negliya que quele, printed Christmas quartet, accompanied; Que dulze que suaue mas que un Jilguero, Sacrament solo; Siola helmano Flacico, Christmas quartet; Vaya pues rompiendo el ayre la jacarilla de garbo, Christmas accompanied solo. Items 1, 3, and 4 are in A minor.

59. Al compas airesillos, Christmas a 4 with harp; Al oceano de gracias, Sacrament a 3; Descansen los sentidos del Riguroso afan, Sacrament a 4 in B flat; Duerme Rosa y descansa, G minor duo; Por que Penas fatiga, Sacrament a 4 (like Bolcanes de amor this villancico in the Sucre archive is dated "Sevilla. 1683" [see n. 2 above]); Quando muere el Sol Triste luto arrastran, Passion and Sacrament a 4.

BIOGRAPHICAL DATA

JUAN GARCÍA (de ZESPEDES)
Born (presumably at Puebla) c. 1619; died
there shortly before August 9, 1678)

At their chapter meeting of August 16, 1630, the Puebla Cathedral canons argued whether to put the soprano choirboy Juan García on a regular monthly salary. [1] After consulting with Gutierre Bernardo de Quiroz (ruled Puebla diocese 1627-1638) they decided August 21, 1630, to allot 50 pesos for his choir robes, but to await his demonstrated progress in the art before putting him on the regular payroll. [2] Thus spurred, he made such strides that on January 17, 1631, he was named tiple at 80 pesos annually and on March 9, 1632, raised to 150. [3]

The duties of the master of the boys (a subordinate to the chapelmaster, Juan Gutiérrez de Padilla) included in this epoch a daily one-hour lesson in plainchant, the principles of psalmody, and other musical rudiments. He was also expected to see that they attended the Colegio de San Juan Evangelista where they learned reading and writing. For these services he was paid 100 pesos annually. On October 27, 1634, the presbítero Toribio Baquero succeeded Padre Pedro Simón in the post, [4] and on June 12, 1645, Padre Melchor Alvares succeeded Juan García. [5]

After the spending orgy at dedication ceremonies in 1649, the cathedral lacked funds to continue paying musicians their accustomed high wages. Therefore the chapter decided August 18, 1651, to slash salaries. [6] Juan García's for singing fell from 150 to 120 pesos. But three years later, June 19, 1654, he more than recuperated when he agreed for an added annual 70 pesos to give the choirboys and suitable adult singers daily lessons in both plainchant and polyphony, as well as bass-viol playing. [7] Since the teaching of canto de órgano customarily fell to the maestro de capilla in all Spanish and New World cathedrals throughout this century, García thus permitted himself to be groomed by Gutiérrez de Padilla for the higher post. Even in 1658 and 1660 when the chapter tried forcing Gutiérrez de Padilla to resume polyphonic instruction himself, rather than by deputy, García continued. [8]

Gutiérrez de Padilla's death, announced at the chapter meeting of April 22, 1664, [9] left the post open for his favorite pupil. As usual, the chapter distributed edictos inviting any qualified contenders in Mexico to compete for the post. But by June 6, 1664, closing date for applications, only García's had been formally received. A word-of-mouth application sent by Antonio de Mora, chapelmaster of the cathedral in what is now Morelia, was refused. [10] On August 12, the chapter formally named licenciado Juan García acting chapelmaster, [11] six years later elevating him to maestro en propiedad.

As an example of his taste, one of García's first recommendations after appointment August 12, 1664, was the purchase of los librillos de Motetes de Palestrina. Contrary to the un-

informed judgment on his composing abilities passed in Hispanic American Historical Review, XXXV/3 (August, 1955), 371, García composed excellently in every vein from the learned (Salve Regina a 7 [Tiple Tenor Alto, Tiple Alto Tenor Bajo, Arpa] dated 1673 in the Puebla Cathedral archive) to the folkloric. His guaracha in the private possession of Dr. Saldívar Silva [12] (facsimile privately published as Christmas greetings in 1963) is the earliest known example of this supposedly afrocubano dance type.

But like many other veteran maestros, García took liberties toward the close of his career. On February 23, 1672, the Puebla chapter ordered him to bring back immediately "all the violones [= bass viols], paper and books" that he had borrowed. [13] He grew lax in his teaching and on July 12, 1672, had to be scolded for not teaching two boy tiples plainchant and counterpoint. [14] On August 12, of the same year García certified as a good job the book for cathedral instrumentalists copied by José de Burgos, músico desta Santa Iglesia. [15] Toward the close of 1676 the cathedral desperately needed new singers and blamed García for not recruiting good prospects and for preferring instrumentalists. [16]

NOTES

1. Puebla Cathedral, Actas Capitulares, IX (1627-1633), fol. 180^V:"se cite a cauildo para tratar y determinar . . . el que se a de señalar a Ju^o garcia moço de coro desta Yg^a. Por cantor tiple della. Para lo qual se trayga el boto y pareçer del s.^{r} obispo."

2. Ibid., fol. 181^V:"y que para lo benidero sabiendo cantar y meresiendolo sele señalara salario."

3. Ibid., fols. 214 (Juan Garcia monasillo) and 271. On February 17, 1632 (fol. 270), both Simon Martines bajon and Juan Garcia tiple petitioned for the pay raises that were granted March 9.

4. A.C., X (1634-1639), fol. 32:". . . con obligacion de doctrinarlos y enseñarlos canto llano, verssos . . . . dandoles licion vna ora Todos los dias de Trauajo y Cuidando de que bayan a la escuela Para que les enseñen a leer y escreuir."

5. A.C., XI (1640-1647), fol. 267:"Que sea maestro de los mozos de choro el p^e Melchor Aluares Con el salario q̄ tenia Ju^o Garcia."

6. A.C., XII (1648-1652), fol. 354 (reuaxa de salarios).

7. A.C., XIII (1653-1656), fol. 132^V:"Hauiendose citado ante Diem Para el Salario que Pide Joan Garcia musico desta Santa Yglessia se comfirio y boto sobre ello y se Resoluio el nombrarle como se le nombra al Sussodho setenta Passos de salario mas en fabrica espiritual con calidad Y obligacion de enseñar canto de organo y llano y los Violones a los monasillos que ay Tiples y a los demas Cantores que conuiniere enseñar Y que aya de Dar licion todos los dias en la Yglesia Y que le apunte las fallas que hiciere como se acostumbra con los demas."
García's successor in this post was licendiado Carlos Palero(A.C., XV [1663-1668], fol. 417^V).

8. A.C., XIV (1657-1662), fols. 129 (August 9, 1658) and 277 (May 21, 1660).

9. A.C., XV (1663-1668), fol. 115.

10. _Ibid._, fol. 124[V]: "que atento a estar Cumplidos los edictos para la Prouision de la plaza de Maestro de Capilla y no hauer hauido mas que vn opositor a ella se cite para el primero Dia de Cauildo para dar forma en el exsamen que se ha de hacer, y se declara no auer lugar de admitir lo pedido por Domingo Pereira Ministril en nombre de Antonio de Mora Maestro de Capilla de la S.[ta] Yglesia de Mechoacan en rasson de la oposision que pretende hacer a dicha plaza de Maestro de Capilla."

11. _Ibid._, fol. 144[V]: "que se le nombran al Liz[do] Joan Garcia Musico desta Yglesia ciento y sinquenta Pessos mas de salario sobre el que tiene de cantor con la obligacion de Regentear el officio de Maestro de Capilla por el tiempo de la voluntad deste cauildo y que se le de Media parte mas en las obenciones."

12. Address in 1970: Calle Diez 27, San Pedro de los Pinos, México 18, D. F.

13. _A. C._, XVI (1669-1675), fol. 171[V]: "Que se le notifique al Maestro de Capilla trayga y ponga en el lugar que solian estar todos los Violones papeles y libros que pertenecen a esta Santa Iglesia para el primer Cabildo." Once returned, all this material was to be completely inventoried, the chapter demanded.

14. _Ibid._, fol. 195: "Que el Maestro de Capilla ponga todo cuidado en enseñar dandolos licion assi en el canto llano como en contrapunto." At the same meeting the chapter voted that the two tiples be placed on stipend in royally endowed local schools.

15. _Ibid._, fol. 199.

16. _A. C._, XVII (1676-1680), fol. 73[V].

FRAY GERÓNIMO GONZÁLEZ [= GONÇALVES de MENDONÇA] (Flourished at Madrid and Seville, 1633)

A one-leaf imprint headed Discvrso del Maestro Pontac, re-metido al Racionero Manuel Correa bound as folio 55 in the manuscript anthology catalogued F. G. 2266 (olim H-5-11) at the Lisbon National Library, begins with Diego Pontac's letter dated June 22, 1633, in which he boasts of having taught "Licenciado Geronimo Gonçalez, Capellan de su Magestad en las Descalças de Madrid, y electo Racionero de Seuilla."[1] However, instead of becoming a Sevillian prebendary, González turned friar.

Both his liturgical music and his villancicos so greatly pleased the royal melomane John IV of Portugal that he bought González's music avidly. At the ducal place in Vila Viçosa, the Maundy Thursday music in 1641 included a Miserere by Victoria with harp accompaniment and the Good Friday a Miserere by fray Gerónimo González for three choirs (first choir with harp accompaniment, second supported by the cornamusa, third with charamella [= shawm]).[2] According to the dean of the chapel at Vila Viçosa, António de Brito de Sousa, the singers (led by Gaspar dos Reis) performed m[to] bem (very well). This identical Miserere Do quinto tom, a 12. a 3. coros shows up at page 391 of the Primeira Parte do Index da Livraria de Mvsica do mvyto alto, e poderoso Rey Dom Ioão o IV. Nosso Senhor (Lisbon: Paulo Craesbeek,

1649).[3]

On the same page of this catalogue are listed a Tone V Miserere a 7 and Tone V a 8 by "Fr. Ieronimo Gonçalues de Mendonça," on the next page various lamentations,[4] and at 450 a Dixit Dominus a 7 and a 8 by "Frey Ieronimo Gonçales." Throughout, the composer's name veers between Spanish and Portuguese forms. That they were one and the same can be proved from the prefatory Table of Contents which lists the psalm at 450 as by "Gonçalvez." But at page 450 itself, the name shows up as "Gonçales." The six leading Peninsular villancico composers of the period, if the Table of Contents is to be trusted, were: Gabriel Dias, Fr. Francisco de Santiago, Juan de Castro y Malagaray, Estêvão de Brito, Carlos Patiño and Fr. Gerónimo González. The latter's 61 Christmas villancicos[5] listed at pages 251-253 and 334-336 include four gallegos, two negros, two ensaladas, a gitano, a jácara, and a portugués. They range from 3 to 12 parts, with the instruments occasionally supporting solo voice. At least 22 more of González's villancicos turn up elsewhere in the catalogue[6] and at pages 386-389, 392, and 431 fourteen Latin works.

Apart from the Sánchez Garza collection, González's jaunty festival pieces turn up also in at least three other New World archives—those at Bogotá Cathedral, San Antonio Abad Seminary in Cuzco, and Guatemala Cathedral. For details, see Stevenson, Renaissance and Baroque Musical Sources in the American (Washington: General Secretariat, Organization of American States, 1970), pages 15, 43, and 85.

NOTES

1. Reprinted with small variants in Joaquim de Vasconcellos, El-Rey D. João o 4.º (Oporto: Typographia Universal, 1905), p. 28. Pontac claims to have taught at Saragossa, Madrid, Salamanca, and Granada. Since the last pupil of whom Pontac boasts is Gerónimo González, the licenciado may have belonged to Pontac's Granada class.

2. Biblioteca da Ajuda [Lisbon], Do Governo de Portugal. Provizões Cartas e Alvaras Reaes, MS 51-VIII-3, fol. 343.

3. Facsimile edition published by Academia Portuguesa da História, Lisbon, 1967, with preface by Damião Peres.

4. The Lamentation a 12 "tem hum coro de hũa voz com tres instrumentos" ("has one choir consisting of a solo voice plus three instruments").

5. Ernesto Vieira, Diccionario biographico de musicos portuguezes (Lisbon: Mattos Moreira & Pinheiro, 1900), I, 477, lists a total of 78 Christmas villancicos in the John IV catalogue. However, Vieira's presumption that Gonçalez = Gonçalvez was of Portuguese descent still remains unsubstantiated.

6. Primeira Parte do Index, pp. 219, 237, 238, 239 (three), 243 (three), 244 (three), 265, 277, 295, 296 (two), 314, 320 (three), 322. Page numbers silently corrected.

JUAN GUTIÉRREZ de PADILLA
(Born at Málaga c. 1590; died at Puebla between
March 18 and April 22, 1664)

The Baroque composer in Mexico who has been thus far most transcribed, studied, and performed is Juan Gutiérrez de Padilla. In his 1949 Harvard University Ph.D. dissertation, Steven Barwick first called attention to the extant repertory of this Puebla Cathedral maestro — at pages 93-94 of Part I noting the survival in the cathedral archive of four double-choir Masses (a 8) and a ferial Missa a 4 in the first 110 folios of Choirbook XV, of approximately thirty miscellaneous liturgical compositions ranging from 4 to 8 voices in the second 144 [= 149] folios of the same libro de facistol, and the presence of four sets of loose-sheet Christmas villancicos dated 1651, 1652, 1653, and 1655 in the same archive. At pages 234-244 of his Part II, Barwick transcribed Padilla's Palm Sunday Passion (which consists of 20 short settings a 4 of the crowd utterances in the Matthew narrative), using for his source the copy of this Passion found at the close of Puebla Cathedral Choirbook I. My Music in Mexico: A Historical Survey (New York: Thomas Y. Crowell, 1952; Apollo Editions, 1971, pp. 127-130), compared three excerpts with corresponding sections from Heinrich Schütz's Matthäus-Passion of 1666.

Availing herself of microfilms taken in 1949 at Puebla Cathedral by George Smisor (who acted on Steven Barwick's suggestion), Alice Ray [Catalyne] transcribed the four Masses a 8 in Puebla Choirbook XV for Volume 2 of her 1953 University of Southern California Ph.D. dissertation, "The Double-Choir Music of Juan de Padilla."[1] Hispanic American Historical Review, XXXV/3 (August, 1955), 363-373, included a biographical article exclusively devoted to him, "The 'Distinguished Maestro' of New Spain: Juan Gutiérrez de Padilla." Die Musik in Geschichte und Gegenwart, X (1962), columns 564, 564-565,[2] included Padilla articles unraveling the confusion hitherto existing, because the maestro who died at Puebla in 1664 had been confounded with the homonymous maestro Juan de Padilla (born at Gibraltar in 1605; died at Toledo December 16, 1673). At Schoenberg Hall, University of California, Los Angeles, Roger Wagner on April 20, 1961, conducted the premieres of Juan Gutiérrez de Padilla's Missa Ave Regina coelorum, Salve Regina, and Exultate iusti, all a 8. The next year he edited the Exultate iusti (Psalm 32:1-6) for Lawson-Gould Music Publishers, New York City, and in 1966 recorded the same work for Angel (S 36008).

Although by March of 1966 no further proof was needed, still my discovery of Juan Gutiérrez de Padilla's will at the Puebla notarial archive in that month neatly confirmed the fact that the Toledo maestro Juan de Padilla who was the son of Gregorio de Padilla, a native of Ronda, and of Juana Espinosa, a native of Gibraltar,[3] should never have been confused with the

Puebla maestro. Juan Gutiérrez de Padilla's last will and testament sworn to before Nicolás Álvarez, Notario Real y Público, on March 18, 1664, can now be consulted at the Archivo General de Notarias del Estado de Puebla, in Testamentos 1664, at folio 48 (both sides). The Puebla Cathedral capitular acts, Volume XV (1663-1668), folio 115, witness to his death before April 22 of the same year.[4] He therefore waited until at death's door before executing his will.

The will begins with the usual invocation of Deity, then identifies the testator as el liz[do] Juan Guttierres de padilla clerigo presvitero maestro de capilla de la ssancta yglessia cathedral desta Ciu[d] de los angeles donde soy vezino hijo lexitimo de Juan gutierres de padilla y de doña catalina de los rios vezinos de la ciudad de malaga en los reynos de Castilla de donde soy natural. Next, the will states that, although mortally sick abed, the testator is in his right mind and appoints el doctor don Joseph de carmona tamaris[5] rasionero de la dha ssanta yglessia persona de quien tengo entera satisfasion as his executor.

No more fitting executor could have been named than another scion of the distinguished family already known to students of Gutiérrez de Padilla's biography, because it was the executor's brother Antonio Tamariz de Carmona whose Relacion y descripcion del Templo Real de la Civdad de la Puebla de los Angeles, a book of 110 leaves published in 1650, had been the first imprint to laud him as an "insigne Maestro" at folio 20 and again as the "insigne Maestro licenciado Iuan de Padilla" at folio 31. "Joseph de Carmona Tamaris," as the will spells the name of Antonio's brother who was a Puebla prebendary, is instructed in the final paragraph of the March 18, 1664, will to distribute alms and do such other charitable acts as Padilla's estate makes possible on his decease.[6] His body is to be interred in the cathedral, accompanied to the grave by the Brothers of St. Peter's Congregation and also the Brothers of St. Philip Neri — in which brotherhoods Padilla himself claims membership. Bachiller Joseph Coronado, el contador Juan de la Mesa, and Francisco de Araujo, all residents of Puebla, witnessed the will.

Now that Gutiérrez de Padilla's birth at Málaga and early training under Francisco Vásquez (maestro de capilla there from 1586 to 1613) are assured, several other facts gleaned from the capitular acts of both Málaga and Cádiz Cathedrals fall into their proper places. On February 16, 1613, the canons of Málaga Cathedral met to decide the winner of a five-man contest for the then vacant chapelmastership.[7] After scrutinizing his background, the Málaga chapter gave the post to Estêvão de Brito, a native of Évora, Portugal.[8] Brito was already highly experienced, whereas Padilla cannot have been much over 23. As early as February 8, 1597, Brito had been elected maestro of Badajoz Cathedral,[9] and on June 1, 1597, his salary had there been fixed at the respectable annual sum of 40,000 maravedis. Moreover, Brito had been ordained in

1608.[10] All this — his age, ordination, and his previous musical successes — gave Brito the edge over the young, as yet unordained, Juan Gutiérrez de Padilla, then still a green maestro at the collegiate church in Jérez de la Frontera.[11] Nonetheless, Padilla won the judges' overwhelming (15-2) vote as their second choice. The three other candidates were all respectable musicians: Francisco de Ávila y Páez, maestro of Descalzas Convent at Madrid, Francisco Martínez de Ávalos from Úbeda, and Fulgencio Méndez Avendaño from Murcia.

Encouraged by this near success, Padilla next presented himself at Cádiz Cathedral, where on March 17, 1616 — now Ju⁰ gutierrez de padilla presbytero — he succeeded Bartolomé Méndez in the chapelmastership.[12] On that same day the Cádiz canons ordered every singer to appear for daily practice under the new maestro's watchful direction. Up-to-date music, as well as established classics, formed the musical diet at Cádiz during Padilla's régime. On September 2, 1616, he recommended buying Philippe Rogier's Missae sex published at Madrid in 1598, as a book muy provechoso pᵃ esta yglia[13] (very worthwhile for this cathedral). Four months later, January 10, 1617, he succeeded in getting the canons to order that the cathedral instrumentalists attend evening as well as daytime fiestas, on pain of dismissal.[14] Also, at the same chapter meeting, he was granted leave and expense money to bring all his possessions from Jérez de la Frontera where they had continued in storage after his departure the preceding spring. Apparently Bartolomé Méndez and Padilla had merely exchanged posts, because on September 15, 1615, an exchange scheme had already been broached at a Cádiz Cathedral chapter meeting.[15]

To jack up lagging discipline, the chapter on April 7, 1617, enjoined the chapelmaster and all his musical subordinates to arrive henceforth at canonical hours and Mass promptly, and to remain the full designated time.[16] On August 31, 1618, Padilla's petition for a month's leave to visit Málaga was granted on condition that before the trip he leave behind in Cádiz the already composed chanzonetas for Blessed Teresa of Ávila's feast, and that he return in time to conduct them on her special day.[17] In recognition of his excellent service during the next year and a half, the chapter on February 3, 1620, raised his pay by ten ducats annually.[18]

A sizable gap between Books III (1618-1620) and IV (1630-1642) of the Cádiz Cathedral acts prevents our now fixing the precise moment that he finally decided to cast his lot henceforth in the New World. But by October 11, 1622, he had already arrived in Puebla — for on that day he officially became coadjutor maestro.[19] Back of him at that time stretched at least a decade of highly successful service in the southern Spanish milieu. Before him there beckoned a 42-year career of as brilliant musical adventure and achievement as was anywhere to reveal itself in Baroque America.

Not the least of his achievements during his first seven years was his successful cooperation with the titular chapelmaster, Gaspar Fernandes, who much outlived expectation. Fortunately for their relations, Fernandes shined as much on the organ bench as at the conductor's stand. What friction does surface in the capitular acts came about always because the singers resented Padilla's getting such a lion's share of the lush tips regularly paid for funerals and other special events. On December 6, less than two months after Padilla's initial appointment, the chapter confirmed his right to double and triple what the other singers took from obenciones, because although titled a "singer" he had in advance been promised a maestro's salary and cut from the tips.[20] Later that same month, the chapter warned Fernandes not to steer from the course charted for distributing tips, no matter how restive the veteran singers and instrumentalists became.[21] Much to the annoyance of the true cantores who saw themselves thereby defrauded, their "pot" continued so late as three months before Fernandes's death being still skimmed for Padilla's benefit.[22]

Not only did Fernandes play, but also he fixed organs. For this, he was paid extra — as, for instance, on January 10, 1623, when the chapter voted him 100 pesos for repairing and overhauling the cathedral grand organ (he received another 100 for expenses).[23] Like every other principal cathedral in Spanish dominions, Puebla in Padilla's epoch hired a substantial corps of instrumentalists to shore up singers, provide instrumental verses in psalms and other alternating music, play in processions and at all festive events. On August 22, 1623, was engaged for 200 pesos annually a new ministril sacabuche named Benito de Padilla.[24] Juan Gutiérrez de Padilla meanwhile drew an annual 500 until granted the next year an extra 100 pesos for teaching polyphonic music to the choirboys and any other potential trebles.[25] On October 2, 1625, Puebla lured temporarily from Mexico City Cathedral the 50-year-old former slave Luis Barreto (now an ordained priest), who in the period 1609-1615 ranked as the best sopranist in the capital.[26] The Maestro de los moços de coro at Puebla throughout Padilla's first seven years was Melchor Álvarez, who however preferred to beef up his income by correcting and caring for the cathedral choirbooks to his assigned duties as choirboy disciplinarian.[27]

In 1627 the Confraternity of the Blessed Sacrament proposed that Ascension be celebrated henceforth with expensive illuminations and elaborate polyphonic music "to augment the devotion of the faithful."[28] The next year still another four days were added to the polyphonic music calendar, December 8 and the following jubileo triduum.[29] Among the more important appointments in 1629 was the one made February 23 of Pedro Simón presbítero to be cantor contralto (200 pesos) and capellán (100 pesos).[30] Gaspar Fernandes died shortly before

September 18 of the same year. [31] A week later the chapter unanimously confirmed Padilla's succession to the post, simultaneously guaranteeing him all its emoluments and fringe benefits. [32] His 500-peso yearly salary was to continue, but was now to be augmented by another forty each year for composing the chanzonetas, having them copied, and delivering them to the cathedral archive. There they were to be safely stored against the day of any possible future reuse. On the same September 25 Luis Eslava — specially recommended by the bishop — was hired as singer at 100 pesos a year, and Padilla enjoined to teach him with care because of his exceptional voice. Lastly, the chapter appointed on September 25 a special commission to review the Constituçiones y ordenanças tocantes al offic⁰ de sochantre maestro de capilla y cantores adopted in 1585 during Bishop Diego Ossorio Romano's episcopate, in order that the succentor, chapelmaster, and singers might be more exactly apprised of their traditional rights and duties. [33]

For playing the organ, the deceased chapelmaster Gaspar Fernandes had been paid an extra 300 pesos annually since September 26, 1606. [34] Funds for this had come from the organ prebend, title to which was held for more than a quarter century by the nonperforming Puebla Cathedral Racionero Juan de Ocampo. [35] On June 18, 1630, Pedro Simón inherited the same post of sostituto del órgano at the same 300-peso annual salary, payable against the organ prebend still titularly held by the sexagenarian Ocampo. [36] Simón also agreed that day to keep the organs in tune for the same yearly 60 pesos that Fernandes had been paid for their tuning and repair.

To offset in a measure the plural salaries Fernandes had received, the Puebla chapter decided August 21, 1630, to raise Padilla's take for chapelmastering to 600 pesos annually — without however setting a precedent for future holders of the office. [37] By a curious coincidence, the chapter voted at the same meeting to place on an annual 50-peso salary the choirboy Juan García who did 34 years later succeed Padilla as chapelmaster. Not only this choirboy but others in Padilla's tutelage were around 1630 making such fast strides that the chapter had good reason to be pleased. Only Padilla's slackness in providing copies of all his chanzonetas for special feasts annoyed the cabildo in 1630 to such a degree that the canons ordered withheld Padilla's annual salary supplement for paper and copying assistance until he complied. [38]

During the next triennium the chapter continued to raise musicians' salaries — that of Simón Martínez bajón from 200 to 250 pesos annually March 9, 1632, and of the just mentioned Juan García from 70 to 150 the same day, for instance. [39] On January 11, 1633, the chapter voted a special gift to Padilla for his exceptional services December 8 and 25 of 1632. [40] The canons decided October 31, 1631, to entrust the current master of the choirboys Pedro Simón with general overhaul of the grand organ and the building of a new organ case. Simón spent

1632 at the job and on January 25, 1633, was voted another 500 pesos to continue. [41] At last, the longtime titular organ prebendary Juan de Ocampo (1568-1633) died (shortly before June 21, 1633 [42]), leaving the cathedral his universal legatee and bequeathing a substantial sum to promote polyphonic singing. [43]

However, this many-barreled good fortune suddenly threatened to go sour the next summer. On Tuesday August 1, 1634, the Puebla chapter all at once fired both Padilla and the cathedral bass player Simón Martínez for some misdeed of theirs the preceding Sunday. [44] As interim chapelmaster until a new maestro could be found, the canons appointed the veteran priest-musician Francisco de Olivera, whom by a secret vote the chapter had elected cathedral succentor as long ago as January 11, 1619. [45] At the same August 1, 1634, meeting the canons decreed that Padilla must immediately turn over "all the polyphonic and plainchant books and folders of music" in his possession to competent cathedral authority. [46] Only because the bishop not present at the meeting was a great music lover were the culprits able to creep back into their wonted posts six weeks later.

On September 9 the canons agreed to reconsider their dismissal at the next chapter meeting. Three days later Canon Juan Rodríguez brought with him Bishop Quiroz's suggestion that both be rehired at their former rates. [47] In the margin of the September 12 minutes appears the proviso: "The chapelmaster and choir [shall] assist at conventual Blessed Sacrament feasts and at nuns' burials." [48] But this does not clarify the reasons for the chapter's sudden dismissal of Padilla and Martínez August 1. Meanwhile the pair had lost six weeks' pay.

At last on January 12, 1635, even this loss was made good when the chapter voted to restore them everything deducted the preceding summer "in appreciation of their great services at the feasts of December 8 and 25." Again it was Bishop Quiroz who sparked the generosity. [49] Another musician whose services December 8 and 25 of 1634 inspired the special recognition of a 20-peso gift was Hernando López Calderón, "harpist and resident of this city." [50] This same harpist crops up again in the Puebla Cathedral acts of 1643, on December 11 of which year the chapter rewarded him for playing December 8. [51] The importance of harp accompaniments in the Padilla repertory comes even more clearly to light in 1643 when the chapter placed on the regular cathedral payroll Nicolás Grinón, a recognized harp virtuoso. [52]

Pedro Simón — to whom overhaul and rebuilding of the grand organ had been entrusted October 31, 1631 — still continued at work in 1634. On August 25 of the latter year the chapter therefore voted to call from the capital the cathedral organist Fabián Ximeno to assess the value of Simón's improvements. [53] After this visit Ximeno agreed January 30, 1635, to send from Mexico City someone competent to help Simón hasten toward a conclusion.[54] The following March 15 the chapter felt confident enough of Simón's prowess to pay him another 500 pesos for finishing the job.[55]

But the efforts of a local bell maker who was an Indian ended less happily. The large bell cast under his supervision having cracked when hoisted into place, the cabildo voted May 4, 1635, to reexamine the agreement with the yndio campanero in the hope of recovering advance payments.[56] Since the bell maker in New Spain then able to guarantee results was the outsider Juan Montero, the chapter felt obliged later that year to sign with him a new contract for the tower's bourdon bell.[57]

Padilla himself successfully operated an instrument-making shop during these years. According to one source, he was selling as far afield as Guatemala the instruments made in this shop with the aid of Negro helpers during the early 1640's. Backed with the reputation of having successfully refurbished the Puebla Cathedral grand organ, Pedro Simón was on August 1, 1642, granted a long leave to do organ repair work in the Oaxaca vicinity.[59] In the meantime new instrumentalists continued being hired regularly in Puebla Cathedral: for instance, Domingo de Pereira sacabuche (sackbut) and Manuel de Correa bajón (bassoon) on October 25, 1641. Both of these probably Portuguese players, who "came from Veracruz," were hired at a yearly 200 pesos for playing their instruments and another 100 for singing at times when instruments were not used or allowed.[60]

Simón could the more easily take off on long trips after December 17, 1641, because as organist and bassoonist earning a yearly 400 pesos the chapter hired on that date a musician destined for glory, the bachiller Francisco López [Capillas].[61] Hired "at the pleasure of the chapelmaster," López Capillas substituted for Simón during such long periods as September 1, 1643, to January 15, 1644, several more months before July 15, 1644, and May 11, 1646, to January 11, 1647.[62] Already by September 13, 1645, López had become so indispensable an organist (and singer when not presiding at the organ) that the chapter dispensed him from henceforth playing the bassoon, except during Advent and Lent when organs were prohibited.[63] Still earning 400 pesos annually in 1645 (200 for playing the organ, the other 200 for singing), he was paid an extra 200 for taking Simón's place at the organ bench during the eight months before January 11, 1647.[64] Four more days elapsed and on January 15, 1647, the chapter regularized his status by naming the now licenciado Francisco López organist at a yearly 600 pesos.[65] Of the 600, half was to come from an account budgeted for a singer. All expenses connected with organ repairs were to be the responsibility of the cathedral, not López. Simón—whom the chapter had already dismissed once (July 15, 1644)—could not personally protest his second dismissal January 15, 1647, because he was again out of town fixing organs elsewhere. When he did return, the chapter would at first do nothing for him except rehire him July 24,

1647, as organ tuner.[66]

This was not enough to please Simón, who managed to get back all his former jobs January 17, 1648.[67] The chapter yielded because he had made himself too valuable for Puebla Cathedral to exist any length of time without him. Not only had he become the indispensable cathedral organ tuner, repairman, and builder, but also he had been constructing the violones[68] (bass viols) and other instruments constantly needed by the Puebla musicians as their old wore out. Reinstating Simón meant also substracting something from López, in this case the 100 pesos extra being paid López for playing bassoon in Advent and Lent when organs were prohibited.[69] Now thoroughly disillusioned with his on-again, off-again status, López decided that he must look elsewhere for a post that would not fluctuate. On May 2, 1648, the famous Mexico City Cathedral organist-choirmaster Fabián Ximeno received a 200-peso gratuity for inspecting the new big organ in Puebla Cathedral and discussing construction of its twin.[70] On July 29, bachiller Ygnacio Ximeno succeeded López (who had already left May 15 [71]), but at only 400 pesos annually. On the same July 29, this pliant relative of the great Fabián Ximeno agreed to Simón's henceforth siphoning off not only the tip money (obenciones) due for cathedral funerals and the like, but also to Simón's earning a pro rata share of the regular organist's salary any time that Simón felt inclined to mount the organ loft and play.[72]

López of course bettered himself by leaving. From 1654 to his death January 18, 1673, he served as organist-choirmaster of Mexico City Cathedral, meantime filling the cathedral archive there with an array of Masses, Magnificats, and other liturgical works unmatched in quality or quantity by any other Mexico City maestro between Franco and Zumaya. For his early rise he had Padilla to thank, because it was Padilla who engineered his entry at Puebla without a formal competition, who protected him during his seven years there, and then helped him find better employment elsewhere. If to (1) López are added (2) the succentor Francisco de Olivera, (3) the bajón Simón Martínez, (4) Padilla's successor, García, (5) Juan de Vaeza, and (6) García's successor, Salazar (born 1650, resident of Puebla)—all of whom are represented in the Sánchez Garza archive — Padilla emerges as the head of an important school of composers and not merely as a solitary light.

On April 18, 1649, Puebla Cathedral was finally consecrated, the prime mover in its completion being the great bishop and viceroy Juan de Palafox y Mendoza. At the ceremonies, which extended throughout the entire week, ecclesiastical dignitaries representing even Manila in the Philippines were present, the total number of attending clergy reaching some 1,200. The Puebla Cathedral, which was actually completed before the Mexico Cathedral, was so luxuriously appointed that it was immediately named the templo de plata ("cathedral of silver") and was aptly called el mayor, y mas sumptuoso Templo que se conoçe en estos Reynos de la America; y que sin encareci-miento compite con los mas insignes, y memorables templos de Europa ("the biggest and most sumptuous known in the Americas, and without exaggeration comparable with the noblest and most memorable European structures").[73]

After the orgy of money-spending and more particularly after Palafox y Mendoza was translated to the Peninsular see of Osma, a reaction in the direction of economy set in. On August 18, 1651, Padilla's salary was slashed from 740 pesos annually to 640, with, however, a concession relieving him from the duty of teaching polyphonic music.[74] At the same time, many of his adult subordinates were reduced corres-ponding amounts. Among his thirteen adult aides listed on that date, only these three emerged scatheless: the licencia-dos José de la Peña cantor and Pedro Simón organista y can-tor, whose salaries stayed at 400 and 300 pesos annually; and Nicolás Grinón arpista, whose pay remained at 200. The rest of the adult capilla included two classed as singers pure and simple, licenciado Andrés Xuárez (reduced from 150 to 130) and Alfonso García (150-120). Five members of the capilla doubled as cantor y ministril — singing or playing their in-struments alternately as occasion demanded: Manuel Correa (400-300) [first hired as bajón upon arrival from Veracruz October 25, 1641]), Alfredo Marcelo (300-230), Simón Mar-tínez (400-300 [fired August 1, 1634, but reinstated six weeks later]), Antonio de Mora (400-350),[76] and Blas de Mora (300-200). The recently hired Ygnacio Ximeno del Águila took a 100-peso cut (500-400). Rather than face a like reduction two of the other musicians, Domingo Pereira (hired as sacabuche October 25, 1641) and Juan Muñoz (corneta rewarded with an extra 50 pesos January 17, 1648), had scurried off to Mexico City.[77] Of course, these thirteen adults did not begin to com-prehend the entire capilla, which included a roughly equal number of choirboys throughout Padilla's epoch.[78] But the large proportion of adult instrumentalists and of singers who could double on instruments deserves underlining.

On June 19, 1654, Juan García (who was to succeed Padilla a decade later) agreed to teach the choirboys plainsong and polyphonic music, and to give lessons in bass-viol playing to all those in the choir — adults as well as youths — who showed aptitude.[79] With money so tight, the scramble for tips (oben-ciones) kept growing worse. Therefore the chapter allowed Padilla a ten-day leave beginning August 31, 1655, to look for the original decrees in the cathedral archive declaring how tips should be distributed.[80] On February 8, 1656, the chap-ter asked Padilla to provide the warden in charge of cathedral property with his 1655 sets of villancicos, any sets missing from previous years, and an inventory of all the cathedral polyphonic treasure entrusted to his care.[81] Having in the interim restored his salary to its pre-1651 level, the chapter on August 9, 1658, asked him to resume teaching the choirboys

polyphonic music.[82] Again two years later, on May 21, 1660, his teaching obligation was reviewed by the cabildo, which now asked him to hold daily classes in plainsong and polyph-ony as had been custom many years previously — not only for the benefit of the choirboys but also the adult cathedral singers.[83] On May 21, 1660, the chapter also asked him to search more actively for new boys with fine voices.[84]

Already the year before he died the cabildo recognized that his oeuvre was now substantially complete and that the time had come for a Gesamtausgabe. Therefore on October 2, 1663, the canons ordered recopying where necessary, binding of the Latin works in stoutest form possible, and organization of the villancicos in convenient folders.[85] On January 11, 1664, he was sick and an extra 50 pesos were appropriated to meet the costs of his illness.[86] Meanwhile discipline among the choir members had so deteriorated that the cabildo fined the entire group, singers and instrumentalists, to bring them to their senses. Only Padilla himself escaped the universal fine levied against musicians February 1, 1664.[87]

The single most important surviving Gutiérrez de Padilla source still remains Choirbook XV at Puebla Cathedral, first inventoried by Barwick. Consisting of two separately foliated halves, this libro de coro contains Masses, motets, psalms, Marian antiphons, lamentations, responsories, hymns, a litany, and a Matthew passion — but strangely enough, no Mag-nificats. The Puebla archive does still include an abundance of Magnificats by Morales, Navarro, Vivanco, and other Peninsular giants. Until a new Padilla source turns up, we may assume that he chose not to cross swords with such al-ready acknowledged masters on their own best ground. Even his Masses do not challenge Morales, Guerrero, and Pales-trina — who rarely or never wrote Masses for double choir. In the alphabetical list of Padilla's Latin works to follow, arabic numerals in parentheses after a title refer to the folio number in the upper right-hand corner of the first opening, and a or b refers to first or second foliation in Choirbook XV.

> Adiuua nos a 5 (7b), Arbor decora a 4 (57b), Ave regina coelorum a 8 (140b), Ave Rex noster a 4 (48B) Christus factus est a 4 (30b), Circumdederunt me a 6 (148b) [= Libro de coro III (31)], Dies irae a 8 (Libro de coro III, 54) [also in loose sheets],[88] Dixit Dominus a 8 (96b), Domine ad adiuuandum a 8 (92b), Domine Dominus noster a 8 (104b), Exultate iusti in Domino a 8 (78b), Felix namque es sacra virgo a 8 (117b), Joseph fili David a 8 (61b), Kyrie eleison, Letania de Loreto, a 2 and a 8 [loose sheets], Lamentatio, Feria VI, a 6 (18b), Lamentatio, Feria VI tenebrarum, a 4 (26b), Mirabilia testi-monia a 8 (66b), Miserere mei Deus a 8 (134b), Missa Ave regina coelorum a 8 (2a), Missa Ego flos campi a 8 (22a), Missa ferialis a 4 (108a), Missa Joseph fili David a 8 (74a), Missa sine nomine a 8 (49a), O Redemptor sume carmen a 4

(52b), Passio secundum Mattaeum a 4 (8b) [=
Libro de coro I, 8 unnumbered folios at close],
Pater de coelis a 10, letania (119b) [duplicated in
mss partbooks], Pater peccavi a 8 (38b), Psalm
Tones a 4 [Tones I-VI] (70a), Quo vulneratus a
4 (54b), Responde mihi, lectio pro defunctis, a
4 (46b), Salve Regina a 8 (85b) [duplicated in mss
partbooks], Sancta et immaculata a 8 (115b), Sicut
cervus a 4, ad benedictionem aquae (53b), Stabat
Mater a 4 (36b), Tantum ergo a 4 (33b), Transfigi
dulcissime Domine a 4 (44b), Tristis est anima
mea a 4 (59b), Velum templi scissum a 4 (31b),
Veni Sancte Spiritus, alternating choirs a 4
[loose sheets], Versa est in luctum cithara a
5 (146b) [Libro de coro III, 29], Vexilla Regis
a 4 [loose sheets], Victimae paschali a 8 [loose
sheets], Vidi turbam magnam (50b)

Sets of villancicos from at least the following seven years
survive in Puebla Cathedral (loose sheets): 1651, 1652, 1653,
1655, 1656 (a 8), 1657 (a 8), 1658 (a 7).[89] The Sánchez Garza
collection boasts thirteen items by Padilla, all except one in
the vernacular. To date, no search has been undertaken for
his works in Guadalajara or Morelia Cathedrals, but Guatemala Cathedral in 1966 still held at least two of Gutiérrez de
Padilla's Christmas villancicos: (1) En vn portal mal cubierto
llora Dios, A 4. Ti A Te B. Dorian mode, an exquisitely sen-
sitive setting. (2) Que tiene esta noche que admira y suspende.
Ti A Te B. "Pregunta" heads each part. At top left of Bajo:
"los dedos dela primera mano"; at bottom "abierto el bajon
esta."

It goes without saying that none of his Latin, much less vernacular music reached print during his lifetime. However, in
conformity with prevalent custom throughout Spanish domains
where any local press existed, the texts of the villancicos
composed by him were published annually. At Indiana University in Bloomington, Lilly Library today counts among its
rarities the booklets in which were printed the Christmas villancicos sung at Puebla Cathedral 1649, 1652, 1659, and in
addition three booklets with the texts of the villancicos sung
December 8, 1654, 1656, and 1659. Catalogued W. 173, 173a-
e, all six villancico sets follow the usual pattern: with the
three villancicos assigned to the first and to the second nocturns, two and a concluding Te Deum to the third nocturn. The
1649 set includes such local color delights as an Aztec tocotín,
a guasteco, and a negrilla. Also, the 1652, 1654, and 1656
sets contain negrillas. Among other types, these six booklets
include kalendas (1649 and 1659 [December 25]), ensaladillas
(1649 and 1652), a batalla (1652), jácaras (1652 and 1659
[December 25]), and juguetes (1659 [December 8 and 25]).

In the negillas of 1649 and 1654, the blacks (singing in dia-
lect) promise to dance a porto rrico = puerto rico. In the
negrillas of 1654 and 1656, natives of the Congo, of Guinea, of
Angola, and of São Tomé are pictured as vying with one another
in the dancing and in the other festivities. The negrilla text
of 1649 (pp. 5-6 of the booklet) divides the blacks into a leader
and a chorus who answer each other in a dialogue the sense of
which can be thus conjectured: "Greetings, kinsmen." "What

does your black lordship want?" "That we go to the little door
to give the Child a present." "Yes, let's all go at once before
the shepherds arrive." "And when we find the Child, what if
he cries for fright?" "To lull him asleep we shall dance, and
the dance will be the puerto rico, lay, lay, lay, lay, lay, lay."
Copla. "We black folk celebrate the Birth playing instruments, and to court the Child we repeat this refrain, lay, lay,
lay, lay, lay, lay."

Negrilla

1 A palente a palente
2 Que que le señol neglico
1 que bamo a lo portalico
   á yeva a niño plesente,
2 vamo turu de repente
   ante que vaya pastora
1 y si à lo niño que yora
   le pantamo que halemo?
2 vno bayle baylemo,
   y sera la puelto rico
   le, le, le, le, le, le.
   que la niño duerme

Copla
   Lo neglo venimo
   le, le, le, le, le, le
   à la nacimenta,
   le, le, le, le, le, le
   tocando trumenta
   le, le, le, le, le, le
   y à niño seluimo,
   le, le, le, le, le, le
   copriya decimo
   le, le, le, le, le, le.

NOTES

1. Cf. Abstracts of Dissertations for the Degree of Doctor of
Philosophy and the Degree of Doctor of Education 1953 (Los
Angeles: University of Southern California Press, 1953), pp.
3-5. The information in last five lines of page 3 and the first
three of page 4 applies to the homonym who died at Toledo, not
to Juan Gutiérrez de Padilla.

2. In the same volume of Die Musik in Geschichte und
Gegenwart, see plate 14 (between cols. 608 and 609). This is
Gutiérrez de Padilla's Adiuua nos, a 5, photographed from the
opening, fols. 6v-7, in the second part of Choirbook XV at
Puebla Cathedral.

3. Further data in Hispanic American Historical Review,
XXXV/3, 365-366 n. 4.

4. "Que se pongan edictos en esta ciudad y la de Mex. co con
termino de treinta Dias, para la Provision de la plaza de
Maestro de capilla desta S. ta Yglesia, que esta Vaca por
Muerte del Liz do Joan Gutierres de Padilla su ultimo Possehe-
dor y que dello se de quenta a su ssa Illma el S. or Obispo."

5. The Carmona Tamaris = Tamariz Carmona clan bulked
large in the civic and ecclesiastical affairs of colonial Puebla.
Diego de Carmona Tamaris, already juez diputado, became

regidor September 3, 1606 (Actas Capitulares XIV, 1606-1612 [secular cabildo], fol. 20). He is also mentioned in the Puebla Cathedral capitular acts as having been "mayordomo y administrador del conbento y cassa delas Recogidas desta ciudad" (died October, 1618). Juan de Carmona Tamaris, father of Padilla's executor, became depositario general of the city July 16, 1610 (secular cabildo, capitular acts, 1606-1612, fol. 147), and later regidor.

6. At fol. 48ᵛ of Testamentos 1664 (Nicolás Álvarez, notary), Padilla assigns all his "vienes derechos y aciones Para que el dho doctor don Joseph de Carmona tamaris lo distribuya en haser bien por ella en limosna y sufragios y lo demas que le Paresiere sin que se le pida quenta de su distribucion Por que esta es mi voluntad."

7. Ibid., fol. 48: "Y quando su diuina magestad ffuere servido llebarme desta pressente vida se de a mi cuerpo sepoltura en la dha ssanta ygla cathedral desta dha ciudad y le acompañen los Hermanos de la Congregacion del bien abenturado San Pedro de·que soy congregante, y los hermanos de la concordia del glorioso San Phelipe neri de quien soy hermano y en lo demas a la dispusision de mi alvasea. = Y Nombro por tal mi alvasea testamentario al dho doctor don Joseph de Carmona tamaris a quien doy Poder Para el vsso y exersisio del dho cargo con general administracion en cuya virtud proseda a la venta y rrecaudasion de mis vienes judicial o estrajudicialmente aunque se a passᵈᵒ el termino de la ley = "

8. Málaga Cathedral, Actas Capitulares, 1609-1615, fol. 246ᵛ. Brito took possession May 8, 1613 (fol. 247ᵛ). Badajoz Cathedral, Actas Capitulares, 1596-1600, fol. 16ᵛ (November 22, 1596), identify him as "esteuam de Brito portuges vezino de la Ciudad de Euora del Reino de portugal."

9. Badajoz called Brito without edictos, convinced by his reputation alone that he was the maestro to succeed the deposed Cristóbal de Medrano.

10. Badajoz, A.C., 1606-1610 (Pleno / Libro q.ᵉ comenzo en 2 de Agosto de 1606 y finaliza en 1 de Marzo de 1610), fol. 120ᵛ (January 30, 1608): "dieron liçençia a Estevan de brito maestro de Capilla para se yr a ordenar por los dias que tuviere necesidad."

11. Málaga, A.C., 1609-1615, fol. 234, lists him as "Juᵒ Guttierez mᵒ de Capilla de Xerez."

12. Cádiz Cathedral, Acuerdos Capitulares, 1610-1617, fol. 335ᵛ: "Estos SS.ᵉˢ vnanimes y conformes Recibieron por maestro de capilla de la ygᵃ a Juᵒ gutierez de padilla presbytero con el salario q̄ tenia brᵐᵉ mendez su antecessor y se le encarga q̄ tenga cuydado de hazer q̄ los cantores hagan exerçiçio todos los dias y que el q̄ no quisia venir pᵃ aprender lo q̄ le hordenare q̄ fuere necessᵒ de quenta al cabᵒ. . . . "

13. Ibid., fol. 350: "Luego se presᵗᵉ vna petᵒⁿ del maestro de capᵃ dize q̄ ha venido vn hombre q̄ trae vn libro de canto de organo de missas de felipe Rogier muy provechoso pᵃ esta yglia." Puebla Cathedral owns this same 1598 edition, and in addition incomplete partbooks (Legajo 36, Cantus I and Tenor) with two Rogier Masses (Inclita stirps Jesse and Ego sum qui sum) and two psalms a 8, Laudate Dominum and Super flumina Babilonis. Choirbook XIX contains at folios 93, 97, 99, 102, and 106 five textless and untitled canciones or cancinas a 5 by Rogier.

14. Ibid., fol. 363.

15. Ibid., fol. 309: "tratose assimismo como se dezia q̄ el mᵒ de capilla dela igla se queria yr a xerez y el de alli dezian q̄ venia aqui y que tratauan de hazer este trueco."

16. Ibid., fol. 369ᵛ. At the same meeting the chapter authorized buying a new baxón = bassoon for Melchor de Loaysa. Mateo Gonçales was playing sacabuche = sackbut for a yearly 70 ducats according to the act of July 6, 1615 (fol. 298).

17. A.C., 1618-1620, fol. 32.

18. Ibid., fol. 103ᵛ. The Cádiz organist 1619-1632 was Pedro Deça Maçuela. Diego de Palacios, formerly of San Salvador Collegiate Church at Seville, became Cádiz maestro de capilla November 17, 1644 (A.C., VI [1643-1653], fol. 94).

19. Puebla Cathedral, Actas Capitulares, VII (1613-1622), fol. 327ᵛ: "En el dicho dia y Cauildo con pareçer y boto de su s.ᵃ Ylluss^a del señor obispo [Gutierre Bernardo de Quiroz, eighth bishop of Puebla, ruled the diocese 1627-1638] q̄ le embio con los dhos canonigos dᵒʳ don Juᵒ de uega y dotor gaspar moreno se Reciuio el m̄ʳᵒ Juan gutiᶻ de padilla Por cantor desta santa /fol. 328/ Yglessia con salario de quinientos Pessos en fabrica en cada un año con obligacion de cantar en la capilla y fuera della Todolo q̄ se ofreciere Y de lleuar el compas cada y quando q̄ se le mandare Por el presidente y estubiere ausente o ocupado El m̄ʳᵒ de capilla desta yglessia [Gaspar Fernandes] y haçer y poner las chançonetas quando sele encargare sin mas salario del que le esta señalado y traerlas pasadas con los demas cantores y asimismo con obligacion de enseñar canto de organo y haçer exerçiçio a los cantores y moços de choro q̄ son o fueren desta Yglessia que se Ynclinaren a ella Y lo quisieren sauer dandolas liçion Puᶜᵃmente Todos los dias de Trauaxo vna ora entera desde las diez a las onçe. Y que le corra el salario desde primero deste mes de otuᵉ. "

20. Ibid., fol. 337 (December 6, 1622): "Mando que en las obençiones q̄ tubieron que distribuir el maestro y cantores de la capilla desta cathedral le den y rrepartan su parte a juan gutierrez de Padilla Presuitero cantor desta dha cathedral a Raçon de quinientos Pessos que son los q̄ tiene de salario segun y como se le dan en las dhas obençiones a gaspar fernandez Maestro de Capilla lo qual se guarde y cumpla por agora y en lo tocante a los demas cantores se guarde y cumpla a la letra el auto que en Raçon desta esta Proueido Por Su Sᵃ Illᵐᵃ obispo y dean y Cauildo en catorce dias del mes de septiembre De mill y seis ciᵗᵒˢ y doçe años Y asimismo se mando se les notifique a todos los dhos cantores dela dha capilla acudan cada y quando que fueren llamados Por qualquiera Delos dhos maestros gaspar fernandez o Juan gutierrez de padilla a passar prouar y poner las chançonetas y las demas cosas Necessarias Y tocantes al seruiçio del choro sopena de que la primera vez que faltare auiendolos llamado se les pondran doce Pessos y ala segunda vez seran despedidos del seruicio desta santa Yglessia /fol. 337ᵛ/ Notifique luego en sus perssonas a cada uno delos dhos maestros y cantores. "

21. Ibid., fol. 339ᵛ (December 20, 1622): "que se diga al m̄ʳᵒ de capilla gaspar fernandez que hasta que pasen estas pascuas y dean y mande por El cauiᵈᵒ otra cossa no ynoue de la costumbre que asta aqui a auido en rrepartir las obençiones a los cantores y ministriles y para las que a de lleuar El m̄ʳᵒ Juᵒ gutierrez padilla guarde El auto que en Raçon della le esta notificado. "

22. A.C., IX (1627-1633), fol. 105ᵛ (June 12, 1629): "que dhos señores canonigo Liçençiado don Luis de Gongora y Racᵒ Juᵒ de ocampo bean y determinen lo que an de lleuar los maestros de capilla de esta Ygᵃ en las obençiones que ganan en ella y fuera della Por quanto todos los Cantores dela Capilla se sienten muy agrauiados en las partes que hasta aqui an lleuado. . . . "

23. A.C., VIII (1623-1627), fol. 1.

24. Ibid., fol. 28. On this same page is mentioned a former collector of cathedral tithes named Francisco de Padilla. Several other ministriles were hired during Padilla's first seven years.

25. Ibid., fol. 72 (July 16, 1624): "con parezer y boto de su sᵃ Illᵐᵃ el señor obispo se acordo y mando que al maestro Juan gutierrez de Padilla se le den Por vn año solamente cien ps de salario por quenta de fabrica Por el trauajo y ocupaçion que a de tener en enseñar canto de organo a los moços de

choro y otros muchachos y personas que a ofreçido /fol. 72^V/
enseñar que tienen voz de tiples P^a la Capilla desta santa
Yglessia de que ai gran nezesidad dellos con declaraçion q̄
visto el fruto y prouecho que se saca delos dhos muchachos y
que ai discipulos que yr enseñando porque cada dia van mudan-
do las Vozes delos dhos tiples y es necessario enseñar de
nueuo ottros se continuara el dho salario adelante el tiempo
que fuere la voluntad de su s^a Illma delos señores obispo
dean y cauildo y que los dhos cien ps corran desde Primero
deste mes de jullio = "

26. Puebla started him at 450 pesos annually (ibid., fol.
134). In 1615 Mexico City Cathedral was paying him only 300
(Revista Musical Chilena, XIX/92 [April-June, 1965], 13
n. 18).

27. A.C., VIII, vol. 110 (January 7, 1625). On August 11,
1626, the chapter voted "Al P^e melchor aluarez 100 pesos de
salario Por la correçion delos libros de Canto . . . y porque
cuide de uerlos enmendarlos y aderesarlos con todo cuidado.
. . ." The previous choirbook custodian, Bartolomé de Salas,
had departed for richer realms — "los rreynos del piru." On
September 18, 1629, the chapter rebuked Álvarez for his
sloth.

28. Ibid., fol. 276 (May 7, 1627): "Musica por el aumento
dela deuocion de los fieles. "

29. A.C., IX (1627-1633), fol. 76 (November 7, 1628).

30. Ibid., fol. 92.

31. Ibid., fol. 117^V: "Que para el martes q̄ viene, q̄ se
contaron veinte y cinco deste mes se cite a cabildo Para nombrar maestro de capilla desta Yg^a por hauer muerto El P^e
Gaspar frz q̄ lo fue. "

32. Ibid., fol. 119: "En el dho dia y cauildo con boto y
parecer de su señoria Ylustrisima del S.^{r} obispo que le ynbio
con el ynfraescrito secret^o fue elixido y nombrado Por todos
los dhos señores nemine discrepante al maestro Joan guttierres Padilla Presuitero por maestro de capilla desta dha
catedral en lugar del P^e Gaspar fernandes difunto que lo fue
hasta que murio el qual se nombro segun y dela manera que
el dho difunto Y lo demas maestros sus antesesores al qual
mandaron se le guarden todas y qualesquier honrras Y
preheminençias que son y fueren anejas a su ofiçio con salario
de los quinientos pesos que hasta oy a tenido el dho maestro
Ju^o Guttrz padilla por Cantor Pagados Por q^{ta} dela fabrica Y
assi mismo se le señalaron quarenta p^{os} en cada vn año por
puntar /fol. 119^V/ las chansonetas que se cantaron en esta
Catedral poniendo a su costa El papel tinta y lo demas ness^o
con calidad que todas las a de ir entregando Para que se
pongan en el archiuo desta Ygl.^{a} y se guarden en el Para que
en las ocaçiones que fuere Necesario aprouecharse dellas se
haga. y en quanto a las honrras preheminençias que se le an
de guardar Y las obligaçiones Con que a de exercer el dho
ofiçio de maestro de capilla dauan y dieron comiçion cunplida
al s^r canonigo Doctor don Antonio de seruantes Caruajal Para
que su mr^d vista las que tubo y deuio tener el dho Gaspar frz
Y sus antesesores Y las que conbiniere añadirles se aciente
Con el susodho yendolas al Cauildo. "

33. Ibid., fol. 120.

34. A.C., VI (1606-1612) fol. 24^V.

, 35. Philip III's cedula confirming Ocampo as Cristóbal de
Águilar's successor in the Puebla Cathedral organ prebend
(won in open competition May 18, 1604) was dated at Lerma
June 28, 1605. See Puebla A.C., VI, fol. 19^V. During the
next three decades Ocampo's prebend paid him 350 pesos
annually, but from 1606 onward his substitutes Fernandes and
then Simón took 300 of this.

36. A.C., IX (1627-1633), fol. 174^V.

37. Ibid., fol. 181^V: "cien p^{o}s mas por tal maestro sobre
los quinientos p^{o}s que asta aqui a tenido con los quales Gose
de seisçientos p^{o}s desde prim^o de Jullio deste año Por quenta
de fabrica atento a sus buenos seruiçios y mereserlo no obstante q̄ el salario ordin^o que esta catedral a pagado a sus
antesesores no a subido de quinientos p^{o}s. "

38. Ibid., fol. 177: "que los contadores desta Yglesia no
entreguen al maestro de capilla Ju^o Guttrz de padilla /fol.
177^V/ los libramientos que se cedan Por el papel, Y apuntar
las chansonetas hasta tanto que entregue las que huuiere fecho
en cada seis meses. . . ."

39. Ibid., fol. 271. Simón Martínez not only played bajón
but also composed. His Tone VIII Solo al SS^{mo} Sacramento in
the Sánchez Garza collection beginning "Oygan escuchen" is a
rather conventional da capo piece in fast ternary meter. But
the fact that it was later refitted with two alternate texts
proves that it was well liked.

40. Ibid., fol. 320.

41. Ibid., fol. 323^V. Simón earned an extra 100 pesos
annually for teaching the choirboys plainchant and psalmody
until replaced as maestro de los moços de coro October 27,
1634, by the presbítero Toribio Baquero (A.C., X [1634-1639],
fol. 32).

42. A.C., IX, fol. 344. He was senior racionero when he
died (fol. 340), and extremely rich. Throughout his long
cathedral career he had made a habit of endowing anniversaries with "capilla y música. " He began fittingly with Gregory the Great, endowed September 13, 1619, and July 10,
1620 (principal yielding 175 pesos annually [A.C., VII, 1613-
1622, fols. 203^V and 241]).

43. A.C., IX, fol. 368^V (November 8, 1633). Although
some few anniversaries paid 2,000 pesos, the March 12
anniversary endowed by the "venerable rracionero Lic^{do} Juan
de Ocampo" paid double that, according to Diego Antonio
Bermúdez de Castro's Theatro Angelopolitano ó Historia de la
Ciudad de la Puebla [1746] (Nicolás León edition, p. 131).

44. A.C., X (1634-1639), fol. 21 (August 1, 1634): "En
el dicho dia y cauildo los dichos señores vnanimes y conformes
y de comun acuerdo por Caussas justas que les mobieron dixeron que despedian y despidieron a Juan Gutierrez de padilla
maestro de capilla que a sido desta santa yglesia y desde el
domingo Passado que se contaron treinta de Jullio sese su
salario y no se le Pague assi el de maestro como los demas
que le estan señalados y que en el ynter que se Probee El
dicho off.^{o} llebe el Compas el Padre françisco de olibera
Para este Trauajo que se le de el Terçio mas en las obençiones
de lo que lleba el Cantor que mas gana, y assimismo dieron
Por despedido a Simon Martinez Vajon para que desde el
dicho dia no le corra su salario Por hauer concurrido las
mismas caussas para hecharle de la capilla desta santa
Yglesia y que esto lo trate y comunique con el señor Obispo
el señor Canonigo licen^{do} Gongora Para que con su acuerdo
y Parezer se ponga en execussion. "

45. A.C., VII (1613-1622), fol. 186. Cristóbal de Salas,
the runner-up, was temporarily allowed to serve alternate
weeks as sochantre, but Olivera was guaranteed 200 pesos
against Salas's annual 150. Unlike most succentors, Olivera
also shone as a composer. His soulful Tone IV motet O vos
omnes in the Sánchez Garza collection cannot match the con-
ciseness and overall unity of Victoria's like-named motet,
but everywhere reveals respectable workmanship.

46. A.C., X, fol. 21: "pida ante el s^r prouissor recaudo
bastante paraque el dicho Juan Gutierrez de padilla m^o de
capilla exsioa y entregue Todos los libros que estan en su
poder tocantes a esta ygla assi de canto de horgano como
canto llano y los quadernos de toda la musica que tiene apun-
tada Para ella. "

47. Ibid., fol. 25^V: "En el dicho dia y Cauildo con boto y Pareser de su ss^a Illma del señor obispo que le trujo el dicho señor canonigo D^{or} Juan Rodrigues de leon se rreciuio de nueuo Juan Gutierrez de Padilla Por maestro de capilla de esta yglessia y simon martinez bajon segun y como fueron admitidos Al tiempo y quando entraron a seruir en esta yglessia y con los mismos salarios y obligaçiones no embargante que estauan despedidos Por los dichos señores Obispo dean y Cauildo Por hauerle Pedido y suplicado el dicho Canonigo. "

48. Ibid.: "El m^o y Capilla acudan a las fiestas del ss^{mo} sacram.^{to} delos conuentos de monjas y a los entierros de Religiosas. "

49. Ibid., fol. 44^V: "Que a Juan Gutierrez Padilla maestro de capilla desta yglessia y a simon Martinez bajon della se les de en aguilando [= aguinaldo] Todo lo que montaren los Puntos que caussaron en el Tiempo que estubieron despedidos del seruicio desta dicha Cathedral [= Cathedral] en gratificassion de lo mucho que an trauajado en la fiesta de la concepçion y en estas Pascuas y en los libramientos que se les dieren ganen el dicho Tiempo como si hubieran estado Pressentes el qual dicho Aguilando se le manda dar con voto y Pareçer de su ss^a Illma del dicho señor Obispo que le Trujo el dicho secretario. "

50. Ibid., fol. 52^V (March 6, 1635): "musico de harpa Veçino desta Ciudad. "

51. A.C., XI (1640-1647), fol. 209^V.

52. Ibid., fol. 193 (August 14, 1643). Grinón was received "con cargo de tocar harpa y violon todas las veçes que se ofrecieren y lo mandaron. "

53. A.C., X (1634-1639), fol. 22^V: "que al Padre Pedro simon Cantor y sostituto del horgano 400 Pesos para el aderesso y adouio del. y estando gastados y acauados se llame a fauian ximeno horganista dela sancta yglesia Cathedral de mexico Para que lo bea y tasse y se ajuste la quenta de lo que se a librado. "

54. Ibid., fol. 47. Ximeno received a gratuity of 200 pesos for his inspection trip.

55. Ibid., fol. 54^V.

56. Ibid., fol. 55.

57. Ibid., fol. 86: "Juan Montero estante en esta Ciudad maestro de fundisiones haga y funda la Campana grande de esta Cathedral que esta quebrada y en la Torre della por pareser Persona que lo entiende y que al pressente no ay otra en este rreyno que lo pueda hazer. . . ."

58. Alice Ray Catalyne, "Music of the Sixteenth to Eighteenth Centuries in the Cathedral of Puebla, Mexico, " Yearbook of the Inter-American Institute for Musical Research, II (1966), 84. Although citing no source, she probably shared her information orally with Dr. Efraín Castro Morales, 11 Sur 306, Puebla. Both Indians and Negroes held cathedral posts during Padilla's time. See A.C., XI (1640-1647), fol. 151^V (September 2, 1642).

59. A.C., XI, fol. 146^V.

60. Ibid., fol. 113^V: "Ministriles que binieron de veracruz. "

61. Ibid., fol. 118^V: "Que se reçiue al B^r franc^o lopes por organista y que este a la voluntad del maestro de capilla con cargo que a de tocar bajon con salario de quatro çientos pessos. "

62. Ibid., fol. 194^V (September 1, 1643): "Que fr^{co} Lopez organista toque hasta que venga Pedro Simon Y venido se prouehera lo que conuenga; fol. 214 (January 15, 1644): "Que

fr^{co} Lopez organista Por q^{to} a seruido el tiempo q̄ auia de asistir el Licenciado Pedro Simon se le paguen los quattro meses q̄ ha faltado susodicho a razon Y conforme gana el salario el dicho L^{do} Pedro Simon y que de este auto se de q^{ta} a su Ex.ª"; fol. 231 (July 15, 1644): "Que a fr^{co} Lopez organista se le den ducientos p^{o}s Por lo que a seruido Y se le de en adelante salario con quien se concierte Para lo qual se cite a cauildo = Y que a Pedro Simon se despida Y que desde q̄ se fue no le corra salario Y lo que se le deuiere se Retenga"; fol. 346 (January 11, 1647): "Que al B^r fran^{co} Lopes organista se le den ducientos p^{o}s Por los ocho meses q̄ a seruido Por el P^e Pedro Simon Y para el aumento q̄ pide de salario a respecto de auer quedado solo se traiga p^a el primer Cauildo. "

63. Ibid., fol. 279: "Que se le den a fr^{co} Lopez organista las obenciones de cantor Por quanto tiene ducientos p^{o}s de salario de tal Cantor Y los otros ducientos de organista con cargo de asistir a dhas obenciones no tomando bajon sino fuere en la yglesia, quando le llame el maestro Y si estubiere ocupado en dha iglesia, si hubiere alg^a obencion se le den como si estubiere presente a ganarla ="

64. Ibid., fol. 346. This act still calls him bachiller, but the next makes him a licenciado.

65. Ibid., fol. 347: "Que al 1do fran^{co} Lopez organista se le den Cada año de salario seiscientos p^{o}s los trecientos de cantor y trecientos de organista y que si fuere necess^o aderesar el organo sea a costa dela yglessia. "

66. Ibid., fol. 384^V.

67. A.C., XII (1648-1652) fol. 6^V: "Que se buelua a receuir a P.^{o} Simon por Organista y Cantor = Y porquanto el liz^{do} fran^{co} lopez lleuaua seisçientos p^{o}s de salario y para que se reparta el trauaxo y ocupaz^{on} tocando por Semanas cada vno el dho organo con Salario de tresçientos p^{o}s a cada vno con calidad que el dho P^e Simon aya de templar el Organo, y los gastos que ttuuieren en adereçarlos sea por quenta dela fabrica ="

68. A.C., XI, fol. 194 (August 20, 1643).

69. A.C., XII, fol. 7^V: "Que el Liz^{do} Fran^{co} lopez sirua solo el ofi^o de organista con el Sal^o de tresçientos p^{o}s confirmando el auto que se hizo en el Cauildo de diez y siete deste mes = Y por quanto lleuaua Cien p^{o}s de Salario por tocar el Vaxon quando faltaua el Organo y lo tocaua el liz^{do} Pedro Simon sele releua deste trauaxo para que no toque el dicho Vaxon y solo sirua el ofi^o de Organista con el Salario delos tresçientos p^{o}s como esta mandado. "

70. Ibid., fol. 29: "Al Liz^{do} Gimeno Organista de Mex^{co} duscientos p^{o}s por la Benida q̄ hizo a esta ciudad a ber el Organo que se a comprado y otro grande que se a de hazer para la Yglessia nueua. "

71. The cabildo of October 6, 1648, voted: "q̄ a Pedro Simon Organista se le libre En la Conttaduria lo que monta la ocupaçion que tuuo desde quinze de mayo deste dho año hasta fin de jullio en tañer el Organo en lug^r de Fran^{co} Lopez Organista y sea respetiue de lo que tenia de salario el susso dho."

72. Ibid., fol. 49^V: "Que se Reçiua por Organista desta Yglessia en lug^r del Liz^{do} Fran^{co} Lopez que lo hera a quien se despido al B^r Ygnacio Ximeno con quatrocientos p^{o}s de Salario con cargo que P^o Simon lleue las Obenciones dela Capilla y si fuere a tocar el Organo alguna parte le pague quien lo lleu^{re}. "

73. Tamariz de Carmona, op. cit., fol. 1.

74. A.C., XII, fol. 354: "reuaxa de Salarios//Al Licenciado Ju^o Gutierres de padilla m^{ro} de Capilla Se le quitan çien p^{o}s por la oblig^{on} de dar lesion de Canto de Organo y queda Su Sal^o en seis çientos Y quarenta p^{o}s. Y el Sr Can^o

Domingo de los rios protesto que el dicho Mͬo de Capilla
Deuia bolber todo lo que a lleu^do por esta raçion atento a q̄
no ha enseñado Y ser en perjuiçio de la fabrica Y estar muy
pobre. Y no hauerlos." The protesting Canon Domingo de
los Rios began as a cathedral racionero = prebendary no later
than April 17, 1640 (A. C., XI, fol. 23). On November 23,
1640, and at various times thereafter he is listed in the acts
as doctor (ibid., fols. 67, 116). He took possession of his
canonry ("Possession of vna canongia al Domingo de los
rios") January 30, 1646 (ibid., fol. 296^V). Contrary to
Hispanic American Historical Review, XXV/3 (August, 1955),
368 n. 13, he never made any pretense of being "another"
(es otro should rightly read el dicho) chapelmaster. The rest
of the canons concurred with his protest against Padilla's
having been paid for teaching never done, especially with the
treasury so low.

75. A. C., fol. 113^V. Correa was also a first-class music
scribe to whom the chapter entrusted the job of recopying several books of motets and seeing them properly bound February
8, 1656 (A. C., XIII, fol. 306^V).

76. Evidently from Spain, Antonio de Mora was given permission at the cabildo of July 4, 1648, to fetch his wife from
Veracruz (A. C., XII, fol. 46^V). Blas was perhaps his son.

77. A. C., XI, fol. 355: "Quedaron Despedidos Ju^o Muñoz
y Domingo Pereira ministriles por hauerse ydo a seruir a la
s^ta Yglesia Cathedral de Mexico."

78. Alice Ray [Catalyne], "The Double-Choir Music," I,
181. During the years 1651-1656 fourteen choirboys were enrolled at the Colegio de San Pedro.

79. A. C., XIII (1653-1656), fol. 132^V.

80. Ibid., fol. 257^V: "Que al liz^do Joan Gutierrez de
Padilla maestro de capilla se le conceden diez dias de Termino para buscar en el archivo el auto y decreto fecho en
tiempo del s^r obispo don Alonso de la Mota acerca de las
obenciones y en este tiempo no le pase por juicio lo proueydo
en esta razon."

81. Ibid., fol. 306^V (February 8, 1656): "Que al liz^do Juan
Gutierrez de Padilla mro de Capilla se le notifique asi ms^o
entregue luego en la contaduria /fol. 307/ Todos los Villansicos que hiço el año pasado de 1655 que sean cantado en esta
yglessia como tiene obligazion y asi ms^o los que faltaren delos
demas años antezedentes y aga mem^a y ymbent^o delos libros
de canto de organo motetes y lo demas del seruicio desta
cathedral que paran en su Poder y vno y otro entregue al contador Antonio Lopez de Otamendi Y al s^r ra^o mayor^mo se le
encarga disponga Vno o dos cajones de los que se ban poniendo
en las capillas desta Yglessia para poner todos los dhos libros
deuajo de llaue y toda seguridad y para que no se saquen della
se saque censura y aga not^o al dho mͬo ="

82. A. C., XIV (1657-1662), fol. 129: "que al liz^do Joan
Gutierrez de Padilla mͬo de capilla se le notifique cumpla con
la obliga^on que tiene de enseñar el canto de organo a los monazillos pues tiene salario para esto con aperceuim^to que de
no hazerlo se procedera a lo que conuenga."

83. Ibid., fol. 277: "que se trate en este cauildo y se com-
fiera la forma que a de tener el mͬo de capilla en enseñar la
musica de canto llano y de organo todos los dias a los cantores
y mozos de choro segun la obliga^on que tubiere y se de asiento
a esta materia."

84. Ibid.: "Asimismo que el dho Mro de Capilla tenga
cuydado de buscar los muchachos que tubieren buenas vozes
para que Vistos y examinados por el Sr Chantre a quien toca
nombrar los monazillos lo haga en aquellos que fueren mas
vtiles a seruiçio de la ygl^a."

85. A. C., XV (1663-1668), fol. 70^V: "Y que se trasladen
todas las obras del Mro Ju^o de padilla y los demas papeles de
musica que lo necesitaren y le aderecen los libros maltratados

y que el trasladar sea por tasacion y la dispoçizion della y de
enquadernar lo que fuere conueniente. . . ."

86. Ibid., fol. 92^V: "que al liz^do Jhoan Gutierres de
padilla Maestro de capilla de esta Sta Yglessia se le den y
paguen por El may^mo de fabrica cinquenta p^os que se le dan
de aiuda de Costa. y assi mismo le supla otros Cinquenta p^os
p cuenta de su salario atento a las Necessidades que tiene.
Y enfermedades que padece."

87. Ibid., fol. 97^V: "menos el Maestro de Capilla por
hallarse enfermo. . . ." The cabildo especially resented the
musicians' failure to attend Saturday Lady Masses.

88. Alice Ray Catalyne, "Music of the Sixteenth to Eighteenth Centuries in the Cathedral of Puebla, Mexico," Yearbook, II (1966), 84.

89. J. T. Medina, La Imprenta en la Puebla de los Angeles
(1640-1821) (Santiago: Imprenta Cervantes, 1908), knew personally no villancico booklet published before 1690 (pp. 84-85).
Nor did he know of anything printed earlier than 1654 by Juan
de Borja Infante (p. 24; but see his curious error on p. xviii,
crediting Juan de Borja Infante with nothing earlier than a
1685 booklet). All the more worthwhile is it, therefore, to
list below the titles of the following heretofore unregistered
villancico booklets, usually of eight pages each, in the Lilly
Library.

W 173d Villancicos qve se cantaron la noche de Navidad en la
    Cathedral de la Puebla de los Angeles este año de mil y
    seiscientos y quarenta y nueve. [Woodcut of Mary, Joseph,
    and the Child.] . . . Con licencia del ordinario en la Puebla,
    Por el Bachiller Iuan Blanco de Alcaçar.

W 173 Villancicos qve se cantaron en la Cathedral de la
    Puebla de los Angeles en los maytines, y fiesta de la limpia
    concepcion este año de 1652. . . . En la Pvebla: En la
    Imprenta de Iuan de Borja, Infante.

W 173a Villancicos que se cantaron en la Cathedral de la
    Pvebla de los Angeles en los Maytines, y fiesta, dela limpia
    Concepcion de Nuestra Señora, este año de mil, y seiscien-
    tos y sinquenta, y quatro. [Woodcut of Virgin in oval.] . . .
    Iuan de Borja, Infante.

W 173b Villancicos [same title as preceding], 1656. . . .
    Viuda de Iuan de Borja, y Gandia.

W 173c Villancicos qve se cantaron en los maytines, y fiesta
    de la Limpia Concepcion . . . 1659. [Virgin on half-moon,
    with nopal and palmetto.] . . . Viuda de Iuan de Borja, y
    Gandia.

W 173e Villancicos qve se cantaron la noche buena en la
    Cathedral de la Puebla de los Angeles, este Año de 1659.
    [Angel singing Gloria.] . . . Con licencia En la
    Puebla de los Angeles, Por la Viuda de Iuan de Borja, y
    Gandia.

The following additional sets of villancicos are catalogued
under W 153f, W 153g, and W 173h at the Lilly Library.

[1681] Villancicos, qve se cantaron en la santa Iglesia Cathe-
    dral de la Puebla de los Angeles, en los Maytines de la Nati-
    vidad de Nuestro Señor Jesu Christo, este año de 1681. Com-
    puestos en metro musico por Antonio de Salazar Maestro de
    Capilla de dicha Santa Iglesia. [Woodcut of the manger
    scene, Joseph near an ox.] . . . Viuda de Iuan Borja.

[1730] Letras de los Villancicos, qve se cantaron en la
    Sancta Iglesia Cathedral de la Puebla de los Angeles, en los
    Maytines Solemnes de la Purificacion y Gozos de N^ra S^ra.
    Este Año de 1730. [Statement that these February 2 villan-
    cicos were endowed by the dean, Ignacio de Asenxo y
    Crespo.] Puestos en metro musico, por el Licenciado D.
    Nicolas Ximenes de Zisneros, Presbytero, Maestro de

Capilla de la referida Santa Iglesia. [Crowned Virgin with flowers, arms crossed.] . . . Por la Viuda de Miguel de Ortega, en el Portal de las Flores.

[1767]   Letras de los Villancicos, que se cantaron en la Santa Iglesia Cathedral de la Puebla de los Angeles, en los Maytines Solemnes de Nuestra Señora la Santissima Virgen Maria en el Rosario, Este Año de mil setecientos sesenta y siete. [Endowed by Captain Domingo de la Hedeza Verastegui, Regidor, who died a professed Dominican; woodcut of crowned Virgin; statement that these were set by Maestro Licenciado D. Joseph Joaquín Lazo Valero, cathedral chapelmaster.] . . . Imprenta de Christoval Thadeo Ortega.

JUAN HIDALGO
(Born at Madrid c. 1614; died there March 30, 1685)

The "unsurpassable composer" of the earliest still extant Spanish opera was born at the Spanish capital and baptized in San Ginés parish, the same church in which he was later to be buried. His father was Antonio Hidalgo (baptized at the village of Moraleja la Mayor September 12, 1585), a guitar maker who upon locating in Madrid married Francisca de Polanco. She was one of two daughters of the guitar maker Juan de Polanco, a native of Retorcillo who when still a youth of 13 or 14 came to the capital to ply his trade. Juan Hidalgo therefore grew up in a circle of luthiers. [1]

In 1631, on May 1, 1633, and on April 22, 1637, he gained various appointments to play the harp and "keyed harp" (clavi-arpa) [2] in the Royal Chapel at Madrid. On June 23, 1643, his appointment as Royal Chapel Músico de arpa was renewed, effective March 1, 1644. [3] As such his salary and perquisites in 1644, 1645, and 1647 amounted to 141,388 maravedís annually. On July 6, 1655, he received the further yearly crown grant of 200 ducats payable against the income of the archdiocese of Seville. [4]

While still single he was on July 29, 1638, appointed to the honorary post of familiar del Santo Oficio. To validate this appointment he had to furnish August 7 of the same year 300 reales de vellón for the cost of verifying his identity and family history. The investigation beginning August 21, 1638, took place at his father's and mother's hometowns and those of their parents: Moraleja la Mayor, Moraleja la Menor, San Sebastián de los Reyes, Retorcillo; and also at Madrid. The results proving satisfactory, his title was confirmed November 17. [5] Two years later, February 23, 1640, he was advanced to notario del Santo Oficio. A younger brother named Francisco Hidalgo (born 1620, died before 1676), gained the title familiar del Santo Oficio in the same year that Juan was raised to notario. [6] On March 1, 1644, this younger brother began serving as harpist along with Juan in the Royal Chapel. [7]

The eighteen character witnesses living at Madrid who in 1638 supported Juan Hidalgo's application for the familiar title included three luthiers (Manuel de Argüello, Juan de Roxas Carrión, and Francisco de Guypúzcoa), one of the queen's bass viol (= violón) players (Luys de As), and two other of her

aides, a surgeon-barber, a silversmith, a book vendor, a merchant, a timekeeper for the Royal Chapel, and two Inquisition officials [8] — but no one of very high rank. The whole tedious identification procedure of 1638 did at least save Juan Hidalgo's brother Francisco from its repetition in 1640, and stood Juan Hidalgo's son born c. 1648 (also named Juan) in good stead when the lad applied for a royal scholarship (granted September 11, 1664) to study at King's College (Colegio de el Rey) in Alcalá de Henares University. This son, the composer's only child, died July 11, 1669, [9] and was buried in the same San Ginés Church mentioned above as the church in which the composer was himself baptized and later interred.

The composer's wife (who survived him) was Francisca Paula de Abaunza, daughter of Domingo de Abaunza (born at Durango in Vizcaya) and of Ana López Zedillo. Complaining December 28, 1673, that as a married man he needed more, not less, than an ecclesiastic, he asked that his 44 years of faithful service be rewarded with the income of a full instead of half prebend. Two months later a powerful court advisor, the Duque del Infantado, backed his application, calling him "único en la facultad de la música." [10] But to no immediate avail. When 1676 ended he was still enjoying only a 500-ducat annual income and the emoluments of two places in the Royal Chapel. He did however manage to survive a general slash of palace salaries in July and August of 1677, at which time the Patriarch of the Indies, Antonio Manrique, interceded thus: "He is of superior ability and has at all times merited the highest royal honors; because of all this and of what he has done in chamber music it does seem that he ought not to be reduced." [11]

Finally on January 3, 1679, he gained his request for a full prebend (applied for in 1673). Although forever complaining of insufficient income, he cannot have been really poor in the interim. On February 3, 1678, he and his wife made their joint will at Madrid before the provincial notary, Baltasar Fernández Montero. [12] At his death he and his wife lived in their "own houses" (casas propias) on Magdalena Street. His estate was large enough to endow 200 Masses at 4 reales each, to clothe an unspecified number of poor clergy, and to pay for other charities. On March 31, 1685, the day after his death, he was buried without pomp in the chapel of Our Lady of Remedies (Nra. Sra. de los Remedios), San Ginés Church. José Subirá found the notice of his private burial in the Archivo Parroquial of this church, Abecedario del Libro 12 de difuntos, folio 20, and also a notice of his death in Libro 9 de la Parroquia de San Martín, que va de 3 febrero 1679 a 31 julio de 1689, folio 276. [13] Hidalgo's widow continued collecting arrears in his court pay during 1688 and 1689. [14]

If it were possible to find the music of the entirely sung La púrpura de la rosa (libretto by Pedro Calderón de la Barca) mounted January 17, 1660, at the Buen Retiro in honor of

Louis XIV's marriage to María Teresa (Philip IV's daughter), this would probably rank as Juan Hidalgo's first opera. Ironically, the music composed by Tomás de Torrejón y Velasco for the first New World presentation of La púrpura de la rosa (Lima, 1701) has been found, but not Hidalgo's for the original Peninsular production. However, Hidalgo's complete music survives for Calderón's Celos aun del aire matan, the three jornadas of which can be seen uniquely in the Évora (Portugal) Biblioteca Pública under call number Cod. $\frac{CLI}{2-1}$ (the first jornada embraces forty leaves, the second fifty, the third sixty). José Subirá found a transcript of only the first jornada in the Palacio de Liria of the Duke of Alba, Jacobo Fitz-James Stuart y Falcó.[15] Six years after publishing news of his discovery he edited the music of this one act.[16] Like La púrpura mythological in its subject matter, Celos aun del aire matan had its first hearing December 5, 1660.

After Philip IV's death (1665) several years elapsed before musical productions so elaborate as these were resumed. On December 3, 1679, to honor the entrance of the new queen María Luisa de Orleáns, Ni amor se libra de amor (alternately titled Siquis y Cupido) was mounted at the Royal Palace, text by Calderón, music by Hidalgo.[17] In 1898 Felipe Pedrell published eleven of Hidalgo's fourteen numbers written for Ni amor se libra de amor (Teatro lírico español anterior al siglo XIX). A generation later he repeated Escena XI, "Quedito pasito" (a 4, with continuo) in his Cancionero musical popular español, IV (Valls: Eduardo Castells, 1922), pages 22-28.[18] However, he each time misdated Hidalgo's music, giving 1640 as the date of first production instead of January 19, 1662. When at the age of eighty Calderón accepted 3,400 reales for his last play, Hado y divisa de Leonido y de Marfisa, Hidalgo was again commissioned to write the music. Premiered Sunday March 3, 1680, in the sumptuous Buen Retiro theater, this Calderonian swan song enlisted the services of two dramatic companies. For teaching the women of the first company Hidalgo's music, Gregorio de la Rosa received 1,000 reales; for teaching the women of the other company, Juan de Cerqueira was paid 500. For composing the music of both the play and prefatory loa, Hidalgo was rewarded with 1,500 reales.

Just as all but one singing role in Celos aun del aire matan was allotted a woman — even when characters enacted were males — so also in this last Calderonian play with music, women did the bulk of the singing. Two male instrumentalists were hired to perform on stage, José Benet (800 reales for three days) and Luis López (600). Juan Cornelio received 500 for playing the violin at rehearsals and at the premiere.[19]

Hidalgo's dramatic music has thus far overshadowed[20] his tonos divinos y humanos, scattered widely in Spanish repositories and also abroad in archives from Portugal to Peru. At Évora, keeping company with his unattributed opera, is his attributed Despertad mortales . . . Si quieres saber des-

pierta for SSAT and continuo (Sacrament villancico) in $\frac{CLI}{1-3}$d, N.^{O} 2. At The Hispanic Society of America, New York City, HC 380/824a contains eight Hidalgo tonos in the rich collection assembled by Federico Olmeda of Burgos and sold to the Society by Hiersemann of Leipzig. Antonio Rodríguez-Moñino and María Brey Mariño list the titles of Hidalgo's eight tonos in their Catálogo de los manuscritos poéticos castellanos existentes en la Biblioteca de The Hispanic Society of America (New York: Hispanic Society of America, 1965), I, 289-291. Pero pues no vale-Ay desdichada, item 16 in their list (an accompanied solo), takes for its text lines from Alfeo y Aretusa, Fiesta de Zarzuela (1672) by Juan Bautista Diamante (1625-1687).[21] In contrast with the eight secular pieces at The Hispanic Society, the Munich set of six Hidalgo villancicos (Mus. MSS 2895-2900) all celebrate the Blessed Virgin.[22] The Cantate spagnuole indexed at pages 114-116 in Taddeo Wiel's I codici musicali Contariniani del secolo XVII nella R. Biblioteca di San Marco in Venezia (Venice: F. Ongania, 1888) include two tonos humanos (MS 470 [Classe IV], pp. 8-12, 13-17) identifiable as Hidalgo's from ascribed concordances in the Madrid Biblioteca Nacional MS M. 3880 (53 and 21): En los floridos páramos and Perdone el amor. The tono at pages 81-86, Iuegas Florilla, belongs to Hidalgo's setting of Juan Vélez de Guevara's Los celos hacen estrellas, beginning at line 1064. Pitts's doctoral dissertation identifies 17 excerpts from the loa, two acts, and fin de fiesta of this same zarzuela as items 24, 34, 20, 42, 38, 9, 10, 11, 5, 8, 12, 13, 14, 17, 15, 16, and 19 in the just mentioned Madrid MS M. 3880.[23] Chapter V of the same dissertation (pp. 208-243) discusses Hidalgo's sacred works catalogued by Pedrell in the Barcelona Biblioteca Central[24] Catàlech de la Biblioteca Musical de la Diputació de Barcelona, II [1909], pp. 21, 33, 46, 47, 48, 51 [5], 54 [2], and 55), in Fitzwilliam Museum MS MU-5-1958 at Cambridge University, at El Escorial, the Madrid National Library (M. 3881/11 and 13), and at Munich. Hidalgo's Missa a 5 with both harp and basso continuo survives at El Escorial (tiple 1 is coro 1 and the other parts are coro 2).[25] A catalogue of Hidalgo's extant music in Spain, at Venice, and in New York City runs to 55 excerpts from dramatic works, 21 tonos humanos, 28 tonos divinos and villancicos, and one Mass.[26]

Apart from the Missa a 5 at El Escorial, Latin music by Hidalgo in Spanish archives remains yet to be catalogued. In fray Domingo Ortiz de Zárate's letter to Miguel de Irízar[27] dated January 2, 1675, the Calced Mercedarian friar at Madrid replied to his friend's request for a Miserere thus: "I have asked a friend to do me the favor of looking for a Miserere by [Carlos] Patiño, Matías Ruiz, or [Cristóbal] Galán, because the rest of the composers in Madrid such as Juan Hidalgo and [Juan del] Vado and others of their ilk spend their time only in composing tonos."[28]

Two South American cathedrals own Hidalgo's works, Bogotá

and Sucre. Both boast his F Major Epiphany villancico a 4 Monarcas generosos, the Bogotá copy being dated 1721. Two years later was sung at Bogotá his Sacrament villancico a 5, also in F, Cantarico q̄ bas a la fuente no teme quiebres. His villancico de Miserere, Mas ay piedad a 3 at Sucre inhabits darker regions than are Hidalgo's wont. At Bogotá the bajo of a Missa de Feria survives as the unique New World testimony to anything like a liturgical interest.

NOTES

1. Jaime Moll Roqueta, "Nuevos datos para la biografía de Juan Hidalgo, arpista y compositor," Miscelánea en homenaje a Monseñor Higinio Anglés (Barcelona: Consejo Superior de Investigaciones Científicas, 1958-1961), II, 586-587. Moll found the supporting document at the Archivo Histórico Nacional de Madrid in Inquisición de Toledo, legajo 354, n.º 1.293 (ibid., II, 585).

2. Santiago Kastner, "Juan Hidalgo," Die Musik in Geschichte und Gegenwart, VI (1957), col. 374, surmises that the clavi-arpa was a harp with a keyboard attachment. Concerning the clavi-arpa see also Hans Joachim Zingel, Harfe und Harfenspiel vom Beginn des 16. bis zweite Drittel des 18. Jahrhunderts (Halle [Saale]: Eduard Klinz, 1931), p. 27; Die Musik in Geschichte und Gegenwart, V (1956), col. 1554 (however, the year 1610 is too early for Hidalgo's invention); Marin Mersenne, Harmonie vniverselle, (Paris: S. Cramoisy, 1636-37, III: Traité des instrumens a chordes, Liure Troisiesme, pp. 113-114 ("vne nouuelle forme d'Epinette dont on vse en Italie").
A fellow-member of the Spanish Royal Chapel who was an Italian harpist and instrument maker, Bartolomeo Giobernardi = Jobernardi may have suggested the idea of such a novelty to Hidalgo. As authority for calling Hidalgo the inventor of the clavi-arpa, José Subirá cites Lázaro Díez del Valle y de la Puerta (La música en la Casa de Alba. Estudios históricos y biográficos [Madrid: Hauser y Menet, 1927], p. 70), a native of León who in 1659 while a criado de su Magᵈ (member of Philip IV's household) wrote an Epilogo y nomenclatura de algunos Artifices dedicated to the famous painter Velásquez (first published in F. J. Sánchez Cantón, Fuentes literarias para la historia del arte español, II [Madrid: C. Bermejo, 1933]).

3. José Subirá, "El operista español Don Juan Hidalgo," Las Ciencias, I/3 (1934), 618. These confusing dates, extracted from the Barbieri papers in the Madrid Biblioteca Nacional, can perhaps be reconciled as plural appointments.

4. Ibid., p. 619.

5. Moll Roqueta, op. cit., p. 586.

6. Ibid., p. 587. In footnote 2 Moll cites as his document: Archivo Histórico Nacional, Inquisición de Toledo, Informaciones genealógicas, Leg. 354, n.º 1290. See also, Archivo Histórico Nacional, Catálogo de las causas contra la fe seguidas ante el Tribunal del Santo Oficio de la Inquisición de Toledo (Madrid: Tip. de la Revista de Archivos, Bibliotecas y Museos, 1903), p. 486.

7. Las Ciencias, I/3, 620. Francisco Hidalgo, who predeceased his elder brother, left a widow named Juana Vélez. In 1676 she was collecting an annual pension of 730 reales.

8. Moll, op. cit., pp. 588-589.

9. Las Ciencias, I/3, 619. In 1669 the Hidalgo family was living in Madrid "en la Puerta Cerrada en casas de Don Juan Pardo Monçon."

10. Ibid., p. 620.

11. Ibid.: "Es de superior habilidad, y ha merecido los mayores honores de SS. MM. en todos tiempos; con que respecto a esto y a lo que ha servido en la cámara, no parece que se le rebaje nada de cuanto goza."

12. Ibid., pp. 616-617 (date in last line of p. 616 should read 1678, not 1687; he died in 1685).

13. Hidalgo was living within bounds of San Martín parish when he died, but wished burial in the church where he had been baptized and where his son lay. Subirá found the son's death notice in a libro de óbitos containing 1669 (fol. 167) from San Justo Church that in 1934 was preserved at the Madrid Iglesia de las Maravillas (ibid., p. 619).

14. Las Ciencias, I/3, 621.

15. La música en la Casa de Alba, pp. xix, 57-82. Facsimile of title page opposite p. 60. The Madrid copy, though only of one jornada, identifies Juan Hidalgo as the composer (Musica dela Comedia Zelos aun del Ayre matan = Primera Jornada = Del = M.º Juan Hidalgo =); the Evora does not identify the composer (Zelos aun del Ayre matan Comedia de D. Pedro Calderon Muzica de [blank]).

16. Celos aun del aire matan. Ópera del siglo XVII, Texto de Calderón y música de Juan Hidalgo (Barcelona: Institut d'Estudis Catalans. Biblioteca de Catalunya, 1933). Subirá left the unfigured basses unrealized, thus effectively discouraging any attempts at performance.

17. Emilio Cotarelo y Mori, Ensayo sobre la vida y obras de D. Pedro Calderón de la Barca, Parte primera (Madrid: Tip. de la "Rev. de Arch., Bibl. y Museos," 1924) p. 327. At p. 314 Cotarelo dates the absolute premiere at the Retiro January 19, 1662.

18. Concerning the now lost manuscript from which Pedrell copied these numbers, see Ruth Eleanor Landes Pitts, "Don Juan Hidalgo, Seventeenth-Century Spanish Composer," George Peabody College for Teachers (Nashville) Ph.D. dissertation, June 1968 (University Microfilms 68-16,348), p. 5.

19. Ibid., pp. 342-344, for all details in this paragraph.

20. Next to Celos aun del aire matan the Calderón play for which Hidalgo wrote the largest amount of still extant music was La estatua de Prometeo (c. 1669). See Pitts, op. cit., pp. 27-31. José Subirá, who kept promising a complete, performable edition of Celos, never mentions La estatua, even when discussing Hidalgo's dramatic music in his latest essays: for instance, "La ópera 'castellana' en los siglos XVII y XVIII (Tema con variaciones lexicográficas)," Segismundo. Revista Hispánica de Teatro, no. 1 (Madrid, 1965), at p. 25 of which he lauds the "música del notabilísimo compositor e insigne arpista Juan Hidalgo." Nor does Subirá discuss Hidalgo's music for Juan Vélez de Guevara's zarzuela Los celos hacen estrellas (1672), excerpts from which Pedrell published in his Teatro lírico español, IV, 1-13. Hidalgo provided the music also for Antonio de Solís's three-act fiesta, Triunfos de Amor y fortuna, celebrating on February 21, 1658, the baptism of Felipe Próspero. Three musical excerpts survive, according to Pitts, op. cit., pp. 36-37. See also Emilio Cotarelo y Mori, "Ensayo histórico sobre la zarzuela," Boletín de la Academia Española, XIX/95 (December, 1932), 761.

21. Cotarelo y Mori, "Ensayo," p. 763; Pitts, op. cit., pp. 38-39.

22. Titles in Jul. Jos. Maier, Die musikalischen Handschriften der K. Hof- und Staatsbibliothek in Muenchen, Erster Theil (Munich: Palm'schen Hofbuchhandlung, 1879), p. 101 (= Cod. 156-161). Cod. 158 and 159 adjust the same music to different texts.

23. Pitts, op. cit., pp. 43-49.

24. En la mesa del altar, a 4 with continuo (top part missing), discussed at pp. 226-227, arrived in the Barcelona Biblioteca Central after Pedrell's catalogue was published. See Pitts's p. 9 n. 4.

25. Ibid., pp. 238-242.

26. Ibid., pp. 287-293. When Hidalgo's works in Latin America are added, the list will grow considerably (Stevenson, Renaissance and Baroque Musical Sources in the Americas [Washington: General Secretariat, Organization of American States, 1970], pp. 19, 86, 244).

27. After serving the collegiate church at Vitoria, Irízar on August 21, 1671, became maestro de capilla at the cathedral in Segovia, where he apparently died in August of 1684. See José López Calo, "Corresponsales de Miguel de Irízar," Anuario Musical, XVIII-1963 (1965), 198.

28. Ibid., p. 200: "tengo encargado a un amigo me haga favor de buscarme un miserere de Patiño o Matías Ruiz o Galán, porque los demás son que hay en Madrid como Juan Hidalgo y Vado y otros así, no se ocupan si no es en hacer tonos. . . ."

JOSÉ de LOAYSA y AGURTO
(Flourished at Mexico City 1647-1695)

Isabel Pope [Conant] happily discovered among manuscripts in the Biblioteca Nacional, Madrid (Manuscritos de América: 251, Tomo III, 23. Signatura 3048, fols. 176-179) an itemized list of all the musicians hired by Mexico City Cathedral in 1647. Signed May 20 of that year, this list begins with the chapelmaster, L[do] [licenciado] Luys Coronado, earning a yearly 500 pesos. His deputy L[do] Melchor de los Reyes earned half that amount. The salaries of the named nineteen choir members ranged from 300 down to 50 pesos annually. The five staff instrumentalists earned 150, 200, or 250 pesos. Joseph de Loaysa comes sixteenth in the list of nineteen cathedral choristers, with an annual salary of 100 pesos. This document, published in Nuestra Música, VI/21 (1er Trimestre, 1951), pages 22-23, forces us to place Loaysa y Agurto's birthdate not much later than 1625. At the very least, he was therefore in his mid-sixties when in 1688 Antonio de Salazar replaced him as cathedral chapelmaster.

Sometime between 1647 and 1655 Loaysa took a cut of 10 pesos in his annual pay. For almost a year after Francisco López Capillas became maestro de capilla April 21, 1654, he and his other subordinates who had suffered cuts kept besieging the Mexico City cathedral chapter for salary raises. When on April 30, 1655, Joseph de Loaysa added his petition for an annual 30 pesos above the 90 that he had been just previously receiving, the chapter acceded but also announced that henceforth absolutely not a single other musician's request would be entertained, because of "la mucha necessidad de la fabrica" ("the [cathedral] foundation's severe economic plight").[1]

After López Capillas's death January 18, 1673,[2] the chapter waited several years before naming Loaysa maestro de capilla. In 1676 when providing the music for the August 15 villancicos by Sor Juana Inés de la Cruz (1651-1695) he remained merely "Br. [bachiller] Joseph de Agurto y Loaysa, Maestro de los villancicos de dicha S. Iglesia."[3] The title page of the December 8 villancicos published that same year calls him "Br. Joseph de Agurto y Loaysa, M[o] Compositor de dicha S. Iglesia."[4] This latter rank recurs on the title page of the villancicos for August 15, 1677.[5] His Assumption set for 1683 denominates him merely "Maestro de dicha Santa Iglesia."[6] At last, in the 1685 and 1686 Assumption sets the title pages call him "Maestro de Capilla de dicha Santa Iglesia,"[7] as does also the title page of the 1688 St. Peter set.[8] On all three title pages of the latter sets, he reverses the order of his apellidos, becoming now el "Br. Joseph de Loaysa, y Agurto."

Villancicos were so much his forte that he composed the music for no fewer than five of the canonical sets by Sor Juana — those for Assumption in 1676, 1679, 1685, for Conception in 1676, and for St. Peter in 1683.[9] As if these were insufficient, he composed the music also for the anonymous 1677 and 1686 Assumption villancico-sets which Méndez Plancarte attributes to Sor Juana on internal evidence.[10] Against this impressive record of collaboration with the Tenth Muse, Antonio de Salazar composed the music for one canonical set and six "attributed" sets, Miguel Mateo de Dallo y Lana[11] wrote for three canonical and one "attributed," and Mateo Vallados[12] for one canonical.[13]

Wearied with the eternal problem of choirboys, who in 1681 were being boarded and clothed by Juan Santos, their underpaid teacher for plainsong and polyphony, Loaysa on January 11 applauded the archdeacon's proposal to reduce their number to no more than twenty — less if possible.[14] Loaysa also welcomed in 1684 the easier solution of entrusting the soprano lead henceforth to a castrato, Bernardo Melendes.[15] Castrati were nothing new to the Americas in 1684. Francisco de Otal at Guamanga = Ayachucho in 1614 and at La Plata = Sucre in 1618 provides an earlier example.[16] At Seville, the mother cathedral of the Indies, castrati were engaged as early as 1620.[17]

After the layman Antonio de Salazar became Mexico City cathedral maestro de capilla September 3, 1688, Loaysa y Agurto still continued on the roll of cathedral musicians. On January 7, 1695, he heads the list thus: "B[r] Joseph de Loaysa Pres[bro]"[18] According to the act of September 3, 1688, Loaysa lived at Toluca.[19]

NOTES

1. Mexico City Cathedral, Actas Capitulares, XII (1652-1655), fol. 197[V]. Probably he had been a cathedral seise to begin with; he earned less in 1654 than in 1647.

2. Documentos para la Historia de Méjico, Tomo II (Mexico City: Juan R. Navarro, 1853), p. 154: "Jueves 18 de enero, murió el Lic. D. Francisco López Capilla, maestro de

la catedral, en que fué hombre insigne, racionero entero de esta iglesia." See also pp. 70 (September 1668) and 114 (September 1671) in this volume, which contains a modernized transcript of Antonio de Robles's Diario de Sucesos Notables [1665-1703].

3. Sor Juana Inés de la Cruz, Obras Completas, II (Villancicos y letras sacras), ed. by Alfonso Méndez Plancarte (Mexico-Buenos Aires: Fondo de Cultura Económica, 1952), p. 355.

4. Ibid., p. 365.

5. José Toribio Medina, La Imprenta en México (1539-1821) II (Santiago: Impreso en Casa del Autor, 1909), p. 492: "Compuestos en Metro musico, por el B[r] Ioseph de Agurto, y Loaysa, Maestro Compositor de dicha Santa Iglesia."

6. Ibid., pp. 553-554.

7. Ibid., III (1908), 9 and 22.

8. Ibid., p. 41.

9. Obras Completas, ed. Méndez Plancarte, II, 355, 388, 401, 365, 397.

10. Ibid., pp. 469, 499.

11. Appointed Puebla Cathedral chapelmaster December 17, 1688, at 600 pesos (Actas Capitulares, XVIII [1681-1689], fol. 386[V], he died there September 1, 1705 (A.C., XXI [1703-1711], fol. 118[V]). Dallo y Lana's music is more widely dispersed in Western Hemisphere archives than that of any other Puebla maestro.

12. A native of Oaxaca (Oaxaca Cathedral, A.C., I [1642-1673], fol. 262[V] [March 23, 1668]), Mateo Vallados = Ballados was appointed maestro de capilla there with a 260 pesos yearly salary March 23, 1668, "con obligacion de tocar la corneta . conponer billansicos en todas las festiuidades que en esta yglesia se acostunbra cantar en el año las missas y los demas . . . y la de la enseñanza todos los dias de canto llano y de organo assi a los niños como a los que necesitaren de aprender dela misma capilla." On January 8, 1692, the Oaxaca Cathedral chapter raised Vallados's salary for being chapelmaster to 300 pesos annually.

13. See Méndez Plancarte ed. (n. 3 above), II, 427, 479, 485, 489, 494, 512, 517; 408, 413, 419, 506; 431.

14. Mexico City, A.C., XXI (1680-1683), fols. 38 (December 17, 1680), 54 (January 11, 1681). Juan Suárez de la Cámara was archdeacon.

15. A.C., XXII (1682 [sic]-1690), fol. 64:"Despues se leyo vna peticion de Bernardo Melendes Musico castrado en que dize ser Musico de la Santa Iglesia de la Puebla y que pretendia entrar en esta a serlo y para esto se presentaba para ser examinado, y oido a satisfaccion fuesse admitido por vno de los Ministros siruientes en la Musica y se le señalasse salario en que reciuiria bien y merced."
Melendes's salary was again discussed May 26, 1684 (ibid., fol. 125).

16. Stevenson, The Music of Pecu: Aboriginal and Viceroyal Epochs (Washington: Pan American Union, 1960), pp. 184-185, 202.

17. Simón de la Rosa y López, Los seises de la Catedral de Sevilla (Seville: Francisco de P. Díaz, 1904), p. 137.

18. A.C., XXIII (1691-1695), fol. 351.

19. A.C., XXII (1684-1690), fol. 318.

ANTONIO de SALAZAR

(Born 1650, place unknown, but a "resident" of
Puebla in 1679; died at Mexico City c. 1715)

When filing application June 20, 1679, to compete for the post of Puebla Cathedral chapelmaster left vacant by Juan García's death the preceding summer, Antonio de Salazar called himself a "resident of Puebla."[1] In the interim since García's death, the acting chapelmaster had been licenciado Carlos Valero.[2] The chapter of June 30, 1679, named Valero, Francisco [de] Vidales (cathedral organist, 1656-1702), and three others a committee to test the candidates. Examine them in every facet of their art, urged the chapter.[3] However, Valero protested against the chapter's allowing two candidates to be examined — Salazar and the bachiller Agustín de Leiva — because neither one was in ecclesiastical orders. By disqualifying them he probably hoped for a "no winner" outcome that would leave him acting chapelmaster.

The report, ready for chapter consideration July 11, 1679, covered these points: (1) the motet and villancico the candidates were required to compose while shut up alone and cut off from outside contact, (2) their ability to harmonize at sight a melody picked at random from a polyphonic partbook, (3) their readiness in improvising a counterpoint to a given plainchant, (4) their skill in setting straight a singer who had strayed from his part.[4] Among those present at the examination and who confirmed the 29-year-old Antonio de Salazar as justly the winner were two outsiders, the choral-vicars of the Dominican and Augustinian houses in Puebla.

In deeding Salazar the post July 11, 1679, the chapter stipulated that he must give a daily one-hour lesson in canto de órgano (polyphonic music), morning or afternoon, to all cathedral music staff. Also, the chapter made him promise that he would deposit in the cathedral archive a copy of each new piece composed by him. (As extra pay for copies of the chanzonetas already written for the preceding December 8, the chapter simultaneously offered him 40 pesos, and for the villancicos adorning the same day 24 pesos.) As a third condition the chapter asked him to guarantee a certain flexibility in accepting any new conditions that the canons in future might wish to impose for the betterment of Puebla Cathedral music.[5]

Fortunately for Puebla, his zeal matched demand. Latin motets[6] and hymns, Spanish villancicos, and instrumental music showed how versatile he could be. Six of his Latin hymns, one for March 19, two for June 29, one for July 25, and two for August 15, still survive in Puebla Cathedral Choirbook V.[7]
His villancico-sets continued delightfully bizarre, with eight or nine distinct numbers in a set. The four suites published at Puebla (texts only) 1680-1684 with poetry credited to Sor

Juana Inés de la Cruz contain no fewer than 33 individual movements, the titles of which range from foliás, jácara, calenda, and negro, to ensaladilla. [8]

His fluency served him well when the time came for him to compete at Mexico City. The preliminaries to this appointment can be traced back to May 28, 1688, on which date Canon José Vidal de Figueroa suggested that the chapter revert to so time-honored a method of choosing the next chapelmaster as a competition publicly announced throughout New Spain. [9] Wednesday, August 11, was declared the closing date for applications to compete. [10] One week later, 19 chapter-members met to decide how the competition should be run. [11] The next morning, after the conventional tests in canto llano y contrapunto, all five candidates were handed the texts of a Latin motet and of a Spanish villancico — which they were required to set before three the next afternoon. Between Friday afternoon and the next Wednesday, August 25, the voting members of the chapter had heard all the compositions performed and were ready to cast their ballots. The scrutiny gave Salazar eight votes, but his nearest contender only three. [12] His salary, which came up for consideration next, was set at a yearly 500 pesos — exactly the salary with which he had started at Puebla in 1679 — but with the added sweetener of 1 real in every peso of the obenciones. In addition, the chapter promised him sufficient music paper for all his compositions and, at Canon Lope Cornejo de Contreras's instance, copying assistance so that "his works can be placed in the archive, as was done at Puebla."[13]

Fortunately for Mexican musical history, Salazar's interest in archives embraced not just his own oeuvre but also the works of his predecessors. Already before Friday, September 3, when his appointment was formally read, he had called the chapter's attention to the maltreatment and dispersal of the Mexico City Cathedral musical patrimony. No one knew just where the polyphonic books had fled, some thinking them to be in Toluca at the house of the former maestro Joseph de Agurto y Loaysa, others claiming that Maestro Carrión had them. When the latter surmise proved correct, the whole lot of polyphonic books was found to be in such bad condition that none could be used without costly repairs. [14] These were ordered, after which they were to be placed in a new and separate archive, to which Salazar alone would have the key.

According to Dr. Gabriel Saldívar Silva, [15] Salazar's output of masses, motets, hymns, Te Deums, [16] and villancicos, exceeds quantitatively that of every other colonial Mexico City maestro de capilla. [17] Two of his villancicos for January 23, 1691 (Feast of St. Ildephonsus), first published in Dr. Saldívar's 1934 text, pages 109-108 [sic], 110-111, also enter my Music in Mexico: A Historical Survey (New York: Thomas Y. Crowell, 1952), pages 143-147. Even more intriguing would be his entire villancico-sets for August 15, 1690, June 29, 1691, and June 29, 1692, when Sor Juana provided the poetry. [18]

Her 1690 set closes with an ensalada that incorporates a juguete [19] and a jácara. In the jácara, Salazar cites the well-known folktune Yo voy con toda la artillería to give flavor at the outset. [20] For the intermezzo opening the third nocturn of her 1691 set, Salazar assembled no fewer than fifteen instruments. These played short solo passages in the following order: bugle, trumpet, sackbut, cornett,[portative] organ, bassoon, violin, shawm, marine trumpet, bass viol, cittern, vihuela, small rebeck, bandore, and harp. [21]

Although not enough of Salazar's works have yet been scored to validate any critique, the milestones of his Mexico City career can at least be posted. His first five years in the capital saw the installation of a new grand organ, built at Madrid by the famous Jorge de Sesma. To insure scrupulous fulfillment of the contract with the Madrid builder, the Mexico City chantre spent several months in Spain (1689-1690) and there engaged Don Tiburcio Sanz de Izaguirre, his brother Félix, and another assistant to accompany the organ to Mexico City. [22] This trio arrived at Veracruz in October 1692. [23] Two years later Don Tiburcio could report to the chapter completion of the organ case, chambers for the pipes, two bellows, an added octave for the corneta de éco stop, and the tuning of all pipes a half-step higher than when they had left Spain — because Mexico City pitch was a semitone above homeland pitch. For all these services, 4,000 pesos of a contracted 12,000 were still owing October 1, 1694.[24]

Before final settlement the chapter insisted, of course, on inspection. The five-member inspecting team consisted of (1) a musically knowledgeable prebendary named Dr. Juan de Narbáez, (2) Joseph [de] Ydiáquez, principal cathedral organist from no later than 1673[25] to at least 1699, [26] (3) Francisco de Orsuchi[1] an assistant organist and tuner since 1656, [27] (4) Diego de León, a cathedral chorister who was a boy choirboy in 1673, [28] (5) Joseph de Espinosa de los Monteros, a cathedral bassoonist. [29] Orsuchil's sealed report of May 17, 1695, asked several searching questions. His queries, those of Dr. Narváez, and the replies of the bigamous organ builder Don Tiburcio throw welcome light on the imported organ, its registration, tone colors, sonorities, and mechanism. [30]

Having spent so much on the new grand organ, the chapter next grappled with the problem of training organists. After Salazar certified that a choirboy named Cristóbal Antonio de Soña was taking daily lessons from Ydiáquez, the chapter placed the youth on a 20-peso yearly salary to help clothe him. For each daily lesson missed, he was to be fined. [31] May 25, 1694, the dean recommended that Manuel de Zumaya, another cathedral choirboy, be given 30 pesos for clothing expense and placed on a yearly salary of 50 or 60 pesos while taking daily lessons with Ydiáquez and assisting in cathedral services when required. [32] As reasons for this generosity the dean voiced his desire to restrain so musically talented a lad from becoming a friar and the obligation of the cathedral authorities to train suitable candidates for each office. Zumaya proved the happiest possible choice for such generosity when in 1715 he succeeded Salazar as maestro de capilla and in 1711 distinguished himself by composing the earliest North American opera for which the libretto survives, La Parténope.[33] Still another youth selected by the chapter to study organ with Ydiáquez after having shown special talent as a seise was Juan Téllez Xirón. On January 5, 1697, this former seise was appointed Ydiáquez's ayudante at 80 pesos annually on condition that he henceforth come to coro properly surpliced and that he continue taking a daily lesson with the now valetudinarian Ydiáquez.[34] According to the cathedral act of February 9, 1700, Téllez had by then been settled on as Ydiáquez's successor, showing what fruit the chapter's investment in him had yielded.[35]

Like Ydiáquez, Salazar took pupils supported by the chapter. José Pérez de Guzmán, an exceptionally gifted ex-choirboy, began private lessons with Salazar on January 10, 1696. The chapter subsidized the lessons and paid the youth at the rate of 50 pesos annually.[36] By 1708 Pérez de Guzmán had made sufficient progress to be selected a chapelmaster at Oaxaca.[37] Another notable pupil was the bachiller Manuel Francisco de Cárdenas, who arrived from Guadalajara July 6, 1700, with a four-month leave to prepare for sochantre under Salazar. Possessor of a muy buena voz, he was invited to stay in Mexico City permanently, where a decade later the cathedral was paying him 200 pesos annually while he continued to study privately "at Salazar's house."[38]

On January 10 of the latter year, Salazar petitioned the chapter to excuse him henceforth from teaching the boy choristers in the choir school. "Not all the choristers need know counterpoint," he averred. However, "he would be glad to continue teaching counterpoint to any prospective succentors who would come to his house." Now sixty, he claimed to be almost blind and in bad health.[39] The chapter agreed to free him from his choir school duties but not to allow counterpoint instruction there to lapse. Instead, the canons deputed Zumaya to teach counterpoint in the choir school every Monday and Thursday, "as required by statute."[40] When Zumaya was selected also to substitute for Salazar in the cathedral, the bachiller Francisco de Atienza protested February 11 and June 27, 1710, against allowing anyone so junior to him as Zumaya to conduct, more especially since in 1703 he had already served as Salazar's substitute.[41] What is more Atienza had stood third in the list of cathedral musicians as long ago as 1695.[42] Still, the majority preferred Zumaya's genius to Atienza's talent and therefore brushed aside his suggestion on February 11, 1710, that the celebrant be allowed to say who should conduct at each mass. Piqued at not having his way, Atienza departed for Puebla not long thereafter.[43]

Zumaya repaid his teacher's faith in him not only by be-

coming "el gran músico de México," as Jesús Estrada calls him in Excelsior, March 23, 1970, page 11A ("Rescate de 300 Años de Música Virreinal"), but also by carrying his mentor's music to Oaxaca where even today survive three vernacular works and two Latin by Antonio de Salazar — Aues flores luces fuentes, a Christmas villancico a 11, Toquen toquen a fuego a 4, and Viua Pedro Diuino, a June 29 Tone VIII villancico; a Tone VIII Magnificat a 12, and Joseph fili David, an accompanied motet a 8 (SATB SATB). In 1966 Guatemala Cathedral still owned Salazar's Mi Dios si llorais, a Christmas accompanied duo, Primores amantes, a Sacrament accompanied duo, and Vengan Corriendo, another Sacrament accompanied duo.

Zumaya and Salazar also cooperated in four extremely beautiful Latin hymns now to be seen in Choirbook V at Mexico City Cathedral, second foliation. Pars I is by Salazar and II by Zumaya at folios 3^V-8 and 12^V-14: Salazar's partes being entitled Egregie Doctor Paule, Christe Sanctorum decus, Miris modis repente liber; pars secunda of the hymn at 8^V-10 is also by Salazar, O Crux ave spes unica. At the Viceroyal Museum, Tepotzotlán, a choirbook dated 1717 (copied by Simón Rodríguez de Guzmán) opens with Vespers music by Zumaya but continues at folios 22^V-26 with Salazar's O sacrum convivium a 8 (Corpus Christi).

The latter work, filmed from another copy at Mexico City Cathedral, joins the following responsoria (all a 8) in Rollo III at the Museo Nacional de Antropología e Historia, Mexico City: Benedictus Dominus Deus, Euge serue bone, Hodie concepta [nata] est Beata Virgo Maria, Inueni David, Quis Deus Magnus, Vidi Dominum. The only one of these just cited responsoria thus far published, Quis Deus Magnus, appears at pages 110-118 in Lincoln B. Spiess and E. Thomas Stanford's An Introduction to Certain Mexican Musical Archives.

Choirbook V at Puebla Cathedral contains six Salazar hymns, two each for June 29 and August 15, one for July 25, and one for March 19.

NOTES

1. Puebla Cathedral, Actas Capitulares, XVII (1676-1680), fol. 243^V: "Se Vbo por oppuesto a la Plaza de M.^{o} de Capilla Antt.^{o} de salazar reçidente en esta Ciu^d y lo firmo el s.^{r} Dean."

2. Ibid., fol. 195 (August 12, 1678).

3. Ibid., fol. 245^V. The chapter also solicited written questions on every phase of theory and practice from the paid cathedral musicians. But the musicians had to swear that they would not allow prejudice or favoritism to sway them in deciding which candidate answered their written question best.

4. Ibid., fol. 247 (July 11, 1679): "el Motete y Villancico q̃ se les mando hazer e hizieron solos y enserrados en la sala de Cauildo y delo demas que obraron en preçençia de los Musicos señalados tapandoles en vn Libro de Canto de Organo vna Voz p^a que la supliesen, y en otro de Canto llano hechando Contrapunto y haziendo perder vno delos Musicos para Ver si

lo metian en el tono que deuia. "

5. Ibid., fol. 247^V.

6. Having grown lax during García's term, both singers and instrumentalists resented being forced to learn new Latin motets — preferring a small group of already known motets by Padilla and other earlier maestros. To remedy this, the chapter issued an ultimatum February 20, 1681, threatening with dismissal any musician who demurred at mastering new motets. In part this ultimatum in A. C., XVIII (1681-1689), fol. 11, reads: "Que se notifique al Maestro de Capilla que en estas Festiuidades de los Apostoles varie los Motetes que hubiere de los demas Maestros, o los componga nuebos, sin repetir vno mismo en estas fiestas, y que en las dominicas post Epiphaniam, despues de alzar en la Missa, se canten motetes y si no los hubiere compuestos, los haga de nuebo. Y esto mismo en las demas Dominicas que se ofrecieren Haziendo a todos los Musicos que asistan a esto y a todo lo demas que les ordenan sin replica ni contradiccion alguna y de el que la hubiere, de luego noticia a este Cabildo. "

7. Stevenson, "Sixteenth- and Seventeenth-Century Resources, " Fontes artis musicae, 1954/2, p. 76.

8. Sor Juana Inés de la Cruz, Obras Completas, II, Villancicos y Letras Sacras, ed. Alfonso Méndez Plancarte (Mexico City: Universidad Nacional Autónoma, 1952), pp. 262, 266 and 299, 270, 276, 289.

9. Mexico City Cathedral, Actas Capitulares, XXII (1682-1690), fol. 303.

10. Ibid., fol. 312.

11. Ibid., fol. 313.

12. Ibid., fol. 315. Girón (first name not given) was his closest contender.

13. Ibid.: "que haga lo que en la Puebla, que ponga en archivo sus obras, y se le de para papel. "

14. Ibid., fol. 318: "Que se haga diligencia con el M^O Loaisa. Toluca. Y que no pareciendo los Libros Musicos que faltan Se saquen censuras para cobrarlos. Y se nombrase Vn s^{or} Capitular para que reciba por inuentario. Entro el M^{ro} Carrion. Y dixo que los libros de Canto llano y Canto figurado auian sido a su cargo. Se determino que los libros de Canto llano, los guarde como asta hora. Y que los libros de Canto figurado Los tenga el M^O de Capilla con inuentario, y que se haga vn archivo aparte. de que tendra la llaue. /fol.318^V/ Que los ss^{res} Jueces Hacedores manden Libres el costo para el adereço de los libros de canturia de organo y Musica figurada y se le encarge al m^o de capilla este adereço. Y que se haga vn armario . . . y Cajones para papeles sueltos. "

15. Historia de la música en México (Épocas precortesiana y colonial (México: Editorial "Cultura, " 1934), pp. 108-109.

16. Francisco Sosa, El Episcopado Mexicano, 3d ed. (Mexico City: Editorial Jus, 1962), II, 57, 62, 66, quotes contemporary descriptions of cathedral ceremonies November 13, 1701, and January 29, 1702, that included Salazar's Te Deums.

17. Otto Mayer-Serra, Música y Músicos de Latinoamérica (Mexico City: Editorial Atlante, 1947), II, 877, repeats this claim.

18. Méndez Plancarte ed. (see n. 8 above), II, 148-163, 330-342, 342-353. José Toribio Medina registered the imprints in La Imprenta en México (1539-1821), III (Santiago [Chile]: Impreso en Casa del Autor, 1908), at pp. 68, 82, and 96 (nos. 1482, 1504, and 1530). According to the title pages, the University of Mexico professor who endowed each of these sets was Simón Esteban Beltrán de Alzate y Esquivel.

19. Juguetes were as popular in Peru as in Mexico throughout the 1690's. But Tomás de Torrejón y Velasco, Lima chapelmaster 1676-1728, wrote a letter to a Cuzco colleague (found by Rubén Vargas Ugarte in the Seminario de San Antonio Abad library at Cuzco), warning him to abandon such "jocular music" if he hoped to please an austere archbishop elected in 1703. See Stevenson, The Music of Peru: Aboriginal and Viceroyal Epochs (Washington: Pan American Union, 1960), p. 107. When they crept back into favor at Sucre=La Plata c. 1772, juguetes took the form of gay sung playlets (ibid., p. 205).

20. Méndez Plancarte ed., II, 161. Such popular touches came usually at the close of the last nocturn.

21. Ibid., pp. 339-340, 516. Andrés Sas offered data on the contemporary use of many of these instruments at Lima in "La vida musical en la Catedral de Lima, " Revista Musical Chilena, XVI/81-82 (July-December, 1962), 23-32.

22. Mexico City Cathedral, A. C., XXII (1682-1690), fol. 394 (January 17, 1690). The dean thought Don Tiburcio's prospective wages should be set before his leaving Spain, but Joseph Vidal de Figueroa, cura of the Sagrario, doubted that this could be intelligently done.

23. For the biography of the tall, blue-eyed ruddy-complected Tiburcio Sanz de Izaguirre (recte Izaguerri), born c. 1655 near Saragossa, Spain, see Archivo General de la Nación, Ramo de Inquisición 693, fols. 453-479. He fell afoul Holy Office authority at Mexico City when it came out that on July 5, 1694, he bigamously married there a fourteen-year-old orphan, whom he had violated. Sixteen years earlier (fol. 470) he had already married at Málaga a woman still alive in 1695.

24. A. C., XXIII (1691-1695), fol. 331 (October 1, 1694). Desperate for money after his recent bigamous marriage, he said that he needed immediately the 4, 000 pesos still owed him by the chapter. Unaware of what was causing his difficulty, the canons heard patiently the memorial of "Tiburcio Saenz de Isaguirre M^{ro} de Organista que ha armado el nuevo Organo, que hiço Don Jorge de Sesma en Madrid, Y que acabo el suplicante, Diciendo que se examino y entrego al Sr. Chantre Don Alonso Ramirez difunto para conducirlo a estos Reynos, a donde se le auia entregado de orden de Su Señoria los Sres Dean y Cabildo, con obligacion de hacer la Caxa, segun la traça por precio de quatro mill pesos, y de hacer secretos, y doz fuelles, y afinarlo en el tono que auia venido de España por precio de ocho mill pesos, y que auiendo echado muchas mejoras en dha Caxa . . . y auer subido dho Organo medio punto por auto de este I11^{mo} Cabildo, y echado vna octaua en la corneta del eco, reducido las ocho Contras fuera de dho Caxa. . . ." The canons thereupon agreed to pay him the outstanding 4, 000 pesos, but after inspection by "los mas cientificos. "

25. A. C., XVIII (1670-1673), fol. 368 (January 10, 1673). Already a licenciado on that date, he won a pay raise from 50 to 100 pesos because he was doing so well.

26. Ibid., XXV (1698-1701), fol. 32^V (January 9, 1699). May 9, 1698, the chapter dispensed him to take hot baths.

27. Ibid., XIII (1656-1660), fol. 116 (December 19, 1656). Hired at 50 pesos to play when the ayudante Alonso Fernández could not come, and to tune, Orsuchil still hung on in 1699 (A. C., XXV [1698-1701], fol. 72^V), but had always been a poor player. February 16, 1700, someone proposed diverting 60 pesos of his pay to the up-and-coming teenage organist Juan Téllez Xirón (fol. 154), but the more humane solution of retirement on full pay was accepted.

28. A. C., XVIII, fol. 369 (January 13, 1673).

29. A. C., XXIV (1695-1697), fol. 26^V. As vajonero he doubtless switched from bassoon to bass viol and other bass instruments at will.

30. See Stevenson, "Mexico City Cathedral Music: 1600-1750," The Americas, A Quarterly Review of Inter-American Cultural History, XXI/2 (October, 1964), 129-130, for details. Throughout this article, the magazine editor without author's permission changed "shawm" to "shawn."

31. A.C., XXIII, fol. 132^V (January 9, 1693). Soña was "quinto seyse y Infante del Choro, que estaba aprendiendo de organo, y que parece iba aprouechando."

32. Ibid., fol. 297^V: "Leyose la Peticion de dho Manuel de Sumaya En que se despide y pide licencia para salir a aprender organo y pide la ayuda de Costa — El Sr Dean Dijo, que se le den los treynta pesos de ayuda de Costa ordinaria para Vestuario, y que para detenello y que no se vaya a meter frayle, Y yr criando en cada officio personas para qualquier frangente; que se le den cinquenta, sesenta pesos de salario al año para Vestuario Clerical y aprenda a Organista Con el Mro Ydiaquez todos los dias y entre en el Choro Con sobrepelliz, y asista al organo siempre que lo tocan su Mro y que le pongan en quadrante y le apunten. los demas Sres que sele de la ayuda de Costa de treinta pesos que le acostumbra — y asi quedo resuelto."

33. Bilingual libretto (Italian by Silvio Stampiglia, Naples, 1699) in Mexican National Library, Rare Books, call-number 17. M4 PAR. Three years earlier Miguel de Rivera printed El Rodrigo, the music of which Zumaya composed to celebrate Luis Fernando's birth. See Medina, op. cit., III (1908), p. 398; also Juan José Eguiara y Eguren, Bibliotheca Mexicana, MS B 015. 72 EGU. b, in Mexican National Library, p. 271.

34. A.C., XXIV (1695-1697), fol. 197: "Juan Tellez seyse del Choro por ayudante de organista con salario de ochenta pesos al año en fabrica, y que entre con sobrepelliz en el Choro, y asista todos los dias en casa de su M^o B^r Ydiaquez a aprender organo."

35. A.C., XXV (1698-1701), fol. 150. Ydiáquez had meantime been retired on his full salary of 600 pesos annually (ibid., XXXVI [1741-1744], fol. 35^V, act of January 30, 1742). On February 10, 1742, Téllez Xirón retired on an annual 400 pesos, after 49 consecutive years of cathedral service.

36. A.C., XXIV, fol. 110^V; salary mentioned at fol. 197 (January 5, 1697). The three students being taught by Salazar in 1692 are named in A.C., XXIII (1691-1695), at fol. 37^V (January 8, 1692).

37. A.C., XXVI (1706-1710), fol. 157^V (February 28, 1708). On the same day, the chapter obligated each of the three cathedral organists — Zumaya, Téllez, and Esquivel — to teach a talented choirboy polyphonic composition so that the stream of new candidates for important positions would not dry up.

38. A.C., XXV, fol. 211 (July 6, 1700); XXVI (1706-1710), fol. 337 (January 10, 1710).

39. A.C., XXVI, fols. 336^V-337 (January 10, 1710): "Leido un escrito de Antonio de Salazar M^{ro} de capilla de esta Sta Ig^a representando el que se le dispense en lo mandado sobre que asista ala escoleta a la enseñanza el Canto figurado, y contrapunto a todos los Musicos, y alos Niños Ynfantes, y aun a dos Sujetos, para el ministerio de Sochantre, por las rasones que espresa en dicho /fol. 337/ escrito su corta salud, y no ser necesario que todos los Cantores ayan de sauer contrapunto para ser diestros, hallarse con sesenta años de hedad, y casi siego, y que los sujetos que sele señalasen para que los enseñase para sochantres, seles mande bayan a su Casa, para con mas continuacion enseñarlo, como lo aria tambien a el que se aplicase a aprender el Contrapunto."

40. Ibid., fol. 337: "Y que por sus ausensias, y enfermedades, asista, como Mro, D^n Manuel de Sumaya Presbytero por su conosida Sufisiensia, y que lo haga en la escoleta todos los lunes, y Juebes del año como esta mandado a la enseñanza

del Contrapunto. y haga toda la musica necesaria para el Culto de esta Sta Yg^a y que sele despache titulo con calidad de que no pueda pedir salario ni cosa alguna por rason de esto."

41. Ibid., fol. 376. At their June 27, 1710, meeting three canons did confirm Atienza's claim to have conducted in 1703. Moreover they agreed that no organist can properly conduct from the bench.

42. A.C., XXIII (1691-1695), fol. 351. This January 7, 1695, list of 22 cathedral músicos begins with the maestro de capilla. Next comes B^r Joseph de Loaysa Pres^{bro} whose musical service dated back to 1647. OnApril 30, 1655 (A.C., XII, fol. 197^V), he had been raised from 90 to 120 pesos annually, and he had preceded Salazar as chapelmaster. Don Augustín de Leiva Pres^{bro}, third on the 1695 list, had served "more than ten years" March 16, 1684 (A.C., XXII, fols. 37^V-38). On that date the archbishop had recommended that since he was a widower whose wife's death the cura of Zacatecas had certified (fol. 34) he be now permitted to take sacred orders. His voice, that of a tiple fixo, entitled him to 300 pesos in the archbishop's opinion (March 16, 1684). Leiva it was who in 1679 had been Salazar's only worthy competitor for the Puebla chapelmastership. After Leiva on the 1695 list comes Don Fran^{co} de Atienza Pineda Pres^{bro}, then B^r Pedro Moreno Pres^{bro}. None of the other 17 musicians on the 1695 roster seems to have been a priest: Diego de León (a cathedral seise January 13, 1673 [XVIII, fol. 369]), Francisco Astasio (senior cornettist [XXV, fol. 234]), Pedro de la Cruz (a sackbut player earning an annual 100 pesos, he was given 50 extra in 1677 because "he was poor" [XX, fol. 86]), Joseph de Espinosa de los Monteros (senior cathedral bassist [XXIV, fol. 26^V]), Guillermo de Carvajal, Carlos de Águilar (master of the boys, he taught them plainchant and insured their proper behavior at church functions [XXIII, fol. 351^V]), Nicolás Bernal (admitted as Ministril de Bajón June 17, 1681 [XXI, fol. 111]), D^n Gerónimo de Zárate, D^n Juan Marsán de Pasi (married bassist given permission to bring his wife from Spain April 1, 1700 [XXV, fol. 171^V]), Tyburcio Vásquez, Bartholomé de Poblete, Manual Dias, Antonio de Soto, Antonio de Oropesa, Manuel Francisco, Diego Dallo, Miguel de Rosas. In a later hand, the list is augmented, "y los demás ministriles," without naming "the other instrumentalists." The low musician on the totem pole, Miguel de Rosas had gained the certificate of proficiency in plainchant and polyphony that permitted him to enter the cathedral choir as recently as January 8, 1692 (XXIII, fol. 37^V).

43. On January 15, 1712, after examination he was appointed maestro de capilla there (Puebla Cathedral, A.C., XXII [1712-1718], fol. 3). He died in March of 1726. J.T. Medina inventoried twelve sets of villancicos for which Atienza composed the music between 1715 and 1722. Copies of the printed texts survived in the Biblioteca Palafoxiana when Medina published La Imprenta en la Puebla de los Angeles (Santiago: 1908), pp. 184, 185, 187, 189, 191, 194, 195, 201, 202 [twice], 206 [twice]. His name on the title pages of these villancicos is always Francisco de Atienza y Pineda presbítero.

FRAY FRANCISCO de SANTIAGO

(Born c. 1578 at Lisbon; died October 5, 1644 at Seville)

Diogo Barbosa Machado called fray Francisco de Santiago "one of the most famous musicians who flourished in his epoch."[1] Ernesto Vieira, who counted the works of this Lisbon-born[2] composer in King John IV's library, discovered the staggering total of 538 villancicos — plus an uncounted multitude of Masses, Psalms, responsories, and motets — thus making Francisco de Santiago the most heavily represented

Portuguese composer in the entire royal archive. [3]

While still a hotheaded youth using his family name of Veiga=
Vega because he had not yet taken Calced Carmelite vows, he
spent five months (February 16, 1596, [4] to July 15 [5]) as maestro de capilla of Plasencia Cathedral. That he was still in his
salad days when appointed can be inferred from his being
labeled at the Plasencia chapter meeting of July 15, 1596, a
mere "boy" lacking the maturity needed to gain his singers'
respect. Probably he was only 18. (On February 16 the Plasencia chapter stipulated that he must take holy orders within
six years; 24 was the canonical minimum age for the priest-
hood.) If only 18, he joins the company of two other Peninsular celebrities who gained their first chapelmasterships at 18
and 17, respectively, Francisco Guerrero (Jaén Cathedral,
1546) and Diego Pontac (Hospital Real, Saragossa, 1620).

On February 19, 1596, after only a month in the post, the
Plasencia canons had already found reason to fault the im-
petuous Veiga. He must not start motets at festal Masses before the chalice is raised, they warned ("hasta q̄ este alçado
El calix"). Since at Plasencia, as everywhere else in Spain
and Portugal, instruments constantly supported voices, new
replacements for worn-out shawms and cornetts frequently had
to be bought. The first needed in Veiga's short period was a
contralto chirimía ordered bought February 23.

Among reasons for dismissing him so soon, various chapter
members cited not only his youth but also his argumentative
nature and a spat with Doctor Busto. Four days after the broken tie vote letting him go with a mere 100-real gift to cover
travel home, the chapter did agree to vote again on his case.
So close was the vote this second time that the chapter sent
the pertiguero to canvass all sick canons at their houses. [6]
Arguing for another chance, one humane canon proposed letting him at least try again. However, the Plasencia maestro
just before Veiga had killed a priest (act of October 30, 1595)
and the majority of the canons now wanted nothing so much as
a mild successor. Smarting from the injustice of being denied
even a puny second chance, Veiga convinced the diocesan provisor that he deserved legal redress. The next day after the
second close vote a notary named Francisco García therefore
"notified the chapter of an order staying the dismissal of the
chapelmaster. "[7] Annoyed by Veiga's cheek, the chapter now
threatened a full-scale battle that would bleed white any liti-
gant. Two months later (September 16, 1596) they had their
new maestro, Antonio Ordóñez. Hired at 90,000 maravedí
and 2 cahizes of wheat annually, Ordóñez so endeared himself
that on January 24, 1597, the chapter responded with any extra
cahiz annually.

Between July 15, 1596, and May 14, 1601, Veiga joined the
Calced Carmelites at Madrid. His choice of this order can
hardly have been accidental. To it belonged in his epoch also
the nonpareil Portuguese composers Manuel Cardoso (1566-
1650) and Manuel Correa (died at Saragossa c. August 1, 1653).

In both Italy and Spain the order had long favored more than
any mere plainsong. Unlike Observant Franciscans and some
other strict mendicants, the Calced Carmelites had since at
least 1312 endorsed part-music at Lady Masses and other
principal feasts. Benedict Zimmerman's "La Cultura Musicale nell'Ordine dei Carmelitani, " published in Rivista
Storica Carmelitana, I (1929-1930), [168]-182, dwells not only
on early legislation allowing "falso bordone" ("motetos" are
already mentioned in the 1324 Constitutions of the order) but
also lists by name 22 reputable Carmelite organists and singers at Florence alone before 1500. To this order belonged
John Hothby and the teacher of Gaffurius, Johannes Bonadies=
Goodendag (Die Musik in Geschichte und Gegenwart, II, 102-
105).

That the youthful Veiga was by no means the first Portuguese
melomane to seek refuge in a Spanish Carmelite house is also
documented by Zimmerman (page 179). Around 1567, while
still a subdeacon in the house, the Portuguese Carmelite
Gaspar de Évora had twice run off "for no other purpose than
to study singing and the violin" ("non per altro scopo che
quello di studiare il canto e il violino, " Reg. n. 113 Ávila,
April 1567 [Registri del Generale Giovan Battista de Rossi,
1564-1578]).

At Easter of 1601, eager at last to atone for having peremp-
torily dismissed him five years earlier, the Plasencia canons
invited back Veiga, now fray Francisco de Santiago, for special services. The evidence survives in the act of May 14,
1601. At that session the Plasencia canons argued "whether
the Carmelite father Veiga, formerly Plasencia Cathedral
chapelmaster, should be paid 200 reales for what he has done
here recently. [8] At the same May 14 session the chapter voted
that Tomás Luis de Victoria be paid 100 reales "for the eight
small books [Madrid miscellany published in 1600] and two
large song books" brought from Madrid by Veiga for Plascen-
cia chapter appraisal.[9]

When seven years later Victoria sent for Plascensia's ap-
proval his next and final publication, the letter accompanying
the Officium defunctorum stated the exact occasion for which
he had composed this now extremely famous work: "las
honrras dela emperatriz. " His letter was read at the chapter
meeting of May 16, 1608. [10] On June 20, 1608, the Plasencia
chapter voted to send someone after "Joanico El Capon Seise
que se fuè a Salaman^ca [11] — an important piece of evidence re-
futing the hitherto accepted idea that rich Seville was in 1620
during the epoch of Veiga=fray Francisco de Santiago the first
Spanish cathedral to hire castrati. [12]

From 1601 until shortly before his appointment to succeed
Alonso Lobo (who died at Seville April 5, 1617), Veiga =
Francisco de Santiago continued maestro de capilla of the
of the Calced Carmelites at Madrid. Even the sacristy of
their church in the capital was provided with vn monachordio
and vn organo in 1595, [13] and as early as 1574 the Madrid

BIOGRAPHICAL DATA

Calced Carmelites boasted of a respectable library of music books and of sheet music bought for festivals by El Maestro mariano.[14] A favorite retreat for rich youths inclined toward religion, the Madrid house received as a sample bequest May 29, 1607, a fifth interest in all income from rented public transportation in the capital.[15] So far as his seniority in the house is concerned, Santiago stood seventh in a list of twelve July 21, 1608.[16] Two years later, December 15, 1610, the same house enrolled fourteen friars.[17]

His reputation in the capital triggered the invitation dated October 7, 1616, to compose the chanzonetas needed at Seville Cathedral for the December 8 and 25 celebrations that year.[18] So well did he please everyone, not only with his music for December 25 and January 6 but also with the way he coached the choirboys for their performances, that on January 11 the Sevillian Cathedral chapter voted to write an official letter offering him the succession to the mortally ill Alonso Lobo.[19] New singers were needed and to ferret them out the chapter asked him January 23 to start canvassing likely prospects by mail.[20] A week later the chapter discussed which seat to give Santiago, the new acting maestro de capilla.[21] Immediately upon Lobo's death April 5,[22] Santiago became titular chapelmaster.[23]

Still the largest city in Spain when Santiago began there, Seville counted about 2,000 Portuguese families among its 125,000 inhabitants in 1640[24] (on December 1 of which year Portugal declared her independence from Spain after sixty years of Spanish rule). The most important Portuguese singer in the Seville Cathedral choir during Santiago's 27-year term was the prebendary Manuel Correa. Not to be confused with his Portuguese homonym who was a Calced Carmelite and who died as Saragossa Cathedral chapelmaster, our Manuel Correa [del Campo[25]] occupied Media Ración no. 8 in Seville Cathedral from July 22, 1617, until his sudden death January 6, 1645,[26] at the age of only 52. A superb contralto singer,[27] he was but one of the many prize musicians[28] bagged by the tireless searcher for excellent performers, Francisco de Santiago.

Santiago traveled far and wide to capture them. On June 30, 1617, the chapter refused to hire a contralto who had journeyed from Plasencia and made three other candidates wait until news came from Santiago "who has gone searching for voices."[29] He was back by August 23, on which date the canons voted him 100 ducats for travel expenses during his search for boy and adult singers.[30] A decade later he journeyed as far afield as Logroño and Ciudad Rodrigo looking for a bass, tenors, and choirboys.[31]

During this same trip he captured for Seville Cathedral a soprano castrato who was an Augustinian friar.[32] Prior to the Augustinian friar, Seville Cathedral had engaged tres seisçicos acolitos que vinieron caponçitos May 11, 1620. At least seven castrati were hired before 1635.[33] On June 28, 1641, the chapter ordered Xptoual, e Valero capones tiples que an

sido seisses paid their due from the prebends reserved for estudiantes. This, and other evidence, justifies our believing that a new brilliant timbre added excitement to Sevillian cathedral music in Santiago's epoch.

Every five years — in 1625, 1630, 1635, and 1640 — the chapter allowed him a long enough leave to revisit Lisbon. The first leave had to be extended because he needed an extra twenty days to finish his business there.[34] Subsequent three-week leaves were granted June 17, 1630, and September 3, 1635.[35] His leave granted June 15, 1640, lasted two months,[36] so that he could take the baths at Caldas da Rainha which his great benefactor the Duke of Bragança (who became King John IV of Portugal later that year), generously helped pay for.[37] Not many Portuguese singers can have been scouted during these home leaves, however. Already in 1619 the Sevillian chapter had begun fearing a Portuguese overload. On July 5, 1619, a new bass (cantor contrauajo) from Portugal named Vasco Diaz was given forty days to fetch his belongings from home,[38] but a fortnight later the chapter heatedly argued whether to name any further prebendaries from Lisbon whatsoever.[39] The chapter preferred tiples from Segovia and Palencia August 7, 1624, and May 9, 1625, a tenor from Santiago de Compostela November 10, 1625, and a contralto from Zamora October 15, 1629,[40] to any more Portuguese pretenders to the posts.

One legitimate complaint against hiring "foreigners" occupied the Sevillian canons at their chapter meeting of April 28, 1625 — the great cost of investigating "foreign" candidates' antecedents. Although the excellent report on Santiago's family connections, early life, and conduct on Portuguese soil completed at Lisbon July 29, 1624,[41] had reassured the Sevillian canons of his fitness in every respect, the expense of obtaining such certified information on "foreigners" served as their excuse for sticking henceforth with "nationals."

Also, the Portuguese may not always have exercised tact. If the Racionero Manuel Correa's attitude was typical, the Portuguese liked to vaunt themselves as inherently better singers than the Spaniards in this epoch — thus piquing Spanish pride.[42] They also hung together. For instance, Correa substituted for Santiago during the chapelmaster's prolix illness. While admitting that Correa was a magnificent musician, the chapter wished to stop his substitute conducting October 3, 1642, perhaps for fear that they would be committed to another Portuguese maestro de capilla after Santiago's imminently expected decease.[43] Although paralyzed, Santiago clung to life two more years. Meantime the Sevillian canons could not be deterred from finding his successor in the person of Luis Bernardo Jalón, whom they called from Toledo to become director of the Colegio de San Isidoro February 22, 1644,[44] after having made him acting chapelmaster with right of succession January 1.[45] Jalón, purely Spanish, was a canon at Burgos when Cuenca tried to call him as maestro de capilla

May 2, 1634 [46] (succeeding Vicente García).

During Santiago's term, the Seville Cathedral chief organists were Francisco Pérez (died December 23, 1640)—who obtained the media ración del órgano June 18, 1613, more as a reward for his faithful substituting during Francisco de Peraza's epoch (May 18, 1586–June 24, 1598) than for his unique personal gifts — and Andrés Martínez (appointed December 15, 1642; died October 13, 1652). [47] The organist of the nearby collegiate church of San Salvador was from September 1, 1599, to his departure for Jaén Cathedral March 31, 1636, the probably Portuguese Francisco Correa de Arauxo. Not only organ but shawms, sackbuts, cornetts, bassoons, and other instruments supported or alternated with voices in Seville Cathedral throughout Santiago's epoch. Bernardo Luis de Castro Palacios's Regimen, y Gouierno . . . de la Santa Metropolitana, y Patriarchal Iglesia de Seu[a], Tomo Primero (1672), the manuscript of which is in the Biblioteca Colombina at Seville, specifies the times when instrumentalists played in the highly instructive "Cap.[o] 22 de los Ministriles" (pp. 221-222). Among the leading ministriles mentioned in the Sevillian Cathedral capitular acts during Santiago's régime were: Francisco Cano de Albánchez (June 12, 1619); Alonso Ortega and his son Diego (sackbuts, April 2, 1620); Juan de Viedma (sackbut, April 9, 1620); Gerónimo de Quesada (April 5, 1625); Julián de Torres (cornett, March 12 and 21, 1626; August 31, 1635). On April 29, 1644, the chapter discussed the hiring of a harpist to play regularly in the coro.

During his heyday in Seville Cathedral, Santiago made a strange sight in humble friar's white habit conducting all these singers and instrumentalists — reports Castro Palacios. [48] Even stranger must have been the sight, because only he among friars was ever appointed maestro de capilla at either Toledo or Seville in the Renaissance or Baroque periods. But although his case was unique he did not allow subordinates to presume on his Carmelite humility. At the chapter meeting of March 9, 1619, he was empowered to fine any musician who failed to obey, even when the musician outranked him ecclesiastically. When on Saturday, March 7, 1626, the cornettist Julián de Torres challenged Santiago's authority at a function in San Andrés Church, the chapter responded by finding the contumacious ministril a month's pay. [49] On Sunday, January 8, 1640, the chapter dismissed the bass singer Juan Urbano, who had dared strike Santiago. The canons also fined Urbano 100 ducats and forbade his ever celebrating Mass again in any chapel of the cathedral. [50]

What were the libels being circulated by the bass singer that gave rise to their bitter encounter? Perhaps Urbano was calling Santiago a Portuguese spy and traitor. Santiago's three-year correspondence with the future John IV does still survive at the Ajuda Library (Lisbon) in 51-VIII-4 (Do Governo de Portugal, Tom. V. Da Ser. Caza de Bargáça, fols. 85-86 [February 16, 1636], 88 -89 [September 6, 1636], 90-91

[December 13/15, 1636], 96 [March 19, 1639]) to prove that Santiago was serving John well in those years as his "eyes on the Indies." The letters treat of such diverse matters as the amount of treasure being returned in galleons from the New World, [51] ways of communicating with John's unlucky brother Dom Duarte, [52] price returns at Lima, [53] proper courtesy titles for John's Spanish correspondents, [54] changing music tastes at Seville, [55] and musical gossip from the Madrid court. [56] Santiago also bought for John the most envied steed in Seville and purchased mirrors for the palace at Vila Viçosa. [57] When Sevillian busybodies doubted John's loyalty to the Spanish crown in 1639, Santiago stoutly defended his reputation. [58] The Ajuda correspondence also reports the beginnings of the paralysis (letter of December 15/15, 1636) that culminated eight years later in Santiago's death.

Ironically for Santiago's reputation, his works in the Seville Cathedral music archive catalogued by Rosa y López [59] in 1904 and by Anglés [60] in 1947 are Latin, [61] as are also the hymns (first and third a 5, second a 4) discovered by Stevenson in the luxurious Seville MS 115 [62]: Nil canitur suauius-Nec lingua valet dicere (In festo Sanctissimi Nominis Jesu [second and fourth strophes of Jesu dulcis memoria ascribed to Bernard of Clairvaux]), Virginis summę (In festo sancti Gabrielis Archangeli), Nos apunturis liberat (In festo Coronę). These hymns were moreover Santiago's first music to be recorded (Riverside Singers, New York City, September 12, 1966, for Sixth International Colloquium of Luso-Brazilian Studies). Yet it was precisely Santiago's motet a 9, Conceptio tua (first item in Rosa y López, second in Anglés), that aroused the ire of the critic of "modern music" quoted by João Álvares Frouvo in his Discvrsos sobre a perfeiçam do Diathesaron (Lisbon: Antonio Craesbeeck de Mello, 1662), page 86: "Este motete nem serve pera a Igreja, como se o dia, & a letra nam pedira aquelle festejo" ("This motet does not suit the church, nor the day, and the text does not call for that feast" [i.e., December 8]).

Santiago's Latin works listed in the Primeira Parte do Index da Livraria de Mvsica do mvyto alto, e poderoso Rey Dom Ioão o IV. (Lisbon: Paulo Craesbeek, 1649), pages 413-416, 432-435, 447 (recte 417-420, 436-439, 451) include everything credited by Rosa y López and Anglés to the present Seville Cathedral archive, the three hymns found there by Stevenson (pp. 414 = 418, 435 = 439), and in addition four Masses, two Magnificats, fourteen Psalms, seven Lady antiphons, two sequences (Dies Irae and Victimae paschali), and twenty works listed as motets (two of the hymns in MS 115 are here classed as motets).

Of the four Masses, the catalogue designates only one as a parody — Ego flos campi, a 8. Nicolas du Pont's motet (at p. 377 = 381) is named as Santiago's model. Diego Pontac studied with du Pont in Madrid (du Pont was Philippe Rogier's pupil). Possibly Santiago, like Pontac, took some lessons from du Pont. His three other Masses join Ego flos campi in calling for eight voices: Da Batalha (in common with Victoria's Pro victoria this was doubtless based on Janequin), Benedicam Dominus, and Do Setimo tom ("Tone VII").

Santiago's Magnificats belong to Tones II (a 8) and IV (a 9). Of his three Salves, one calls for 16 voices, another for 8. The third is polytextual. In this, the soprano soloist sings the Salve text, two opposing choruses reply with the Ave Regina coelorum. Throughout his Lamentations Santiago often inserts instrumentally accompanied solo verses, the soloist's part being then elaborately ornamented ("tiple grossado" or "hũa voz grossada").

Vocal solos, instrumentally accompanied, also turn up occasionally in his varied villancico repertory. The John IV catalogue classes his villancicos under such headings as negro, gallego, portugués, asturiano, sayagués, gitana, xácara, ensalada, campanas, cañas, máscara, and calenda—with Christmas villancicos vaunting the widest variety of types. How enchanting the Sevillian public found his polychoral Nativity villancicos can be easily proved from the cathedral capitular acts, which often mention special rewards. Typical of these prizes were the 30,000 maravedís voted him by the chapter January 11, 1627, "for excellent service this past Christmas season," [63] and again January 9, 1629. [64] So fanatical a local following did his villancicos attract that nine for Christmas and another nine for Epiphany ("de Reyes") became the rule during his term as maestro. [65]

For Corpus Christi he began in 1618 mounting playlets with choirboys playing principal roles. These coloquios, acted and sung by the seises, went into rehearsal three months before presentation. To obtain the best texts for Santiago's Corpus Christi and Christmas villancicos, the chapter habitually sponsored contests, the winner receiving a cash prize. [66]

The boarding and household care of the seises fell to the maestro de capilla only now and then in Sevillian cathedral history. [67] Santiago during two distinct epochs accepted the responsibility: from January 1, 1619, to January 1, 1623, and from February 9, 1628, to December 31, 1635. Each time he acquitted himself of the onerous duties with signal satisfaction to the chapter. [68]

Santiago flourished a generation too early for his vernacular works to be heavily represented in surviving New World archives. Nonetheless, Bogotá Cathedral archive yielded in 1966 his Christmas villancico a 4, Tirale, tirale flechas, and his Ascension villancico for two accompanied tiples, Que se ausenta y nos dexa. [69]

NOTES

1. Bibliotheca Lusitana, II (Lisbon: Ignácio Rodrigues, 1747), p. 275: "Foy hum dos mais celebres professores de Musica que florecerão na sua idade." Barbosa Machado does not say with whom he studied. The famous composers at Lisbon in his youth included Duarte Lobo ("mestre da Capella

da Sé de Lisboa" when in 1594 he signed the Parecer recommending Frei Estêvão's Liber Passionum [Lisbon: Simão López, 1595]), Manuel Cardoso (professed in the Lisbon Calced Carmelite monastery July 5, 1589), and Pedro Thalesio ("hum dos maiores talentos que avia neste Reino para ensinar" according to a contemporary report [Theophilo Braga, Historia da Universidade de Coimbra, II (Lisbon: Typographia da Academia Real das Sciencias, 1895), p. 828]).

2. Barbosa Machado called him "natural de Lisboa." For confirmation of this, see Simón de la Rosa y López, Los seises de la Catedral de Sevilla (Seville: Francisco de P. Díaz, 1904), p. 145: "Procedente del reino de Portugal, tuvo que legitimar su situación presentando un excelente informe de vida y costumbres instruido en Lisboa el 29 de Julio de 1624."

3. Diccionario biographico de musicos portuguezes (Lisbon: Mattos Moreira, 1900), II, 271. Primeira Parte do Index da Livraria de Mvsica do mvyto alto, e poderoso Rey Dom Ioão o IV. Nosso Senhor (Lisbon: Paulo Craesbeek, 1649), issued in facsimile by Academia Portuguesa da História (1967), opens with a Table of Contents.

4. Plasencia Cathedral, Actas Capitulares, XVI (1592-1598), February 16, 1596 [no folio numbers in this volume]: "Mandaron Votar qual de los dos opositores q̃ an venido a oponerse al magisto de capilla que esta Vaco en esta sancta yglesia se Proueerã que son El vno Medrano y El otro Vega Portugues. Y ordenaron que si saliere Receuido Vega sea con condicion que dentro de seis años se ordene de orden sacro y sino se ordenare se le an de dar menos Veinte mill mrs de salario q̃ se le señalare los quales se le an de quitar pasados los dhos seis años has que se ordene. E luego mandaron Votar qual de los dhos dos opositores se recibira por maestro de capilla con salario de duzientos ducados y tres caizes de trigo El -a- que se Recibe a Vega Portugues E la R que se reciba a medrano. E Votado y regulados los votos por El arno de plasa Presidente en presa de mi El secreto fueron todas aes y asi le Recibieron al dho Vega Portugues Por maestro de capilla en la forma susodha."

5. A.C., XVI, July 15, 1596: "Mandose si se boluera a Receuir a Vega maestro de capilla El a q̃ se Reciba la R que no. El Raciono botello dixo que propone que atento que El maestro de capilla a estado desconpuesto con El Doctor Busto Ro y es poco suficiente para maestro de capilla en vna Yglesia tan prinçipal como la de Plasencia y es muchacho y le tienen poco Respeto los cantores y suceden cassos cada dia con el y por otras cossas pide se vote Por aes y erres si se despidira o no El -a- q̃ se despida y la R que no." After he lost, they voted to give him "mas cient Reales Para que se Vaya a su trra."

6. A.C., XVI (sin foliar), July 19, 1596: "Mandose votar si se bolvera a recibir Vega por maestro de capilla el a que se reciba la r que se pongan edictos al magisterio. Fue Alvar Nuñez pertiguero a consultar los enfermos. dio fe quel chantre contradice volver a recibir al maestro de capilla. y en lo demas se remite al tesorero. El arcediano de Medellin se remite a Anto de Almaraz y Doctor Alonso Perez que se reciba a que no le den mas partido del que tenia Leon que se reciba con condicion que si fuere distraido la mayor parte le despida y el lo demas se remite al Dr Mateo de la Pila. Francisco de Tamayo se remite en todo al Ardno de Plasa. Pedro Lopez contradice el recibirle ni darle salario y lo demas se remite al tesorero. Votado y regulado los votos por el Ado de Plasa presidente en presencia de mi el secretario huvo mas rs [erres] y asi no le recibieron y cometieron al Ardo de Truxillo y al ardo de Bejar manden poner edictos."

7. Ibid., July 20, 1596: "Entro Francisco Garcia notario y les notifico un mandamiento del prouisor para que voluiesen a recibir al maestro de capilla. . . ."

8. A.C., XVII, fol. 344: "Mandaron consultar si se daran doçientas Rs en fca [fabrica] al padre Vega dela Orden del

Carmen Maestro de Capilla q̄ fue desta Sta Iglesia por lo q̄ en ella a hecho estos dias. "

9. Ibid.: "Mandaron dar çien R^s en f.^ca por los ocho libros pequeños y dos grandes de canto del maestro de capilla Victoria, y q̄ no se den mas. " On May 18 the chapter formally accepted the books (fol. 345).

10. A. C., XVIII (1606-1611), fol. 213^V (May 16, 1608): "Viosè vna carta de Thome de Victoria Cappellan dela emperatriz y maestro de capilla dela Capilla Real con vn libro q̄ embia de Vn off^o para diffunctos q̄ hizo en Canto de Organo para las honrras dela emperatriz y mandaron enquadernar el dicho libro y se trayga a Cab^o y se vea lo q̄ se le a de Responder, y dar por el dicho libro. "

11. Ibid., fol. 221^V.

12. Rosa y López, op. cit., p. 137.

13. Madrid, Archivo Histórico Nacional, Clero 7047 (Ynbentario delas cosas dela Sacristia. ē este monast.^o de N. S.^a del Carmen de Madrid. Año de M. D. lxxiij Años), fols. 52 and 63^V.

14. Ibid., fol. 70 (October 19, 1574).

15. Archivo Histórico Nacional, Clero 3803. This interest had cost María de Torres, the widow of Mancio Blanco, 4, 000 ducats. Their son, likewise named Mancio Blanco, had already joined the Madrid Calced Carmelites before May 29, 1607.

16. AHN, Clero 3796 (Becerro 6°. Memorias de Anibal Cambi. L. 23. N. 20), fol. 355.

17. Clero 3797 (L. 25. N. 37), fol. 1^V.

18. Seville Cathedral, A. C., 1612. 1613. 14. 15. 16., fol. 431^V (Friday, October 7, 1616): "este dia cometio el cau^o al p^e fr fr.^co de Santiago dela orden de nra s^a del carmen m^o de cap^a del convento de la dha orden de m^d [Madrid] que haga las chançonetas neces^as p^a las fiestas de la concep^on de nra s^a y pascua de nau^d deste año q̄ se an de cantar en esta s^ta Igl^ia y assi mismo le cometieron haga dilig.^a para traer a esta s^ta Igl^a muchachos q̄ siruan de seises. y vna boz de Tiple de que tiene notiçia. "

19. A. C., 1617. 1618. 19. 20. 21., fol. 2^V. Two days earlier (Monday, January 9, 1617), the chapter decided to vote on calling him and on the proper pay for his Christmas and Epiphany work ("el Trauajo q̄ a tenido en las fiestas de nau^d y reies y en hauer enseñado los seises").

20. Ibid., fol. 6^V.

21. Ibid., fol. 9 (January 30, 1617).

22. Ibid., fol. 24^V. Lobo died so poor that the chapter gave him a charity funeral ("y atento a la pobreza [fol. 26] con que el dho m^o louo murio que se haga su entierro por quenta del cau^o").

23. Seville Cathedral, Libro delas. Entradas. de Señores. Benefiçiados. En esta Sta iglesia El cual parece corrio en los años desde el de 1500 hasta el de 1700., fol. 74^V: "Subcedio en esta R^on [Ración N.º 20, Magister Puerorum] el m^o frai fran^co de S^tiago fraile Profeso de la orden de nra S^a del Carmen por ser eminentissimo en el arte y benemerito en moribus y bita gana dende el 5 de abrill de 1617 fallecio en 5 de Otu^e de 1644. "

24. Antonio Domínguez Ortiz, Orto y ocaso de Sevilla. Estudio sobre la Prosperidad y Decadencia de la Ciudad durante los Siglos XVI y XVII (Seville: Imprenta de la Diputación Provincial, 1946), p. 47. In 1500 Seville boasted 70, 000 inhabitants (p. 41), in 1565 100, 000 (p. 42), in 1588 150, 000.

25. He thus signs himself in the printed leaflet inserted at fol. 55 in the manuscript miscellany at Lisbon National Library, F. G. 2266 (olim H-5-11).

26. Seville Cathedral, Libro delas. Entradas, fol. 82^V.

27. A. C., 1643-1644. 1645-1646., fol. 1 of second foliation (January 6, 1645): "Este dho dia, acauado la missa mando llamar a cau^o el Sor Dean para tratar del entierro del Rac^o Manuel Correa difunto cantor contralto que fue desta Sta igla. " They decided to bury him in the cathedral near the organ ("sepultura en la nave dela cap^a nra s^ra dela estrella").

He died intestate, and "poor" (on December 9, 1644 [ibid., fol. 47^V] the chapter loaned him 100 ducats)— despite an income from his ración superior to what chapelmasters earned in most cathedrals. An outstanding composer, he preferred to write not vernacular but Latin works some of which still survive in the Seville Cathedral archive. See Anuario Musical, II (1947), 33-34.

28. He began singing before being formally appointed racionero. According to the Seville A. C., 1617. 1618. 19. 20. 21., fol. 54^V, on June 28, 1617, he was granted a 15-day licence to absent himself from the choir ("Manuel Correa musico contralto que por 15 dias pueda salir de casa sin oblig^on de acudir al coro para aiuda a q̄ combalezca de la graue enferm^d que a tenido").

29. Ibid., fol. 56: "q̄ a ido a buscar vozes. "

30. Ibid., fol. 69^V: "niños para seises y cantores para el seru^o desta Sta Igl^a. "

31. A. C., 1626 1627 1628 1629 1630, fol. 192 (August 28, 1627): "Este dia entraron cinco muchachos q̄ el m^o de cap^a a embiado para seises desta s^ta Igl^a buscados en diferentes partes y hauiendoles el Cau^o oido Cantar a todos m^do q̄ se reçiban para seises y se les de todo lo neçes^o. "

32. Ibid., fol. 193. The act of Monday, September 6, 1627, reads: "Este dia hauiendo visto vna carta del M^o de Capilla Fr. Fran.^co de S. Tiago se cometio a la Cont.^a se le escriua q̄. enquanto a los dos Tenores de Ciu^d Rodrigo haga lo que se le tiene ordenado y a tratado con ellos y Enq.^to al Contrabajo de Logroño le ofrezca 10500 Rs para su biaje y ver si contenta y al capon tiple Frayle agustino procure q̄. venga como auisa. "

33. Rosa y López, op. cit., p. 137, gives their names, birthplaces, and dates of entry.

34. A. C., 1624-1625, fol. 112 (October 31, 1625): "Este dia dieron otros v^te dias de licencia al M.^o de Cap.^a para estar ausente atento a q̄ en el tiempo q̄ llevo no a podido acabar en Lisboa el neg^o a que fue. "

35. A. C., 1626 1627 1628 1629 1630, fol. 398; A. C., 1635-1640, fol. 31^V.

36. Ibid., fol. 258^V: "Este dia dio el cau.^o licencia a el Padre maestro de capilla vsando de la licencia que tiene P.^a que haga ausencia de Seu.^a Por dos meses. "

37. Biblioteca da Ajuda (Lisbon), MS 51-VIII-5 (Caderno de despezas Particulares do Seruisço do Duque nosso Senhor que comesou ao pr.^o de Junho de 637. em diante), fol. 17^V: "A^o p^e fr. fran^co de Santiago des mil reis de quarenta de q̄ S. Ex.ª lhe fes m.^e neste mes [July 1640] p^a ajuda dos gastos das Caldas. "

38. A. C., 1617. 1618. 19. 20. 21., fol. 228.

39. Ibid., fol. 232^V (July 18, 1619). He had to be back in Seville before August 15.

40. Ibid., fol. 267^V; A. C. 1625. 1626. 1627., fol. 2; A. C., 1626 1627 1628 1629 1630, fol. 352: "Que se auise

al P^e M^ro que se concierte con el contralto de Zamora que venga a Seuilla p^a oirle. . . . "

41. Rosa y López, op. cit., p. 145.

42. In the Discvrso mentioned above in note 25, Correa calls the singers in Lisbon the best in the entire Peninsula. They are "los mejores cantores de España (que bastara dezir de Portugal)." So eminent a Spanish writer as Hierónimo Román entertained the same high opinion of Portuguese musical prowess in this period. See his, Repvblicas del mvndo (Salamanca: Juan Fernández, 1595, fol. 252 [bk. 4, ch. 18, "Del vso y antiguedad del canto y musica en la yglesia para solemnidad y de los organos y otros instrumentos"]).

43. A.C., 1641 y 1642, p. [sic] 455: "Este dia el don Ger^mo Çapatta Ars^no de Reino y Can^o dixo que por quanto El M^o de capilla esta ynposibilitado de seruir esta yglesia y la capilla esta de la forma que El Cau^o conose y El Ministerio del R^o Manuel Correa no es de Maestro sino de gran musico como lo es. y la asistencia que El Cau^o le dio de M^o es por ausencias Temporales del M^o de Capilla y la que tiene el M^o oy por su enferm^d yncurable es perpetua Requerio a El Cau^o se sirua de Mandarse llamar para ber que forma abra para Gouernar esta Capilla Mientras El p^e M^o uiue Con su enfermedad." Later that month (October 31, 1642 [fol. 479]), the chapter decided to let matters ride until the end of the year.

44. Rosa y López, op. cit., p. 152.

45. Libro delas. Entradas, fol. 74^V. Jalón died at Seville Palm Sunday, April 6, 1659.

46. Cuenca Cathedral, A.C., 1631-1638, fol. 90. Previously he had directed the music at the Real Convento de la Encarnación (Madrid).

47. Libro delas. Entradas, fol. 87^V.

48. Rosa y López, op. cit., p. 145, quoting from an unspecified manuscript treatise by Castro Palacios (fl. 1672-1717) in the Biblioteca Colombina. Castro Palacios served as longtime maestro de ceremonias.

49. A.C., 1625. 1626. 1627., fol. 23^V (Saturday, March 21, 1626): "Este dia auiendo platicado muy a la larga sobre el llamamiento hecho en razon de la determinacion que se haria con Julian de Torres por razon de la descompositura que tuvo en la Yglesia de Sr S. Andres con el Maestro de Capilla se voto por avas . . . y verbalm^te votado le condenaron en 30 d^s para la fabrica. . . . "

50. A.C., 1635 hasta 1640, fol. 216^V: "auiendole el dho maestro [Santiago] reprehendido de algunas Palabras que en desonor suyo auia hablado con demasiado desacato tuuo atreuimiento a Poner las manos, de lo qual informado el Sr. Dean dio quenta a el cau^o de ello y el cau^o mando que quede despidido. . . . "

51. Biblioteca da Ajuda, MS 51-VIII-4, fol. 88^V: "Las flotas de nueua españa vinieron y traen mas de 16 millones de dineros y haçienda sin lo q̄ se a escondido, la otra flota vendra con los galeones (donde tenemos nro Caudal) con el fauor de dios p^a nobiembre."
In his letter of December 13/15, 1636, Santiago adds a postscript (fol. 91) beginning thus: "Oluidoseme de dar quenta a v ex^a de nra encomienda, quanto los galeones lleuaron y las flotas. . . . "

52. Ibid., fol. 86: "Ya se partieron las naues Inglesas p^a Venecia y en vna dellas fue la encomienda p^a su ex^a el s^r don duarte. . . . " Later in his letter of February 16, 1636, he says that the captain of the vessel returned the letters that John wished to send Dom Duarte, whereupon a consul traveling aboard the ship (Camillo Poletti) agreed to take them. In his letter of September 16, 1636, Santiago writes (fol. 89): "por via de Inglaterra puede v ex^a escriuir a su ex^a el s^r don d^te

escriua y todos los meses poco mas tendra v ex^a nueuas suyas en esta ciudad, pues las q̄ tiene el Rey vienen por este Camino."

53. Ibid., fol. 91: "Y asi el q̄ lo lleuo paso con ello a lima donde tendra su preçio y todo lo q̄ se detiene es mejorarlo con el fauor de dios."

54. Ibid., fol. 88: "el Cap^an Alonso de Heredia es Capitan como Obispo de anillo, el s^r duquede Medina se llamaua siempre Capitan y q^do le escriuia tan bien selo llama en el sobre escrito no por q̄ el lo fuese de leua alguno sino q̄ como su ex^a era Cap^an g^al daua estos titulos honrrosos a quien lo merecia, ya si mesmo el patriarcha q^do le escriue y el duque de bejar es de la misma suerte. Agora v ex^a hara lo q̄ mas conuenga, si bien [q̄ marked out] esto es honrrarle."

55. In promising to send on copies of all his most recent villancicos in his letter of December 13/15, 1636, Santiago warned John: "primero q̄ pues esta el gusto de todo el m^do tal q̄ sino son tramoyas no gustan de vill^os." Santiago's business was to keep abreast of the changing tastes. His December 8 villancicos had pleased the public, but he could not yet guarantee the success of his December 25 villancicos because "no los he prouado y me faltan oy tres por haçer. pero la disposicion ya esta en Casa." Evidently he wished always to try out his villancicos in advance with the performers, before forecasting triumph.

56. In his letter of March 19, 1639, he confesses that Maestro Capitán (Mateo Romero) caused him no surprise when he began intrigues against his successor, Carlos Patiño. Although officially retired from directing the capilla flamenca on February 22, 1634, Capitán five years later still sought to conduct at least the chamber musicians "q̄ es delo que el Rey mas gusta. Capitan no puede dejar su condiçion sino con su vida bien lo a experimentado ver q̄ a sido el dauid deste gigante, y quien mas le supo Rendir en el m^do." Antonio de Mendoza, urged on by Capitán, had found an opportunity to speak with the king "acerca del poco donaire de Carlos [Patiño]" (fol. 96^V). For a summary of Capitán's life, including his relations with John IV, see R. Stevenson, Spanish Cathedral Music in the Golden Age (Berkeley and Los Angeles: University of California Press, 1961), pp. 476-478.

57. Ajuda, fol. 85 (February 16, 1636): "Agora entro yo y digo q̄ q^do su carta de v ex^a llego ya tenia echo compra de una haca. sino de g^de Clin excelente en todo . . . de la mas bella Cosa q̄ se a visto muchos dias ha. . . . " He had managed to get the horse for 2,500 reales, though 4,000 had been offered by responsible buyers, and felt extremely proud of his astuteness because "crea q̄ tan lindo animal no a entrado en este lugar, ni q̄ tanto se aya lleuado los ojos de todos." The two mirrors, one for la casa de la sofa at Vila Viçosa, had cost 2,000 silver reales, but were worth at least 3,000 apiece, Santiago assured the Duke. John had given him discretionary authority to buy anything that he thought suitable, costing up to 1,500, but Santiago felt so sure of the great bargain that he risked the 500 extra for the pair of mirrors.

58. Ibid., fol. 96 (March 19, 1639): "Mucho se a dicho en esta ciudad de q̄ v ex^a era general delas Armas de ese Reyno, q̄ todos aplaudieron pequeños y grandes diziendo q̄ donde v ex^a estaua, estaria con seguridad ese Reyno [fol. 96^V] Y que solo su grandeza de v ex^a y de su cuydado se podia fiar este que tanto nos da el enemigo, yo les desengañe a algunos Caualleros diziendo v ex^a no abia açetado esto porque venia con subordinacion a la duqueza de Mantua, y que abia replicado por dos veçes, y q̄ sabia q̄ abiendo ocasion el primero q̄ acudiria a la neçesidad seria v ex^a con todos sus criados y vasallos como soldado, fue bien pareçido a todos y de todos celebrado y dijo vno destos caualleros es mucha cosa vn duque de Bargança p^a yr subordinado."

59. Los seises, p. 145. First and third items correspond with Anglés's second and first entries.

60. <u>Anuario Musical</u>, II (1947), 37, nos. 10 and 11. Anglés did not see the <u>Regina coeli letare a 8</u> (Tone VI) listed by Rosa y López.

61. According to Anglés (<u>op. cit.</u>, p. 37), Santiago's Latin <u>Responsoria tenebrarum a 8</u> (parts for two oboes occupied the ninth and tenth partbooks inventoried by Rosa y López) were freshly copied by Juan Osorio, a Sevillian priestly choir-singer, as late as 1772 — 128 years after Santiago's death.

62. <u>Portugal and Brazil in Transition</u>, ed. Raymond S. Sayers (Minneapolis: University of Minnesota Press, 1968), p. 314.

63. <u>A.C.</u>, 1625 1626 1627, fol. 100^V: "Este dia mandaron dar 30U mrs de ayuda de costa por vna vez en aguinaldo al m^o de Capilla por lo bien que a seruido en ella."

64. <u>A.C.</u>, 1626 1627 1628 1629 1630, fol. 373^V.

65. Bernardo Luis de Castro Palacios, <u>Tratado de algunas Ceremonias</u> (Biblioteca Colombina MS dated 1712), pp. 47-48.

66. <u>A.C.</u>, 1617. 1618. 19. 20. 21., fol. 120 (March 15, 1618): "Este dia se cometio a los ss^{res} d. felix de g^m y d. baltasar de Salablanca vean vn coloquio quel m^o de cap^a dize q' tiene para q' en la fiesta del s^{mo} sacram^{to} los muchachos seises le representen y Canten y si les pareçiere apposito q' lo hagan. determinen lo q' combenga y los mesmos ss^{res} determinen si les pareçiere q' se pongan edictos por q^{ta} de la f^{ca} para el q' mejor villancico hiçiere del sacram^{to} y del nacim^{to} por q' assi habra letras apposito de q' elejir q' se canten."

67. Rosa y López, <u>op. cit.</u>, p. 131: "Como ya hemos tenido ocasión de observar, los cargos de maestro de seises y de capilla unas veces se desempeñaban por la misma persona y otras veces no." Santiago's dates as maestro de seises come in the same footnote, p. 131.

68. Sample year-end clothing and equipment distributions to seises (December 31, 1628) are quoted in Rosa y López's long footnote, p. 130.

69. Stevenson, <u>Renaissance and Baroque Musical Sources in the Americas</u> (Washington: General Secretariat, Organization of American States, 1970), p. 25.

JUAN de VAEZA SAAVEDRA
(Flourished at Puebla, 1662-1671)

Of all the Puebla composers in the Sánchez Garza collection, Vaeza is the one who most openly discloses himself in the annotations scribbled on the covers. All five pieces preserved entire bear exact first performance datés on the covers. These dates range from 1662 (<u>En aquel pesebre</u>) to 1671 (<u>A del coro celeste</u>). Only he among the local composers antedating 1700 in the collection enjoyed the rank of "don." Since not even the seventeenth-century Puebla Cathedral maestros de capilla in the Sánchez Garza collection were "dons," Vaeza has to have been a gentleman of quality.

His name has not turned up in Puebla Cathedral acts. But he obviously resided there, as is revealed by such notes as this on the cover of the romance <u>Pastores velen se abraça</u>: "For Mother Catherine of St. Margaret, chapelmistress of Holy Trinity Convent, composed by Vaeza in 1667"; [1] or this on the

chanzoneta <u>Con suavidad de boses</u>: "Composed in 1667 for the profession of dear little Theresa." [2] The original text of the chanzoneta specifically alludes to Theresa's taking the veil that year in Holy Trinity at the tender age of fifteen. "Marequita la baesa" played the "biolon" part in Vaeza's 1671 calendrical villancico, <u>A del coro celeste</u>. Since the other performers whose names are written on their parts were convent singers, the bass viol player on this occasion may have been the composer's daughter.

Of the four Vaeza items labeled romances, all but the 1662 <u>En aquel pesebre</u> begin with six or seven strophes followed by estribillo. [3] The 1662 lacks an estribillo. His 1671 calendrical villancico ("Billansico de Calenda") has nothing to do with the hot, tropical Negro dance called the calenda, but instead is intended for Christmas Eve at the traditional reading of Christ's genealogy. Every preserved Vaeza piece except Theresa's profession chanzoneta was composed as special Christmas music for Holy Trinity convent use.

NOTES

1. Para la Me Cattalina de S.^{a} Margarita maestra de capi^a del Convento de la SSm^a trinidad año de 1667 — fecit Vaeza.

2. A la profesion de Theresica la chiquita. fecit Vaeza Año de 1667.

3. See Miguel Querol Gavaldá, "El romance polifónico en el siglo XVII," <u>Anuario Musical</u>, X (1955), 111-120, for a fundamental study of the repertory and formal structures of the seventeenth-century romance.

FRANCISCO de VIDALES
(Born [presumably at Mexico City] c. 1630; died at Puebla, June 2, 1702)

According to the Mexico City Cathedral <u>Actas Capitulares</u>, XII (1652-1655), folios 183^V-184 (act of April 6, 1655), Francisco [de] Vidales was the nephew of Fabián Ximeno, Mexico City organist-choirmaster who died shortly before April 17, 1654. How highly the Mexico City chapter esteemed the nephew (who was already a <u>licenciado</u>) can be surmised from the canons' decision April 6, 1655, that Ximeno's successor, Francisco López Capillas, should alternate with Vidales on the organ bench every other week. [1] Only at double feasts did the chapter require that both be present. López Capillas, who had served Puebla Cathedral as organist from December 17, 1641, [2] to July 29, 1648, [3] already rated as one of the great colonial lights. To be placed on anything like a par with him means that Vidales was that early considered a consummate artist.

One year later Puebla Cathedral hired Vidales as principal organist, a post that he retained until death 46 years later [4] (Juan Gutiérrez de Padilla was Puebla chapelmaster when Vidales was engaged). In 1660 the chapter reprimanded Vidales for allowing a small portable organ to go out on loan. [5]

In 1676 he gave the cathedral eight bound music books, presumably of his own compositions, and for these was duly thanked April 17 by the chapter, which voted that they should henceforth be carefully preserved in the cathedral archive.[6] On June 30, 1679, he was appointed one of six judges to decide which contender was best qualified for the vacant Puebla Cathedral chapelmastership.[7] Antonio de Salazar emerged victor July 11, 1679.[8]

Luis de Bomborón, the gachupín who succeeded Vidales in 1703, proved much less tractable — in 1710 raising a row because the cathedral harpist Diego Florentín was both dark complected and a poor performer, in 1712 demanding an inordinate pay raise, and in 1715 departing for Mexico City to write an opera.[9] After Bomborón, whose death is announced in the Actas Capitulares, XXIII (1719-1723), fol. 130 (June 18, 1720), came the B[r] D[n] Miguel Thadeo de Ochoa, whom the Puebla Cathedral chapter appointed Organista Mayor July 29, 1722 (ibid., fol. 390[V]).

NOTES

1. Robert Stevenson, "Mexico City Cathedral Music: 1600-1750," The Americas, A Quarterly Review of Inter-American Cultural History, XXI/2 (October, 1964), 121-122. The Mexico City Cathedral chapter received April 6, 1655 (Actas Capitulares, XII [1652-1655], fol. 183[V]) "las peticiones de Francisco Lopez Capillas Maestro de Capilla desta sancta Yglessia, y organista en ella, y la de Fran[co] Vidal assimesmo ayudante de organista." After discussion, the canons decided that "Francisco Lopez Capillas queda señalado por primer /fol. 184[V]/ Maestro de organo y el Licenciado Francisco Vidal por segundo Maestro de organo." In a later addition to this long act, stretching from fols. 183[V] to 184[V], Vidal's name is expanded to Vidales at the crucial passage on 184[r] establishing López Capillas's yearly salary "por M[o] de Capilla y organista" at 250 pesos, and Francisco Vidales's at 195 for being organist.

2. Puebla Cathedral, Actas Capitulares, XI (1640-1647), fol. 118[V]: "Que se reçiue al B[r] fran[co] lopes por organista y que este a la voluntad del maestro de capilla con cargo que a de tocar bajon con salario de quatro çientos pessos."

3. A.C., XII (1648-1652), fol. 49[V]: "Que se Reçiua por Organista desta Yglessia en lug[r] del Liz[do] Fran[co] Lopez que lo hera a quien se despido al B[r] Ygnacio Ximeno con quatrocientos p[o]s de Salario. . . ." Lopez quit May 15.

4. A.C., XX (1696-1702), fol. 277[V] (June 2, 1702). The act announcing his death refers to him as "Fran[co] Vidales Presbytero organista."

5. A.C., XIV (1657-1662), fol. 277 (May 21, 1660): "Que se notifique al organista desta S[ta] Yglessia que el organo chico se buelua a ella y no lo saque sino fuere para las Yglessias donde este cauildo asistiere como esta mandado."

6. A.C., XVII (1676-1680), fol. 17.

7. Ibid., fol. 245[V].

8. Ibid., fol. 248.

9. Data kindly supplied by Dr. Efraín Castro Morales, 11 Sur 306, Puebla.

FABIÁN [PÉREZ] XIMENO
(Born c. 1595; died c. April 17, 1654, at Mexico City)

According to a table of Mexico City musicians dated December 1, 1623, Juan Ximénez was then first cathedral organist and Fabián Ximeno second.[1] But out of respect for his unique gifts, Ximeno was already in 1623 as second organist being paid more than twice the first's salary. He also added to his income by inspecting organs in other cathedrals. According to the Puebla Cathedral Actas Capitulares, X (1634-1639), folio 47, Fabián Ximeno presbítero received 200 pesos on January 30, 1635, for the trip from Mexico City to look at a new large organ then under construction. When its twin was finished, he received on May 2, 1648, another 200 pesos for services at its dedication (Actas Capitulares, XII [1648-1652], fol. 29).

Although he did not immediately succeed Ximénez, Ximeno is listed as Mexico City cathedral first organist November 28, 1642. On that date he induced the Mexico City chapter to hire as tuner and repairman Joseph Vidal[es].[2] The treasurey was just then so depleted that the following December 23 the chapter met secretly to vote on reducing all musicians' pay. The axe fell publicly March 3, 1643, when the cathedral chapter ordered everyone reduced by ten percent and no new musicians (with the possible exception of an eminent sopranist) engaged until further notice.[3] Because he knew that he was indispensable Fabián Peres [or Pérez] Ximeno — as his full name reads in various acts[4] — contested June 26, 1643, this blanket cut and obtained that same day the promise that the 100 pesos deducted from his own annual salary would be restored.

The previous April 24 the chapter had accepted funds endowing two chaplaincies. This money was bequeathed by the deceased Mexico City cathedral chapelmaster, Antonio Rodríguez Mata (present in the cathedral since September 23, 1614[5]). Rodríguez Mata's successor was Luis Coronado, a mere músico in 1623, but from 1632 chief Mexico City cathedral organist.[6] Coronado lived to enjoy the chapelmaster title only a little longer than five years.

At the chapter meeting of March 31, 1648,[7] the canons learned of Licenciado Luis Coronado's death, whereupon they named Fabián Ximeno to be the new maestro de capilla and Juan Coronado to be his assistant. The promotion to maestro entitled Ximeno to special seating in the choir enclosure and a 50-peso annual salary boost commencing November 26, 1649.[8] Even so, he claimed to be "poor" and because of his long cathedral service deserving of more money, which on May 2, 1651, the chapter refused him.[9] At the same chapter meeting "was read another petition of the said maestro, in which he asks dissolution of certain choirs, and in particular of one

choir led by a Negro, because of the indecency of their singing,
the nonsense which they utter when assisting at Masses and at
other paid church functions. "[10]

Ximeno next complained that the payments to unauthorized
choirs took bread out of the mouths of the duly appointed
cathedral singers, whose right it was to officiate instead. In
reply, the canons reminded Ximeno that certain poor clergy in
these "nonunion" choirs would be left penniless, were the
cathedral singers to monopolize every paid engagement, and
ended by naming the cathedral provisor, Doctor Pedro de
Barrientos, "well experienced in these wrangles between
choirs, " to resolve their differences with his usual prudence.
In their discussion it is quite evident that the music of the
capilla del negro pleased certain members of the chapter so
well that they were ready to protect the Negro, even at the
risk of offending their most veteran musical staff.

Sensing the need to brighten the sound of his own rather elderly choir, Ximeno next proposed the importation of some
new instrumentalists from nearby Puebla. At their meeting
of May 26, 1651, the Mexico City chapter argued "whether or
not to receive the instrumentalists who have arrived from
Puebla. "[11] The next February 9 (1652) one such player who
had left Mexico City Cathedral a decade earlier was rehired at
an annual 100 pesos — Nicolás Grinón, harpist. [12] This same
harpist, first hired at Puebla Cathedral August 14, 1643, con
cargo de tocar harpa y violon, [13] had been earning 200 pesos
annually at Puebla in 1651. But a general salary reduction
ordered there on August 18, 1651, plus some other problems,
had dissuaded him from continuing. [14] He liked Mexico City
no better this time, quitting the capital after only seven
months. [15]

During Ximeno's last two years, his trying to act as both
chapelmaster and first organist proved too much for him.
Meantime the discipline of his musicians deteriorated. To
steady them in their proper course the chapter was forced to
resort to so time-honored system as fines, refusing to abate
the fines a jot when June 28, 1652, the musicians sent in a
petition. [16] Because certain senior musicians summoned before the chapter acted presumptuous, the canons on October 14,
1653, reminded them to observe due respect. [17] Shortly before
the following April 17, 1654, Ximeno died. [18] Only four days
later the bachiller Francisco López Capillas presbítero was
picked to succeed him both as maestro de capilla and as organist. [19] Any such speedy appointment argues López Capillas's
presence in Mexico City during the previous weeks while
Ximeno's death was being expected.

At the same April 24, 1654, meeting, the chapter agreed to
pay 100 pesos to Juan Coronado, the bachiller who on March
31, 1648, had been named Ximeno's assistant, and another 100
pesos to Ximeno's nephew, Francisco Vidales. Like Luis
Coronado who trained Juan, so also it would appear that Ximeno had prepared his own young nephew.

In the act of April 6, the chapter appointed Francisco Vidales "sobrino del mº fabian Ximeno, " not only to be the new
chapelmaster's "ayudante de organista" but also decreed that
the two should alternate from week to week, except at double
feasts when the attendance of both would be henceforth required. [20] The next year Vidales transferred to Puebla Cathedral, which today still conserves not only Vidales's music but
also his uncle's Missa Quarti toni a 11, Missa de la Batalla
a 8 (Sexti toni), and other works.

NOTES

1. Guatemala City Cathedral, Libro de el 111ᵉ Cabildo de
Sanctiago de Guatemala delos aquerdos . . . que se acen
desde el Año de 1599: en adelante [this is Book II of the Actas
Capitulares and runs to 1650], fol. 149. The Guatemala
Cathedral authorities had solicited a complete list of Mexico
City cathedral musicians (with their salaries) in order to have
a model for a similar musical establishment. Ximeno's sal-
ary of 700 pesos annually struck them as unduly high.

2. Mexico City Cathedral, Actas Capitulares, X (1640-
1650), fol. 199ᵛ. Vidal was to receive the same salary as his
predecessor "por afinador y Maestro de haçer organos. "

3. Ibid., fol. 228ᵛ.

4. Ibid., fol. 248ᵛ (June 26, 1643); Actas Capitulares,
XXXVI (1741-1744), fol. 35ᵛ (January 30, 1742).

5. Actas Capitulares, V (1606-1616), fol. 366ᵛ. On this
date he submitted a royal cedula naming him to a media ración
(half prebend) and to be maestro de capilla. Juan Hernández
successfully protested the chapelmaster title, but from 1618
onward Rodríguez [de] Mata composed the villancicos and
chanzonetas (A. C., VI, 1617-1620, fol. 85 [February 1, 1619],
90ᵛ [February 20, 1619]; A. C., VII, 1620-1625, fol. 48
[May 29, 1620] and from no later than 1632 bore the title of
maestro de capilla (A. C., VIII, 1626-1632, fol. 374ᵛ [May 14,
1632]; A. C., IX, 1633-1639, fol. 159ᵛ [June 3, 1636]).

6. A. C., VIII, fol. 374ᵛ [May 14, 1632].

7. A. C., X, fol. 637ᵛ.

8. Ibid., fol. 749ᵛ.

9. A. C., XI (1650-1653), fol. 33ᵛ.

10. Ibid.: "Leyosse otra pettᵒⁿ del dicho Mº enq̄ pide se
quitten las capillas de musicos, Y en particular, Vna de un
negro, por la indecenssia, conque cantan, y disparates que
diçen enel officiar las missas, Y en otros actos tocantes al
ministerio / fol. 34 / de Iglesia, fuera de que se minoran las
obensiones, dela Capilla dela Cathedral, donde es interessada
la fabrica."

11. A. C., XI, fol. 43:"Mando despachar Cedula para si se
han de recibir o no Los musicos menestriles que vinieron de
la Puebla."

12. Before taking his parents to Puebla in 1642, Nicolás
Grinón had served as Mexico City Cathedral harpist. See
Mexico City Cathedral, A. C. X, fol. 176 (July 8, 1642).
Once there, Grinón was induced to stay (ibid., fol. 198
[November 21, 1642]).

13. Puebla Cathedral, Actas Capitulares, XI (1640-1647),
fol. 193.

14. Puebla Cathedral, A. C., XII (1648-1652), fol. 354
("reuaxa de salarios"). He was also miffed at Juan Gutiérrez

de Padilla, Puebla maestro de capilla, for failing to equalize
"las Obenciones de todos los musicos" (he lodged this complaint with the Puebla chapter March 8, 1650).

15. Mexico City, A.C., XI, fol. 199[V] (September 3, 1652):
"Admitesse el despidimiento de Grinon el musico y Arpista de
la Capilla."

16. Ibid., fol. 172[V].

17. Ibid., fol. 319.

18. A.C., XII (1652-1655), fol. 39[V]:"Mandosse despachar
çedula de ante diem para Nombrar M[o] de Capilla y organista
desta Sancta Iglessia por hauer vacado estas dos plaças con
la muerte del M[o] fauian Perez Ximeno."

19. Ibid., fol. 40[V] [April 21, 1654]:" Nombrasse al B[r]
Francisco Lopez Capillas presbitero por Maestro de la
Capilla de Muzica desta Sta Yglessia, y por organista de ella,
atento a su mucha suficiencia y hauilidad, para dhos minis-
terios, y se señalaron de salario quinientos pessos. . . ."

20. Ibid., fol. 183[V]. In this act Ximeno's nephew is first
called Francisco Vidal, but at fol. 184 Francisco Vidales.

ALONSO XUARES [= JUÁREZ]
(Died at Cuenca, Spain, June 26, 1696)

Although Seville boasted next to the highest income of any
Spanish seventeenth-century cathedral, both Xuares and his
predecessor Miguel Tello (March 28, 1673-October 1, 1674)
quit Seville to return to the cathedrals whence they had come —
Tello to Murcia,[1] and Xuares to Cuenca.[2] But the circumstances of their quitting differed notably, Tello marching off
without any advance warning. After this insult, the Sevillian
cabildo directed Juan de Loaysa (February 27, 1633-May 9,
1709), who was both chapter secretary and Colombina librarian, to offer Xuares the post of maestro de capilla solely on
the basis of his reputation, without the customary competition.

During their correspondence and personal interviews,
Loaysa not only found his professional qualifications fully equal
to report, but also came to admire his vast store of knowledge,
memory, and especially his command of Scripture. The nine
years during which Xuares governed Sevillian cathedral music
(April 29, 1675-May 1, 1684)[3] gave Loaysa daily reason to
applaud Xuares's Latinity, over and above his musical skill
evidenced in motets for every Sunday in Advent and Lent, his
O vos omnes for Friday of the Seven Dolors, Lauda Sion
sequence for Corpus Christi, his Masses, Vespers for first-
class feasts, motets for burial services, and his Misericordias Domini composed for St. Dionysius's day, 1681.[4] So
satisfied were the Sevillian canons with Xuares that Loaysa
dared call him "the one and only best maestro in Spain."[5]

However, Xuares fought continuously with a kidney complaint
while in Seville and went back to Cuenca on medical advice.
His mother, Ana de la Fuente, who kept house for him in
Seville, returned with him, but died soon thereafter — as did
also a sister who was a nun in Guadalajara, Mother Agueda de
San Ildefonso. The bishop of Cuenca from February 18, 1682,

to Xuares's death was Alonso Antonio de San Martín, a natural
son of Philip IV. An enthusiastic devotee of music, he in-
stalled at his own expense a new grand organ in Cuenca Cathedral,[6] and generously rewarded Xuares with a half prebend,
a benefice, direction of the boychoir school, and other com-
modities. Twelve days before his death, Xuares began running a fever, but its seriousness went unrecognized until four
days before decease.

Until the last Monday of his life, every mail to Seville carried his letters to Loaysa. However, his fast admirers there
were not limited to the Colombina librarian. Canons Alonso
del Corro, Ibarburu, Matías de los Reyes, Manuel González,
Ambrosio de la Cuesta, and even a canon absent in Rome,
Luis Federigui,[7] delighted in his ability as a raconteur, his
knowing appraisal of the passing scene, and his successful
prognostication of future events. Even the distance between
Cuenca and Seville did not prevent the master of ceremonies
from seeking his advice on hard problems, as did also two
other Seville cathedral functionaries.

Xuares's generosity became proverbial. He assisted
Sebastián Durón[8] at every stage, not only bringing him to
Seville, but helping him find better posts at Burgo de Osma
and Palencia. He placed his pupil Juan Martínez Díaz in the
chapelmastership of the collegiate church at Jérez de la
Frontera, and later arranged to have Martínez Díaz succeed
him at Cuenca. He also helped nuns needing dowries and
many others in financial straits, so much so that he himself
died penniless. Loaysa therefore paid for his tomb in Cuenca
Cathedral, where he was buried near his mother's grave (before San Antonio altar). The cost of the stone, the inscription,
and the installation ran to 330 reales.

Hilarión Eslava, maestro de capilla at Seville Cathedral
1832-1847, was the first to publish any of Xuares's motets.
Lira sacro-hispana, siglo XVII, I, i, contains his Vulnerasti
cor meum a 8 and Dum sacrum pignus a 9. In 1860 Muñoz y
Soliva recalled Xuares as one of the prime glories of Cuenca
music, mentioning that the same motets lauded by Loaysa
were recopied as late as 1778[9] and in 1860 were still being
sung at Cuenca. In 1947 Higinio Anglés reported that Seville
Cathedral still owned not only the exact same Advent and Lent
motets (9 partbooks, one of them for the accompaniment) but
also Xuares's parody a 7 based on the motet a 7 by his predecessor at Seville Miguel Tello, Missa Sobre Sancte Ferdinandae Rex (13 partbooks).[10]

Thanks to the persuasiveness of Charles II and Queen Mother
Mariana, Pope Clement X on February 14, 1675, declared val-
id San Fernando's canonization processes of 1630 and 1668.
The culminating ceremonies in Seville Cathedral began at 11
in the morning of May 21, 1677, and on this day, when the
royal bones of the "Santo Rey Don Fernando" were accorded a
new place of honor in the cathedral, Xuares's Missa Sobre
Sancte Ferdinandae Rex had its premiere.[11] Probably this

was the same Mass again heard November 10, 1683, when
news reached Seville that the Turks had raised their siege of
Vienna.[12]

At Cuenca, Restituto Navarro Gonzalo's Catálogo Musical
del Archivo de la Santa Iglesia Catedral Basílica (Cuenca:
Instituto de Música Religiosa, 1965) gives Xuares no fewer
than six instrumentally accompanied Masses a 8 (Batalla,
Confitemini, Ecce sacerdos magnus, Regina coeli, Tota pulchra, one untitled), sixteen accompanied Vesper psalms mostly a 8, five accompanied Magnificats a 8, a 9, and a 11, at
least 55 motets, four lamentations, several hymns, various
settings of parts of the Officium defunctorum, and three sequences. For San Fernando, the Cuenca archive has his
Accipe sanctum gladium a 5,[13] for San Julián (bishop of Cuenca) Surge Domine in requiem tuam a 8 dated 1695 and "composed for the placing of a silver urn" in the saint's memory,[14]
and for Santa Filomena a motet a 8 recopied as late as 1849.[15]
His Regina austri a 4 calls for clavicordio accompaniment and
supporting violón.[16] If the date can be believed, his earliest
motet at Cuenca was written in 1651, Delicta juventutis a 7.[17]
The last work dated in his lifetime, Los pastores de Belén a 8,
1698,[18] also enjoys the distinction of being his only vernacular
piece itemized in either Seville or Cuenca music archive.

Obviously, however, he wrote villancicos in quantity. On
January 9, 1676, Jacinto Antonio Mesa (chapelmaster at
Córdoba) daily expected from Seville the texts of the villanci-
cos set by Xuares the previous Christmas season.[19] Juan
Hidalgo, if no other, taught Xuares how to set a "quedito,
pasito" text.[20]

NOTES

1. Simón de la Rosa y López, Los seises de la Catedral de
Sevilla (Seville: Francisco de P. Díaz, 1904), pp. 326-327.

2. Ibid., pp. 154-155, 327.

3. Seville Cathedral, Libro delas. Entradas. de Señores.
Beneficiados. En esta Sta iglesia El cual parece corrio en los
años desde el de 1500 hasta el de 1700, fol. 75.

4. At 7 on the morning of October 9, 1680, an earthquake
threatened to ruin Seville. This being the day of St. Dionysius
the Areopagite, the cathedral chapter decided henceforth to
memorialize October 9 con rito doble. See Diego Ortiz de
Zúñiga, Anales eclesiásticos y seculares de la muy noble y
muy leal ciudad de Sevilla (Madrid: Imprenta Real, 1796), V,
350-353. From 1681 to 1684 both secular and ecclesiastical
cabildos attended the special ceremonies at which Xuares's
Misericordias Domini was annually sung.

5. Rosa y López, op cit., pp. 154-157, quotes verbatim
Loaysa's biographical memoir. Our second through fifth para-
graphs are a condensed paraphrase of this memoir. "Unico y
mejor maestro de España" are Loaysa's words at p. 155.

6. Trifón Muñoz y Soliva, Noticias de todos los Ilmos.
Señores Obispos que han regido la diócesis de Cuenca (Cuenca:
Francisco Gómez é hijo, 1860), p. 319.

7. Luis Federigui succeeded his uncle, who died in 1678
(Ortiz de Zúñiga, op cit., V, 333). In November 1688 he left

for Rome to represent the Sevillian chapter in litigation
against the new archbishop, Jayme de Palafox, dying there
April 26, 1696 (ibid., p. 445).

8. Concerning the 1680 trip to Guadalajara during which
Xuares recruited Durón and Xuares's further favors, see the
Sebastián Durón biography above, pp. 41-42.

9. Muñoz y Soliva, op. cit., p. 502: "De música con
acompañamiento de solo órgano una copiosa coleccion de motetes para despues de la consagracion de las dominicas de
Adviento, Cuaresma, Santos, Difuntos, á cuatro, seis, y ocho
voces por D. Alonso Juarez en 1778, es música de armonías
muy bellas y propias de iglesia. . . . "

10. "La música conservada en la Biblioteca Colombina y en
la Catedral de Sevilla," Anuario Musical, II (1947), 37-38.

11. Ortiz de Zúñiga, op cit., V, 320-324, describes the
day's events.

12. Ibid., p. 378: "En los dias 7, 8, y 9 [November, 1683]
hubo luminarias y repiques, y en los intermedios tocaban los
Músicos de la misma Santa Iglesia varias piezas con sonora
armonía, y el dia 10 saliéron los dos cabildos en procesion
por debaxo de gradas cantando el Te Deum, y de vuelta fuéron
á la capilla de nuestra Señora de la Antigua, adonde hiciéron,
estacion . . . allí se colocó una imágen del glorioso San
Fernando, y se dixo la Misa de accion de gracias con el apa-
rato de primera dignidad, y sermon."

13. Restituto Navarro Gonzalo, Catálogo Musical (Cuenca:
Instituto de Música Religiosa, 1965), p. 157.

14. Ibid., p. 136.

15. Ibid., p. 162.

16. Ibid., p. 289.

17. Ibid., 1631 is a misprint for 1651.

18. Ibid., p. 307.

19. José López Calo, "Corresponsales de Miguel de Irízar
(II)," Anuario Musical, XX-1965 (1967), p. 217.

20. Felipe Pedrell, Cancionero musical popular español
(Valls: Eduardo Castells, 1922), IV, 22-28 (wrongly dated.)

Texts

How quickly villancico texts sung at Puebla blew across the
Atlantic can be proved from surviving printed texts of the
villancicos sung in the Portuguese Royal Chapel that concord
with my numbers 4, 5, and 8 below. During Epiphany and
Christmas matins of 1654 were sung at Lisbon the negro =
negrilla A siolo Flasiquiyo mentioning a black who had been
in Puerto Rico and the jácara A la xacara xacarilla (see
Villancicos Da Capella Real nas matinas da festa dos Reys do
anno de 1654 [Lisbon: Domingo Lopes Rosa, 1654], pp. 17-21,
and Villancicos qve se cantarão na Capella do muyto Alto, &
muyto Poderoso Rey Dom Ioão o IV. N.S. Nas Matinas da
noite do Natal da era de 1654 [Lisbon: Na Officina
Craesbeeckiana, 1654], pp. 17-21). The music for both of
these composed by Juan Gutiérrez de Padilla is for the first
time printed in the present volume, as is also his music for
another villancico sung in the Portuguese Royal Chapel seven
years later, the gallego Si al na[s]çer o Minino se yela (Villancicos que se cantarão na Capella do muito Alto, &
Poderoso Rey D. Affonso VI. N. S. Nas Matinas da noute dos
Reys do anno de 1661 [Lisbon: Antonio Craesbeeck, 1661],
pp. 11-13).

So far as the "quality" of the original villancico poetry is
concerned, none of the verse printed below flashes the sparkle
and genius of Sor Juana's villancico verse. Why should it,
when as Isabel Pope reminds us (Annales Musicologiques, II,
191) so great an authority as Juan Díaz Rengifo in his Arte
Poética Española — first published at Salamanca 1592 — "pref-
aces his discussion of the villancico by saying categorically:
'Villancico es un género de Copla, que solamente se compone
para ser cantado' " ("the villancico is a species of couplet
written for the sole purpose of being sung").

1

Al dormir el Sol en la cuna del alva
con arrullos con halagos con olores
le mezen le aplauden le cantan
los Angeles puros los zefiros gratos
las fertiles flores las liquidas fuentes
las rapidas aves las debiles auras.
Y todos humildes dizen a una voz
roro rororo dormid niño Dios.

Coplas

Los Angeles puros con dulze canzion
la cuna le mezen al dormido amor.
No le disperteis, no, pues su amante voz
el aire repite con leve rumor
roro rororo dormid niño Dios.

Los zefiros gratos con huella veloz
moviendo las plantas no pisan la flor.
No le disperteis, no, pues su acorde union
se inflama y entona con tierno fabor
roro rororo dormid niño Dios.

Las fertiles flores con salvas de olor
perfumes exalan en suave prision.
No le disperteis, no, pues su inspiracion
el catre le mullen cantando una voz
roro rororo dormid niño Dios.

Las liquidas fuentes con musico son
de blandos murmureos le adormeçen oy.
No le disperteis, no, pues en su cancion
con vozes de perlas repiten sin voz
roro rororo dormid niño Dios.

Las rapidas aves con diestro primor
motetes entonan al ynfante sol.
No le disperteis, no, pues en su region
con quiebros repiten trinando el loor
roro rororo dormid niño Dios.

Las debiles auras templado el ardor
le halagan le arrullan con vital mocion
No le disperteis, no, pues su resplandor
el sueño le inspira cantando en union
roro rororo dormid niño Dios.

2

Hermoso amor que forxas
tus flechas de las paxas
Temblando a mis rigores
ardiendote a tus ancias.

De que suerte zeñiido
Podras vibrar las jaras
si te apriçiona el yelo
y te nieua la escarcha

Si no es que dan tus ojos
Rayos que soles fraguan
quando te ven qual niño
con las manos faxadas

Yngenioso artificio
tuuo tu idea rara
en humanas finezas
Por Redimir desgracias

Desde el eterno monte
al valle humilde vaxas
que para hazer fauores
abates glorias y alas.

Suspende los luzientes
harpones de tu aljaua
Pues para que te adoren
esos pucheros vastan

Estri⁰
  Mas ay que disparas
  suspiros ardientes
  que el pecho me abrasan
  Y con lagrimas tiernas
  Rindes las almas

3

Serenissima una noche
mas q̄ si fuera un infante
en lo crespo de diciembre
quiso por dicha estrellarse.
Estrivillo por cruçado tañer el canario

  Ande el baile
  y al sol q̄ a nasido
  por dios verdadero
  oi todos le aclamen

4
Jacara

A la xacara xacarilla
de buen garbo y lindo porte
traygo por plato de corte
siendo pasto de la villa.

A la xacara xacarilla
de novedad de novedades
Aunque a mas de mil navidades
que alegra la navidad

Vaya vaya de xacarilla
que el altissimo se humilla
vaya vaya de xacara vaya
que el amor pasa de rraya

Coplas

1. Agora que con la noche
    se suspenden nuestras penas
    y a pagar culpas agenas
    nace un bello Benjami
    si el Rey me escuchara a mi
    o que bien cantara yo
    como ninguno canto
    del niño mas prodigioso

2. Con licençia de lo hermoso
    Rayos desembayna ardientes
    escuchenme los valientes
    esta verdadera historia
    que al fin se canta la gloria
    y a el la cantan al naçer
    general se vio el plaçer
    quel velo a la tierra embia.

3. Que en los ojos de Maria
    madrugaba un claro sol
    Con celestial arrebol
    mostro la aurora mas pura
    muchos siglos de hermosura
    en pocos años de hedad
    sino sol era deidad
    y el sol es quien la a vestido.

4. Quien como ella le a tenido
    quien como ella le tendra
    Virgen y madre sera
    del ques, sin principio y fin
    Serrana y mas serafin
    que serrana y que muger
    porque Dios quiere nasçer
    Apercive su jornada.

5. La bella bien maridada
    de las mas lindas que vi

bien es que se diga aqui
de su esposo lo galante
El mas verdadero Amante
y el mas venturoso joben
Sin que los yelos la estorven
dentro de una ave Maria.

6. Muerta de amores venia
la diosa de los amores
saludanla rruyseñores
y por madre de la vida
la daban la bienvenida
perla a perla y flor a flor,
A un portal los llevo amor,
y en la noche mas elada.

7. Miran de çierra nevada,
Altos y encumbrados rriscos
En los grandes obeliscos
ya no ay piedra sobre piedra
escollo armado de yedra
Yo te conoci edificio
Ya se miran por rresquisio
las glorias a manos llenas

8. En un rretrete que apenas
se divisan las paredes
esta para haser mercedes
que en su primer arrebol
dividido se vio el sol
en breve espaçio de çielo
Su gloria puso en suelo
Con la voluntad mas viva.

9. Quien liverta descautiva
Quien rroba la voluntad
La noche de navidad
la tierra vio su alegria
Al pie de una peña fria
ques madre de perlas ya
tierno sol mostrando esta
opuesto al yelo y al ayre

10. Valentia en el donayre
y donayre en el mirar
para empesar a pagar
de un criado obligasiones
Bañando esta las prisiones
con lagrimas que derrama
Tiene de campo la cama
del yelo puesto al rrigor.

11. Ay verdad es que en amor
siempre fuistis desgraçiadas
las promesas confirmadas
El mas tosco mas se afila
Y a la gayta baylo Gila
que tocaba Anton Pascual
dejemosle en el portal
con principios de Romançes.

12. Y pues no a de ver mas lançes
y mi xacarilla buela
Acabose y acabela
que era de vidrio y quebrela
Acabela y acabose
que estava al yelo y quebrose
Acabose y acabela
questava al yelo y quebrela.

5

Negrilla

A siolo flasiquiyo
¿que manda siol Thome?
¿tenemo tura trumenta
templarita cum cunsielta?
   Si siolo ven pote
   auisa bosa mise
   que sa lo moleno ya
   cayendo de pularrisa
   y muliendo pol bayla
llamalo llamalo aplisa
que a veniro lo branco ya
y lo niño aspelandosa
y se aleglala ha ha ha ha
con lo zambamba ha ha ha ha
con lo guacambe con lo cascave
   Si siñolo Thome
   repicamo lo rrabe
   ya la panderetiyo Anton
   baylalemo lo neglo al son.

Responsion
Tumbucutu cutu cutu
y toquemo pasito querito
tumbucutu cutu cutu
no pantemo a lo niño sesu
Coplas
1. Turu neglo de Guinea
   que venimo combirara
   A detla e su criara
   Munglave con su liblea
      y pluque lo branco vea

quere branco nos selvimo
con vayal de un tamo plimo
y haleme a lo niño bu.

2. De merico y silujano
    se vista Minguel aplisa
    pues nos culase su clisa
    las helilas con su mano
    bayle el canario y viyano
    mas no pase pol detlas
    de mula que da lasas
    de toro que dira mu.

3. Antoniyo con su sayo
    que tluxo re pueltorrico
    Saldra vestiro re mico
    y Minguel de papangayo
    Y quando yegue adorayo
    al niño le dira asi
    si tu yo lamo pol mi
    yo me aleglamo pol tu.

6
Calenda

Romance
De carambanos el dia
viste y compone los campos
desflorando la esmeralda
porque salga lo escarchado.

El cristal que se divide
rrecoje a fuerça de embargos
para que brille en sus ondas
uno y otro passamano.

No es por lisonga la gala
diuiça del color blanco
sino por lo azul de un çielo
que lo va menos preçiando.

Esta es la niña graçiosa
cuyo vientre soberano
nos a de dar esta noche
a un Dios que va de encarnado.

Caminad Virgen y Madre
le diçe el esposo casto
que la carga es peregrina,
y vuestro mayor descanso.

El Oriente de Belen
No podra llamarse ocaso
que es el fin deste camino
y prinçipio a un bien tan alto

Moved el passo a una dicha
no por goçar del rregalo
que llevais con vos señora
camineis tan paso a paso.

Obligada con el rruego
da nueva embidia a los prados
y derretida la nieve
la rrinden sus alabastros.

Estribillo

Y los cielos al verla
venevolos con tiernos canticos
la çelebran formando
sus disticos perlas al talamo
que Belen le dedica
honorifico a un Dios magnanimo.

7
Juego de cañas

Las estreyas se rien
los luseros se alegran
la luna mas hermosa
su Resplandor ostenta

Arrasimos floresen
los prados y las seluas
los corderiyos saltan
los paxaros gorgean

Sobre Belen se escuchan
dulsisimas cadensias
de boses que sonoras
disen de esta manera.

Estrivillo

Afuera afuera
que bienen cabayeros
a selebrar la fiesta
Aparta aparta
que el cielo se a venido
al aire a jugar cañas.

Coplas

Que galas tan lusidas
que vistosas libreas
que plumas tan bolantes
que garsotas tan beyas

que grabes se apersiben
que atentos se carean
que diestros se prouocan
que corteses se encuentran

que bien que bien se alargan
que bien las cañas fechan
que bien en fin se juntan
que bien corren parejas

Que bien se juegan
que bien se tiran
que bien se emplean
vivas exalasiones
aladas primaveras.
Esta si esta si
ques en toda la nochebuena.

Coplas

Al mejor mayorasgo
del cielo y de la tierra
en su primera cuna
adoran y festejan.

Al prinsipe nasido
y su madre la Reina
les dan presiosas joyas
de aljofares y perlas.

Los de Belen los miran
y con alegres señas
airosos los aplauden
bisarros los selebran.

8
Gallego a 3 y a 4 con instrumentos

Si al naçer o minino se yela
por miña fe que lo prova la terra

Si o fogo tirita
mas si a neve queima
si o solsiño chora
e sua may le enjeita
por miña fe que lo prova la terra.

Si en la neve o menino se abrasa
por miña fe que jas fogo na palla

Si o fogo tirita
mas si a neve queima
si o solsiño chora
e sua may le enjeita
por miña fe que lo prova la terra.

Coplas

1. Si en a palla tirita o minino
    prestale pouco naçer solesiño
    Ay prestale pouco naçer solesiño.

2. Si a la rrisa del alva sollousa
    prestale pouco que nasca da aurora
    Ay prestale pouco que nasca da aurora.

3. Si su mesmo calor no le vale
    prestale pouco que un boy me le abahe
    Ay prestale pouco que un boy me le abahe

4. Si me chora el amor peroliñas
    valeme mais que venir de las indias
    Ay valeme mais que venir de las indias.

5. Si a la terra se abayja la gloria
    valeme mais que a rriquesa da frota
    Ay valeme mais que a rriquesa da frota.

6. Si en a palla o minino se deyta
    valeme mais que lo trigo das eras
    Ay valeme mais que lo trigo das eras.

7. Si los Angeles baijan tan cedo
    yo apostare ques en bayjo lo celo
    Ay yo apostare ques en bayjo lo celo.

8. Si de noite o solçino rrelumbra
    yo apostare que a naçido la luna
    Ay yo apostare que a naçido la luna.

9. Si no medio da noite amaneçe
    yo apostare que jamais anochese
    Ay yo apostare que jamais anochese.

10. Si o solçino se mostra garrido
    querole ven pois me quita lo frio
    Ay querole ven pois me quita lo frio.

11. Si o pastor corderiño suspira
    querole ven pois velando nos silva
    Ay querole ven pois velando nos silva.

12. Si o cordeiro a naçido na terra
    querole ven por la paz que nos deixa
    Ay querole ven por la paz que nos deixa.

Responsion a 4

Si al naçer o minino se yela
Ay por miña fe que lo prova la terra.

9

Al dichoso naçer de mi niño
los çielos la tierra
las aguas el ayre
en feliz armonia rrepitan
ecos ecos suaves.
los angeles los hombres
los brutos y las aues
canten como que lloren
lloren como que canten
pues mi niño se rrie
quando llorando naçe.

10

Vaya vaya de cantos de amores.
Vaya vaya de gustos vaya pastores
al sol diuino que raya de noche.
Vaya de glorias
vaya de fiestas
vaya de gustos pastores
vaya de amores pastores.

Coplas
Sol que a Belen yluminas
en la mitad de la Noche
gloriosamente obstentando
en cada raio mill soles

Enhorabuena tus luçes
yluminen a los hombres
los que a tu Oriente esperaron
y a tu lucimiento adoren

Enhorabuena felice
en sus braços te coloque.
La Aurora candida y pura
a quien por Madre conoçes

Y pues ya canoras aues
en metricas dulçes voçes
de tu Oriente solemnisan
los peregrinos albores.

11

Tarara tarara qui yo soy Anton
ninglito li nacimiento
qui lo canto lo mas y mijo.

Yo soy Anton molinela
y ese niño qui nacio
hijo es li unos la lablalola
li tula mi estimacion.

Tarara tarara qui yo soy Anton.

Pul eso mi sonajiya
cascabela y atambo
voy a bayla yo a Belena,
pultilica y camalon

Tarara tarara qui yo soy Anton.

Milalo quantu pastola
buscando a la niño Dios,
van curriendo a las pultale
pala daye la adolacion.

Tarara tarara qui yo soy Anton.

La sagala chilubina
vistila li risplandor,
las conta sus viyancica,
gluria cun compas y son.

Tarara tarara qui yo soy Anton.

(four more coplas follow)

12

Un ciego que contrabajo
canta coplas por la calle
por alegrar oy la fiesta
es ciego a natibitate

Oyganle oiganle
que viene cantando
y canta del çielo
de tejas abajo

Coplas
Fue la santa navidad,
de Adan hija de verdad,
por via recta
segun su genealogia

Lo demuestra paso a paso,
y fue el caso susedido,

que Adan de Eua era marido
Como çierto Autor lo preua

Y a esta Eua le dio gana
de morder una mançana
Y mordiola que fue culpa
golpe en bola y pecado garrafal

Y fue tal, que alcanso a feas y lindas
pero no la dieron gindas, ni ensalada,
pues quedo ella condenada,
y todo el mundo comun.

Respuesta a las coplas
Tumbe tumbe que tumbe tum,
Tumbe que tumbe tumbe que tumbe.

Coplas
Viendo el sumo consistorio
como dise el reportorio,
por un bocado
todo el mundo condenado.

Dixo el Padre puesto en medio,
buen remedio que el çegundo,
vaia a redimir el mundo
y el dara un remedio fixo.

Que es buen hijo y sino
vera para que naçio nasca,
y muera que no faltara
quien quiera, darle muerte como digo,

Ni un amigo que le benda aunque se ahorque
pero llebara buen porque, su pecado,
pues rebentara el cuidado,
por donde es bueno el atum.

Respuesta a las coplas
Tumbe tumbe que tumbe tum,
Tumbe que tumbe tumbe que tumbe.

13

Ay como flecha la niña
Rayos ermosos penachos del sol
que a sus luces no ai lus que le iguale
ni sombras de nubes jamas se bistio.
Ay que muger ay que blason
fortalesa con alma inbencible
valor que tan tierno salio vençedor.

Coplas
Esta ermosa niña
que Rayos del sol
tan airosa tubo
tan galan vençio
    oi se no conçede
    aurora mejor
    a cuya puressa
    sombra no llego.
Desde cuia esfera
que la encubre oy
al disiembre elado
en abril bolbio.
    Toda es una gracia
    Todo es un amor
    que promete uida
    que afigura a Dios.

14

Por selebrar este dia
Vna cafila de neglos
a el son de sus atambores
cantaron aquestos bersos.

Aunque neglo samo
caravali gente samo
a bogle qui canta aqui
a lo niño rioso qui naze ayi.

li li li li
li li li li
Baylando y cantando
cuacuarani.

Coplas
Sambia punga mariquiya
turu la neglo vini
a la fieza de lo niño
bonito como carmin.

    Suena la tanbore Anton
    tira la chacayia
    qui la enfara tabaco
    a lo ispañol gachupin.

Salga la ninglo Bastolo
monicongo canta aqui li
asiendo los guigorite
mijo lo que pinjil

Pabliyo qui se escondio
detras de Andres
cante la rre mi fa sol
aunque   canto la rre mi.

Lo lensiyo de ginea i cusina
aqui sali piselumble
a lo misias as
de lemos cuatreros mill.

Espelansa mazabique
vini vn poquiya aran
los mulata enbusera
turu amiga veminti.

Luele sia salica fuera
que biene mucho guipidelo
boracho undique la Montesuma
la gintil Montesuma

Turu sali de rrepente
cantando turu vini
aria fiesa y tambole
la ningliyo disi asi.

15

Yntrodusion

Los que fueren de buen gusto
oyganme vna xacarilla nueba
que e de cantar en Belen;
siempre el garbo y la voz
yo la cantare tambien
¿como que? ¿como que?
a que so me toca a mi
el por que que yo me lo se
¿como que? ¿como que?
pues quitemonos de ruidos
y cantemos a las tres
tres a tres y vna a vna
vaya vaya de xacara pues.

En el meson de la luna
junto a la puerta del sol
del cielo de vna doncella
en tierra vn lucero dio.

A ser galan de las almas
el verbo al hielo nacio,
que lo tomo con fineza
pero con poco calor

Sin duda el Jaian diuino
que nasca morir de amor
pues quando se embosa el rostro
me descubre el coraçon.

Por ser de la Trinidad
vino por la redempcion.
Metiose en Santa Maria
ya dado en San Salvador.

Metiose en cuna de niebe
que no es nuebo en su aficion
dexarse llebar del agua
el espiritu de Dios.

Al soberano cupido
desde que naçe le hirio
la flecha que en el desnudo
hiero mas presto el harpon.

A matar vino a la muerte
picado de que el amor
le dio vna herida mortal
y fue porque le encarno.

Que no se caiga el portal
es un milagro de Dios
Bien puede el Jaian haçer
cuenta que a nacido oy.

Se anda perdonando vidas
muy preciado de leon
y le suele haçer llorar
el mas pobre pecador.

El naçer en la campaña
es prueba de su valor
y esperarle cuerpo a cuerpo
es cosa de confesion.

El sangriento açero esgrime
Herodes que en su region
contener mala conciencia
deseaba ver de Dios.

Bien aya la xacarilla
y el padre que la engendro
y a las que tambien la cantan
buenas pasquas les de Dios

16

Ay ay galeguiños
ay ay que lo veyo
mas ay que lo miro
ay que lo veyo
en un pesebriño

Ay ay o filo de Deus
ay ay que a la terra vino
ay ay que lo veyo
en un portaliño.

Copla 1ª
Ay soen gantiñas [gaitiñas]
e dai mil boltiñas
ay tocai las flautiñas
tambem los pandeiros
ay ay que face pucheros
por mis amoriños
                           [D.C.]

Copla 2ª
Ay fagamosle festas
que entre duas bestas
ay que muito le cuestas
naçer sendo nobre
Ay ay no terra tan pobre
por os pecadiños.
                           [D.C.]

17

Venid venid zagales
vereis a un Dios niño
que duerme soñando
tiernos jemidos
quedito pasito no despierten
ojos que lloran dormidos

Coplas
Venid a ver zagales
Al vello amor dormido
que de los llantos sus ojos
suenan los suspiros

venid a ver estrellas
en çielo anocheçido
que mientras duermen dos soles
truecan exerçiços

quedito pasito no despierten
ojos que lloran dormidos

venid a ver influxos
En astros escondidos
que con las luzes que ocultan
rinden   alvedrios

venid a ver los ojos
en llanto humedeçidos
que de las perlas que vierten
siembran dos impireos

quedito pasito no despierten
ojos que lloran dormidos

List of Works Cited

The following list omits music and manuscripts. "Author" entries conform with Library of Congress main entries.

Abreu Gómez, Ermilo. Sor Juana Inés de la Cruz. Bibliografía y Biblioteca. Mexico City: Secretaría de Relaciones Exteriores [Monografías Bibliográficas Mexicanas, 29], 1934.

Alonso, Martín, Enciclopedia del Idioma. Diccionario Histórico y Moderno de la lengua española. Madrid: Águilar, 1958. 3 vols.

Altamirano, Ignacio Manuel. Christmas in the Mountains. Translated with introduction and notes by Harvey L. Johnson. Gainesville: University of Florida Press, 1961.

Álvarez Solar-Quintes, Nicolás. "Músicos de Mariana de Neoburgo y de la Real Capilla de Nápoles," Anuario Musical, XI (1956), 165-193.

_____. "Nuevas obras de Sebastián Durón y de Luigi Boccherini, y músicos del Infante Don Luis Antonio de Borbón," Anuario Musical, XIII (1958), 225-259.

_____. "Nuevos documentos para la biografía del compositor Sebastián Durón," Anuario Musical, X (1955), 137-162.

_____. "Panorama musical desde Felipe III a Carlos II: Nuevos documentos sobre ministriles, organistas y Reales Capillas flamenca y española de música," Anuario Musical, XII (1957), 167-200.

Anglés, Higinio. "La música conservada en la Biblioteca Colombina y en la Catedral de Sevilla," Anuario Musical, II (1947), 3-39.

Apel, Willi. "Secret Chromatic Art in the Netherlands Motet" (review), Musical Quarterly, XXXII/3 (July, 1946), 471-476.

Arnold, F. T. The Art of Accompaniment from a Thorough-Bass as Practised in the XVIIth and XVIIIth Centuries. London: Oxford University Press, 1931.

Artero, José. "Oposiciones al Magisterio de Capilla en España durante el siglo XVII," Anuario Musical, II (1947), 191-202.

Ayestarán, Lauro. "Domenico Zipoli y el barroco musical sudamericano," Revista Musical Chilena, XVI/81-82 (July-December, 1962), 94-124.

_____. "El Barroco Musical Hispanoamericano," Yearbook of the Inter-American Institute for Musical Research, I (1965), 55-93.

Baines, Anthony. European and American Musical Instruments. London: B. T. Batsford, 1966.

Bal y Gay, Jesús, editor. Treinta canciones de Lope de Vega. Madrid: Residencia de Estudiantes, 1935.

Barcelona. Biblioteca de Catalunya. Publicacions del Departament de Música, XI. Celos aun del aire matan. Opera del siglo XVII. Texto de Calderón y música de Juan Hidalgo. Transcription and prologue by José Subirá. Barcelona: Institut d'Estudis Catalans, 1933.

_____. XII. El villancico i la cantata del segle XVII a València. Edited by Vicenç Ripollès. Barcelona: Institut d'Estudis Catalans, 1935.

_____. XVI. Mateo Flecha: Las Ensaladas. Edited with introduction by Higinio Anglés. Barcelona: Diputación Provincial, 1954 [1955].

Barwick, Steven. "Sacred Vocal Polyphony in Early Colonial Mexico." Harvard University Ph. D. dissertation, 1949.

Bermúdez de Castro, Diego Antonio. Theatro Angelopolitano ó Historia de la Ciudad de la Puebla. Escrito en el año 1746. Lo publica por vez primera el Dr. Nicolás León. Mexico City: n. p., 1908.

Bermúdez de la Torre, Pedro Joseph. Trivnfos del Santo Oficio Pervano. Lima: Imprenta Real, 1737.

Bibliotheca Musica Bononiensis. Pedro Cerone. El Melopeo. Tractado de musica theorica y pratica. Facsimile edition with preface by F. Antonio Gallo. Bologna: Forni Editore, 1969. 2 vols. [Sezione II N. 25.]

Boggs, Ralph Steele. "Bibliografía Completa, Clasificada y Comentado, de los Artículos de Mexican Folkways (MF), con Índice," Boletín Bibliográfico de Antropología Americana, VI/1-3 (January-December, 1942), 221-265.

Braga, Theophilo. Historia da Universidade de Coimbra, Vol. II. Lisbon: Typographia da Academia Real das Sciencias, 1895.

Cametti, Alberto. "Orazio Michi 'dell'Arpa', virtuoso e compositore di musica della prima metà del seicento," Rivista Musicale Italiana, XXI (1914), 203-277.

Campos, Rubén M. El folklore musical de las ciudades. Investigación acerca de la música mexicana para bailar y cantar. Mexico City: Talleres Linotipográficos "El Modelo," 1930.

_____. El folklore y la música mexicana: Investigación acerca de la cultura musical en México (1525-1925). Mexico City: Talleres Gráficos de la Nación, 1928.

Carrión, Antonio. Historia de la Ciudad de Puebla de los

Angeles. Puebla: Viuda de Davalos e hijos, 1896-1897.
2 vols.

Chase, Gilbert. A Guide to the Music of Latin America. 2d.
ed. Washington: Pan American Union, 1962.

_____. The Music of Spain. New York: W. W. Norton &
Company, 1941.

Cotarelo y Mori, Emilio. "Ensayo histórico sobre la zarzuela, o sea el drama lírico español," Boletín de la Academia
Española, XIX/95 (December, 1932) to XXI/105 (December,
1934).

_____. Ensayo sobre la vida y obras de D. Pedro Calderón
de la Barca. Parte primera. Madrid: Tip. de la "Rev. de
Arch., Bibl. y Museos," 1924.

Documentos para la Historia de Méjico, II. Mexico City: Juan
B. Navarro, 1853.

Domínguez Ortiz, Antonio. Orto y ocaso de Sevilla: Estudio
sobre la Prosperidad y Decadencia de la Ciudad durante los
Siglos XVI y XVII. Seville: Diputación Provincial, 1946.

"Dulzaina" and "Harfe." Articles in Hugo Riemanns Musik
Lexikon, 11th ed. by Alfred Einstein. Berlin: Max Hesses
Verlag, 1929. Vol. I, pp. 434, 706-707.

Fortún [de Ponce], Julia. Antología de Navidad. La Paz:
Biblioteca Paceña, 1956.

Feijóo [= Feyjóo] y Montenegro, Benito Jerónimo. Teatro
Critico Universal. Madrid: Joachin Ibarra, 1773. Vol. I.

Frouvo, João Álvares. Discvrsos sobre a perfeiçam do Diathesaron. Lisbon: Antonio Craesbeeck de Mello, 1662.

Galilei, Vicenzo. Dialogo della musica antica et della
moderna. A Facsimile of the 1581 Florence Edition. New
York: Broude Brothers, 1967.

Gams, Pius Bonifacius. Series Episcoporum Ecclesiae Catho-
licae. Regensburg: Joseph Manz, 1873.

García Icazbalceta, Joaquín. Bibliografía Mexicana del Siglo
XVI, 2d. ed by Agustín Millares Carlo. Mexico City:
Fondo de Cultura Económica, 1954.

Geiger, Albert. "Bausteine zur Geschichte des iberischen
Vulgaer-Villancico," Zeitschrift für Musikwissenschaft,
IV/2 (November, 1921), 65-93.

_____. "Die spanischen Ccs. 133/199 der Muenchner Staats-
bibliothek," Zeitschrift für Musikwissenschaft, V/9-10
(June-July, 1923), 485-505.

Grebe, María Ester. "Introducción al estudio del Villancico
en Latinoamérica," Revista Musical Chilena, XXIII/107
(April-June, 1969), 7-31.

Grunfeld, Frederic V. The Art and Times of the Guitar.
New York: Macmillan Company, 1969.

Hamma, Walter. Meister italienischer Geigenbaukunst.
Stuttgart: Verlagsgesellschaft MBH, 1964.

Hannas, Ruth. "Cerone, Philosopher and Teacher." Musical
Quarterly, XXI/4 (October, 1935), 408-422.

_____. "Cerone's Approach to the Teaching of Counterpoint,"
in Papers Read by Members of the American Musicological

Society at the Annual Meeting . . . 1937. 75-80.

Harrison, Frank, and Joan Rimmer. European Musical
Instruments. London: Studio Vista, 1964.

International Colloquium on Luso-Brazilian Studies. 6th,
Cambridge, Mass., and New York, 1966. Portugal and
Brazil in Transition, ed. by Raymond S. Sayers. Minne-
apolis: University of Minnesota Press, 1968.

Internationale Gesellschaft für Musikwissenschaft. Documenta Musicologica. Erste Reihe, XI. Fray Juan Bermudo.
Declaración de Instrumentos musicales 1555. Facsimile ed.
by Macário Santiago Kastner. Kassel: Bärenreiter-Verlag,
1957.

_____. Documenta Musicologica. Erste Reihe, XIII. Fran-
cisco Salinas. De Música. Facsimile ed. by Macario Santiago Kastner. Kassel: Bärenreiter-Verlag, 1958.

João IV, King of Portugal. Primeira parte do Index da
Livraria de música de El-Rei D. João IV. Reprodução
facsimilada da edição de 1649. Preface by Damião Peres.
Lisbon: Academia Portuguesa da História, 1967.

Juana Inés de la Cruz, Sor. Obras Completas, II. Villancicos
y letras sacras. Ed. with prologue and notes by Alfonso
Méndez Plancarte. Mexico City: Fondo de Cultura Económica, 1952.

Kastner, Macário Santiago. "Le 'clavecin parfait' de
Bartolomeo Jobernardi," Anuario Musical, VIII (1953),
193-209.

_____. "Harfe und Harfner in der Iberischen Musik des 17.
Jahrhunderts," in Natalicia Musicologica Knud Jeppesen.
Copenhagen: Wilhelm Hansen, 1962. 165-172.

_____. "Juan Hidalgo," Die Musik in Geschichte und Gegen-
wart, VI (1957), 374-375.

Langwill, Lyndesay G. The Bassoon and Contrabassoon.
London: Ernst Benn, 1965.

Launay, Denise. "À propos d'une messe de Charles d'Helfer.
Le problème de l'exécution des messes réputées a capella
en France, aux XVIIe et XVIIIe siècles," in Les Colloques
de Wégimont, IV/1 - 1957: Le "Baroque" Musical. Paris:
Société d'Édition "Les Belles Lettres," 1963. [Bibliothèque
de la faculté de Philosophie et Lettres de l'Université de
Liège, Fascicule CLXXI.] 177-199.

Leicht, Hugo. Las calles de Puebla. Estudio histórico.
Puebla: Mijares, 1934.

López Calo, José. "El Archivo de Música de la Capilla Real
de Granada," Anuario Musical, XIII (1958), 103-128.

_____. "Corresponsales de Miguel de Irízar," Anuario Musi-
cal, XVIII-1963 (1965), 197-222, XX-1965 (1967), 209-233.

Lozano González, Antonio. La Música Popular, Religiosa y
Dramática en Zaragoza Desde el Siglo XVI hasta nuestros
días. Saragossa: Tip. de Julián Sanz y Navarro, 1895.

Machado, Diogo Barbosa. Bibliotheca Lusitana, II. Lisbon:
Ignacio Rodrigues, 1747.

Maier, Jul. Jos. Die musikalischen Handschriften der K.

Hof- und Staatsbibliothek in Muenchen. Erster Theil.
Die Handschriften bis zum Ende des XVII. Jahrhunderts.
Munich: In Commission der Palm'schen Hofbuchhandlung,
1879.

Mayer-Serra, Otto. Música y Músicos de Latinoamérica.
Mexico City: Editorial Atlante, 1947. 2 vols.

Medina, José Toribio. La Imprenta en la Puebla de los
Angeles. Santiago: Imprenta Cervantes, 1908.

_____. La Imprenta en México (1539-1821), Vols. II, III.
Santiago: Impreso en Casa del Autor, 1909, 1908 [sic].

Mendoza, Vicente T. La canción mexicana. Ensayo de
clasificación y antología. Mexico City: Instituto de Investigaciones Estéticas, 1961.

_____. Lírica infantil de México. Mexico City: El Colegio de
México, 1951.

_____. "Música de Navidad en México," México en el Arte,
6 (December, 1948), 21-32.

_____. Panorama de la música tradicional de México.
Mexico City: Imprenta Universitaria, 1956.

Mersenne, Marin. Harmonie universelle contenant la théorie
et la pratique de la musique (Paris, 1636) Édition facsimile.
Vol. III. Paris: Centre National de la Recherche scientifique, 1963.

Mexico City. Cabildo. Terzer libro de las Actas de Cabildo
del Ayuntamiento de la gran cibdad de Tenuxtitlan Mexico
[1532-1535]. Transcribed by Manuel Orozco y Berra.
Mexico City: Edición del "Municipio Libre," 1889.

Mitjana y Gordón, Rafael. "Espagne" in Encyclopédie de la
musique et Dictionnaire du conservatoire. Première Partie.
Paris: Librairie Delagrave, 1920. IV. 1913-2400.

Moll Roqueta, Jaime. "Nuevos datos para la biografía de Juan
Hidalgo, arpista y compositor," in Miscelánea en homenaje
a Monseñor Higinio Anglés. Vol. II. Barcelona: Consejo
Superior de Investigaciones Científicas, 1961. 585-589.

Muñoz y Soliva, Trifón. Noticias de todos los Ilmos. Señores
Obispos que han regido la diócesis de Cuenca. Cuenca:
Francisco Gómez é hijo, 1860.

Myers, Kurtz and Richard S. Hill. Record Ratings. New
York: Crown Publishers, 1956.

Navarro Gonzalo, Restituto. Catálogo Musical del Archivo de
la Santa Iglesia Catedral Basílica de Cuenca. Cuenca:
Instituto de Música Religiosa, 1965.

Núñez y Domínguez, José de J. "La Nochebuena de los
Totonacos," Mexican Folkways, I/4 (December-January,
1925-1926), 22-25.

Orta Velázquez, Guillermo. Breve historia de la música en
México. Mexico City: Manuel Porrúa, 1970.

Ortiz de Zúñiga, Diego. Anales eclesiásticos y seculares de
la muy noble y muy leal ciudad de Sevilla. Vol. V. Madrid:
Imprenta Real, 1796.

Palisca, Claude. Baroque Music. Englewood Cliffs: Prentice-
Hall, 1968.

Paso y Troncoso, Francisco, del. Epistolario de Nueva
España, 1505-1818. Vol. IX. Antigua librería Robredo,
1940.

Pedrell, Felipe. Catàlech de la Biblioteca Musical de la
Diputació de Barcelona. Barcelona: Palau de la Diputació,
1908-1909. 2 vols.

_____. "La Musique indigène dans le théâtre espagnol du
XVIIe siècle," Sammelbände der Internationalen Musik-
gesellschaft, V (1903-1904), 46-90.

_____. P. Antonio Eximeno: Glosario de la gran remoción
de ideas que para mejoramiento de la técnica y estética del
arte músico ejerció el insigne jesuita valenciano. Madrid:
Unión Musical Española (Antes Casa Dotesio), 1920.

Pelinski, Ramón Adolfo. "Die weltliche Musik Spaniens am
Anfang des 17. Jhs. Der Cancionero Claudio de la Sablonara." Inaugural-Dissertation, Ludwig-Maximilian-Univer-
sität. Munich, 1969.

Peralta Barnuevo, Joseph de. Lima trivmphante, glorias de
la America. Lima: Joseph de Contreras y Alvarado, 1708.

Pereira Salas, Eugenio. "Los Villancicos Chilenos,"
Revista Musical Chilena, X/51 (1955), 37-48.

Pérez Pastor, Cristóbal. La Imprenta en Toledo. Madrid:
Manuel Tello, 1887.

Pitts, Ruth Eleanor Landes. "Don Juan Hidalgo, Seventeenth-
Century Spanish Composer." George Peabody College for
Teachers (Nashville), Ph.D. dissertation. June, 1968.
[University Microfilms 68-16,348].

Pope, Isabel. "Documentos Relacionados con la Historia de
la Música en México," Nuestra Música, VI/21 (1er Trimestre, 1951), 5-28.

_____. "Musical and Metrical Form of the Villancico: Notes
on Its Development and Its Rôle in Music and Literature in
the Fifteenth Century," Annales Musicologiques, II (1954),
189-214.

_____. "Villancico," in Die Musik in Geschichte und Gegen-
wart, XIII (1966), 1628-1631.

_____. "El Villancico Polifónico," in Cancionero de Upsala.
Mexico City: El Colegio de México, 1944. 13-43.

Querol Gavaldá, Miguel. "El 'Cancionero Musical de Olot',"
Anuario Musical, XVIII-1963 (1965), 57-65.

_____. "Importance historique et nationale du romance," in
Musique et poésie au XVIe siècle. Paris: Éditions du
Centre national de la Recherche scientifique, 1954. 299-
327.

_____. "La polyphonie religieuse espagnole au XVIIe siècle,"
in Les Colloques de Wégimont, IV/1-1957: Le "Baroque"
Musical. Paris: Société d'Édition "Les Belles Lettres,"
1963. 91-105.

_____. "El romance polifónico en el siglo XVII," Anuario
Musical, X (1955), 111-120.

Ray [Catalyne], Alice. "The Double-Choir Music of Juan de
Padilla," University of Southern California Ph.D. disserta-

tion, 1953.

_____. "Music of the Sixteenth to Eighteenth Centuries in the Cathedral of Puebla, Mexico," in Yearbook of the Inter-American Institute for Musical Research, II (1966), 75-90.

Rego, Pedro Vaz. Armonico Lazo, con que se une una metrica correspondencia de Portugal a Castilla. Évora: n.p., 1731.

Rensch, Roslyn. The Harp. New York: Philosophical Library, 1950.

Robb, John Donald. Hispanic Folk Songs of New Mexico with Selected Songs Collected, Transcribed, and Arranged for Voice and Piano. Albuquerque: University of New Mexico Press, 1954.

Robe, Stanley. Coloquios de Pastores from Jalisco, Mexico. Berkeley: University of California Press, 1954. [Folklore Studies, IV.]

Robles, Antonio de. Diario de sucesos notables (1665-1703). Tomo I. Ed. with prologue by Antonio Castro Leal. Mexico City: Editorial Porrua, 1946.

Rodríguez-Moñino, Antonio, and María Brey Marino. Catálogo de los manuscritos poéticos castellanos existentes en la Biblioteca de The Hispanic Society of America. New York: The Hispanic Society of America, 1965. 3 vols.

Román, Hierónimo. Repvblicas del mvndo. Salamanca: Juan Fernández, 1595.

Rosa y López, Simón de la. Los seises de la Catedral de Sevilla: Ensayo de investigación histórica. Seville: Francisco de P. Díaz, 1904.

Rubio Piqueras, Felipe. Música y Músicos Toledanos. Contribución a su estudio. Toledo: Establecimiento Tipográfico de Sucesor de J. Peláez, 1923.

Salazar, Adolfo. La música de España: La música en la cultura española. Buenos Aires: Espasa-Calpe, 1953.

Saldívar [Silva], Gabriel. Historia de la música en México (Épocas precortesiana y colonial). Mexico City: Ediciones "Cultura," 1934.

Sánchez Cantón, Francisco Javier. Fuentes literarias para la historia del arte español. Vol. II. Madrid: C. Bermejo, 1933.

Sas, Andrés. "La vida musical en la Catedral de Lima durante la colonia," Revista Musical Chilena, XVI/81-82 (July-December, 1962), 8-53.

Schrade, Leo. Review of Monteverdi: Vespro della Beata Vergine (1610). Ed. by Hans F. Redlich. Musical Quarterly, XL/1 (January, 1954), 138-145.

Siemens Hernández, Lothar G. "La Seo de Zaragoza, destacada escuela de órgano en el siglo XVII," Anuario Musical, XXI-1966 (1968), 147-167, XXIII-1968 (1970), 129-156.

_____. "Hispaniae Musica: Masters of the Baroque," Liner Notes for Deutsche Grammophon Gesellschaft Archiv Produktion, 198 453 Stereo. 1968.

_____. "Nuevas aportaciones para la biografía de Sebastián Durón," Anuario Musical, XVIII-1963 (1965), 137-159.

_____. "Nuevos documentos sobre el músico Sebastián Durón: once años de vida profesional anteriores a su llegada a la corte del rey Carlos II," Anuario Musical, XVI (1961), 177-199.

Solar-Quintes, Nicolás A. See Álvarez Solar-Quintes, Nicolás.

Spain. Archivo Histórico Nacional. Catálogo de las causas contra la fe seguidas ante el Tribunal del Santo Oficio de la Inquisición de Toledo. Madrid: Tipografía de la Revista de Archivos, Bibliotecas y Museos, 1903.

Spain. Consejo Superior de Investigaciones Científicas. Instituto Español de Musicología. Catálogo Musical de la Biblioteca Nacional de Madrid por Higinio Anglés y José Subirá. Barcelona: Casa Provincial de Caridad Imprenta-Escuela, 1946-1951. 3 vols.

_____. Monumentos de la Música Española, Vol. XVIII. Romances y letras a tres vozes (Siglo XVII). Transcription and study by Miguel Querol Gavaldá. Barcelona: Casa Provincial de Caridad, 1966.

_____. Monumentos de la Musica Española. Vol. XXVII: Antonio de Cabezón (1510-1566): Obras de música para tecla, arpa y vihuela. Ed. by Felipe Pedrell, corrected by Higinio Anglés. Barcelona: Casa Provincial de Caridad, 1966.

Spiess, Lincoln B., and E. Thomas Stanford. An Introduction to Certain Mexican Musical Archives. Detroit: Information Coordinators, 1969 [1970]. [Detroit Studies in Music Bibliography-15.]

Stevenson, Robert. "The Afro-American Musical Legacy to 1800," Musical Quarterly, LIV/4 (October, 1968), 475-502.

_____. "The Bogotá Music Archive," Journal of the American Musicological Society, XV/3 (Fall, 1962), 292-315.

_____. "Christmas Music in Mexico," Etude, LXVIII/12 (December, 1950), 18-19.

_____. "The 'Distinguished Maestro' of New Spain: Juan Gutiérrez de Padilla," Hispanic American Historical Review, XXXV/3 (August, 1955), 363-373.

_____. "European Music in 16th-Century Guatemala," Musical Quarterly, L/3 (July, 1964), 341-352.

_____. "The First New World Composers: Fresh Data from Peninsular Archives," Journal of the American Musicological Society, XXIII/1 (Spring, 1970), 95-106.

_____. Juan Bermudo. The Hague: Martinus Nijhoff, 1960.

_____. "Mexico City Cathedral Music: 1600-1750," The Americas: A Quarterly Review of Inter-American Cultural History, XXI/2 (October, 1964), 111-135.

_____. "La música en la Catedral de México: 1600-1750," Revista Musical Chilena, XIX/92 (April-June, 1965), 11-31.

_____. Music in Mexico: A Historical Survey. New York:

Thomas Y. Crowell, 1952.

_____. The Music of Peru: Aboriginal and Viceroyal Epochs.
Washington: Pan American Union, 1960.

_____. Portuguese Music and Musicians Abroad (to 1650).
Lima: Pacific Press, 1966.

_____. Program notes in Thirty-third Annual Carmel Bach
Festival Booklet (1970), 29-30.

_____. Renaissance and Baroque Musical Sources in the
Americas. Washington: General Secretariat, Organization
of American States, 1970.

_____. "Sixteenth- and Seventeenth-Century Resources in
Mexico," Fontes artis musicae, 1954/2, 69-78; 1955/1
10-15.

_____. Spanish Cathedral Music in the Golden Age. Berkeley
and Los Angeles: University of California Press, 1961.

_____. Spanish Music in the Age of Columbus. The Hague:
Martinus Nijhoff, 1960.

_____. "Vicente T. Mendoza," Journal of the International
Folk Music Council, XVIII (1966), 79-80.

_____. "Zumaya, Manuel de," Die Musik in Geschichte und
Gegenwart, XIV (1968), 1423-1424.

Subirá, José. "Calderón de la Barca, libretista de ópera,"
Anuario Musical, XX (1965 [1967]), 59-73.

_____. "Dos músicos del Rey Felipe IV: B. Jovernardi y E.
Butler," Anuario Musical, XIX (1964[1966]), 201-223.

_____. Historia de la música española e hispanoamericana.
Barcelona: Salvat Editores, 1953.

_____. "Un manuscrito musical de principios del siglo
XVIII," Anuario Musical, IV (1949), 181-191.

_____. La música en la Casa de Alba: Estudios históricos y
biográficos. Madrid: Casa Hauser y Menet, 1927.

_____. "La música en la Real Capilla madrileña y en el
Colegio de Niños Cantorcicos," Anuario Musical, XIV
(1959), 207-230.

_____. "Músicos al servicio de Calderón y de Comella,"
Anuario Musical, XXII (1967 [1969]), 197-208.

_____. "La ópera 'castellana' en los siglos XVII y XVIII
(Tema con variaciones lexicográficas)," Segismundo:
Revista Hispánica de Teatro, no. 1 (1965), 23-42.

_____. "El operista español Don Juan Hidalgo: Nuevas noti-
cias biográficas," Anales de la Asociación española para
el progreso de Las Ciencias, I/3 (1934), 614-622.

Tamariz de Carmona, Antonio. Relacion, y descripcion del
Templo Real de la Civdad de la Puebla de los Angeles, en la
Nueua España, y su Catedral. Puebla: n.p. 1650 [1649].

Toor, Frances. "Christmas in Mexico," Mexican Folkways,
II/5 (December-January, 1926/1927), 31-43.

_____. "Las Posadas de Vecindad en la Ciudad de México,"
Mexican Folkways, I/4 (December-January, 1925/1926),
16-21.

_____. A Treasury of Mexican Folkways. New York:
Crown Publishers, 1947.

Torre de Trujillo, Lola de la. "El Archivo de Música de la
Catedral de Las Palmas," El Museo Canario, XXV/89-92
(January-December, 1964), 181-242, and XXVI/93-96
(1965), 147-203.

Trueblood, Alan S. "Substance and Form in La Dorotea:
A Study in Lope's Artistic Use of Personal Experience."
Harvard University Ph.D. dissertation, 1951.

Vasconcellos, Joaquim de. El-Rey D. João o 4.to. Oporto:
Typografia Universal, 1900 [1905].

Vega, Carlos. "Un códice peruano colonial del siglo XVII,"
Revista Musical Chilena, XVI/81-82 (July-December, 1962),
54-93.

Vega Carpio, Lope de. La Dorotea. 2d. ed. by Edwin S.
Morby. Berkeley and Los Angeles: University of California
Press, 1968.

_____. La Dorotea Accion en prosa. (Madrid, 1632). Fac-
simile edition. Madrid [Valencia]: Editorial Catalia, 1951.

Vetancurt, Agustín de. Teatro Mexicano. Mexico City: Doña
Maria de Benavides viuda de Iuan de Ribera, 1698 [1697].
New ed., Madrid: Porrua Turanzas, 1960-1961. 4 vols.

Veytia, Mariano. Historia de la fundación de la ciudad de la
Puebla de los Angeles en la Nueva España. . . . Su autor:
el licenciado don Mariano Fernández Echeverría y Veytia.
Puebla [= Mixcoac, D. F.], Imprenta "Labor," 1931. 2 vols.

Vieira, Ernesto. Diccionario biographico de musicos portuguezes. Lisbon: Mattos Moreira & Pinheiro, 1900. 2 vols.

"Villancico." Article in Diccionario de la música Labor.
1954. 2231-2232.

Wiel, Taddeo. I codici musicali contariniani del secolo XVII
nella R. Biblioteca di San Marco in Venezia. Venice:
F. Ogania, 1888.

Zimmerman, Benedict. "La Cultura Musicale nell'Ordine
dei Carmelitani," Rivista Storica Carmelitana, I (1929-
1930), 168-182.

Zerón Zapata, Miguel. La Puebla de los Angeles en el siglo
XVII. Mexico City: Editorial Patria, 1945.

Zingel, Hans Joachim. "Die kreuzsaitige 'Arpa de dos
ordenes'," Die Musikforschung, VII/3 (1954), 335-336.

_____. Harfe und Harfenspiel vom Beginn des 16. bis ins
zweite Drittel des 18. Jahrhunderts. Inaugural-Dissertation,
Friedrichs-Universität, Halle-Wittenberg. Halle (Saale):
Eduard Klinz, 1931.

Index

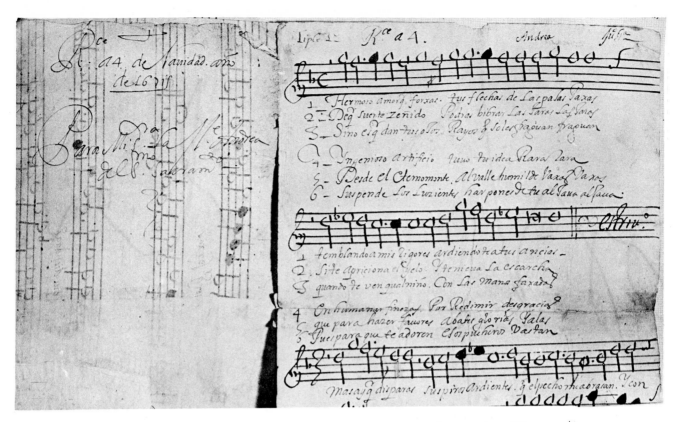

I. Juan García. R.ce a 4. de Nauidad. año de 1671 Para Mi S.ª la M.e Andrea del S.mo Sacram.to

II.   Juan Gutiérrez de Padilla.   Juego de cañas a 3, y a 6   1º chº   mº padiya.

III. Antonio de Salazar. Negro a Duo, de Nauidad.

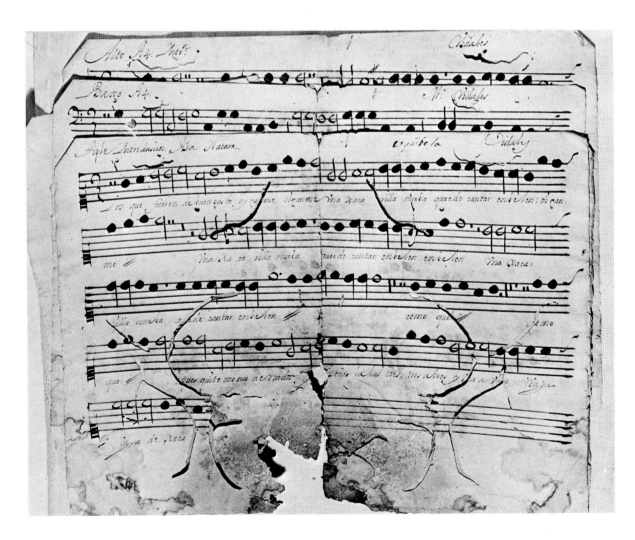

IV. Francisco de Vidales. Tiple Yntrodusion Ala Xacara.

V. Fabián Ximeno. Tiple Solo y con la copilla.

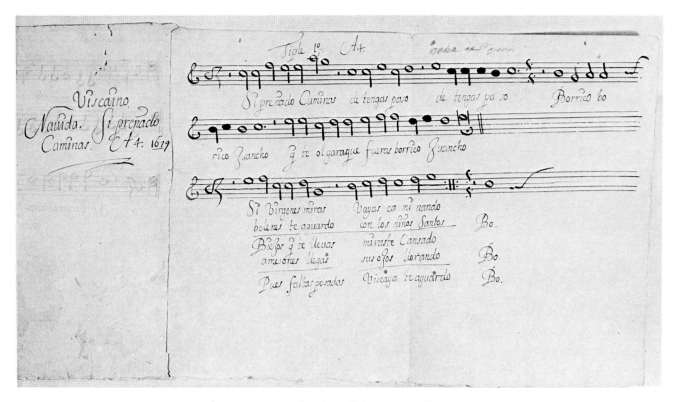

VI. Viscaino. Nauida. Si preñado caminas. A 4. 1679.

VII. Tiple Estri^{llo} a 5. Chanberga.

VIII. Francisco de Olivera. Tiple 1º A 5 Motete de fran^{co} de olibera.

IX. Antonio de Salazar. Letania De Nuestra Señora De Loreto . . . Año de 1690.

X. Francisco de Atienza. Tiple 1.º Missa A, 5 Vo,ˢ del S,ʳ Ma,º D,ⁿ fra,ᶜᵒ Atienza.

Music Transcriptions

Al dormir el sol en la cuna del alva
A 2 con acompañamiento

Sebastián Durón

102

104

me_ _zen al dor_mi_do a_mor,
plan_tas no pi-san la flor,
-za_ lan en sua-ve pri-sion,

no le dis_per_teis, no, no,

_mu_ zeos le a_dor_me_cen oy
-to_nan al yn_fan_te sol,
-rocu_llan con vi_tal mo_cion,

no le dis_per_teis, no, no,

me_ zen al dor_mi_do a_mor,
plan_ tas no pi-san la flor,
-za_ lan en sua-ve pri-sion,

no le dis_per_teis, no, no,

_mu_ zeos le a_dor_me_cen oy
-to_ nan al yn_fan_te sol,
-rocu_llan con vi_tal mo_cion,

no le dis_per_teis, no, no,

45

no pues su a_man_te Voz el ai_ re re_ pi_te con le_ ve ru_
no pues su a_cor_de u_nion se in_fla_ma y en_ to_ma con tier_ no fa_
no pues su inspi_ra_cion, el za_ tre le mu_llen can_tan_do u_ ma

no pues en su can_cion con vo_zes de per_las re_pi_ten sin
no pues en su re_ gion con quie_bros re_ pi_ten tri_nan_do el lo_
no pues su res_plan_dor el sue_no le in_ spi_ra can_tan_do en u_

no pues su a_man_te Voz el ai_ re re_ pi_te con le_ ve ru_
no pues su a_cor_de u_nion se in_fla_ma y en_ to_ma con tier_ no fa_
no pues su inspi_ra_cion, el za_ tre le mu_llen can_tan_do u_ ma

no pues en su can_cion con vo_zes de per_las re_pi_ten sin
no pues en su re_ gion con quie_bros re_ pi_ten tri_nan_do el lo_
no pues su res_plan_dor el sue_no le in_ spi_ra can_tan_do en u_

Hermoso amor que forxas tus flechas

Romance a 4 de Navidad año de 1671

Juan Garcia

Estr°

Mas ay que dis-pa-ras sus-pi-ros ar-dien-tes que el pe-cho me a-

Mas ay que dis-pa-ras sus-pi-ros ar-dien-tes que el pe-cho me a-

10

-bra-san y con la-gri-mas tier-nas Rin- des las al-mas las al- mas

y con

y con

-bra-san y con la-gri-mas tier-nas Rin- des las al-mas las al- mas y con

108

Serenissima una noche
A 4 voces

fr[ay] G[erónimo] G[onzález]

A la xacara xacarilla
Jacara A 4

Juan Gutiérrez de Padilla

*In the basso part, only the first eight notes of the estribillo and of the coplas are texted. Doubtless the estribillo was both played and sung. Such a ♭♮ ligature as that in measure 24 lacks relevance unless the estribillo was sung.

** In the original, f♯ is clearly marked in the original against f♮ in the tiple.

[FINE]

116

* ⁊♭ in original

118

A siolo flasiquiyo

Negrilla

Juan Gutiérrez de Padilla

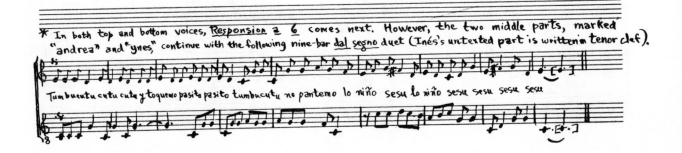

✱ In both top and bottom voices, Responsion a 6 comes next. However, the two middle parts, marked "andrea" and "ynes," continue with the following nine-bar dal segno duet (Inés's untexted part is written in tenor clef).

Tumbucutu cutu cutu y toquemo pasito pasito tumbucutu no pantemo lo niño sesu lo niño sesu sesu sesu sesu

122

3ª Copla

An- to- ni- yo con su sa- yo que tlu- xo- re puel- to- rci- co
Sal- dra ves- ti- ro re mi- co, y Min- guel de pa- pan- ga- yo

An- to- ni- yo con su sa- yo que tlu- xo- re puel- to- rci- co
Sal- dra ves- ti- ro re mi- co, y Min- guel de pa- pan- ga- yo

y quan- do ye- que ado- ra yo al ni- ño le di- ra a- si

y quan- do ye- que ado- ra yo al ni- ño le di- ra a- si

si tu yo la- mo pol mi, yo me a- le- gla- mo pol tu.

si tu yo la- mo pol mi, yo me a- le- gla- mo pol tu.

[D.S al $\mathcal{fg}$]

De carambanos el dia viste
Calenda a 4 y a 6
Juan Gutiérrez de Padilla

* Bottom part textless after first four words in Romance and first seven in Estribillo.

Estrivillo **

** Written in the ubiquitous C₃ mensuration (♩ = ♩ in transcription), the estribillo is entitled "responsion" in one of the two parts not participating in the Romance, but "estrivillo" in Ti A₁ A₂ Te₁ and B.

la çe‑ le‑bran for‑ man‑do sus dis‑ti‑ cos, per‑las, per‑las al ta‑ la‑ mo

la çe‑ le‑bran for‑ man‑do sus dis‑ti‑ cos, per‑ las, per‑ las al ta‑ la‑ mo

la çe‑

la çe‑ le‑bran for‑ man‑do sus dis‑ ti‑ cos, per‑ las, per‑ las al ta‑ la‑ mo

la çe‑

la çe‑

la çe‑ le‑bran for‑man‑do sus dis‑ti‑ cos, per‑las per‑ las al ta‑la‑mo

per‑las al ta‑ la‑mo, per‑las per‑ las al ta‑la‑mo

‑le‑bran for‑man‑do sus dis‑ti‑ cos per‑las al ta‑ la‑mo, per‑ las

per‑las al ta‑ la‑mo per‑las al ta‑ la‑ mo, per‑ las al ta‑la‑mo

‑le‑bran for‑man‑do sus dis‑ti‑cos per‑las al ta‑ la‑mo per‑las al ta‑ la‑mo

‑le‑bran for‑man‑do sus dis‑ti‑ cos per‑las al ta‑la‑mo per‑las

128

Las estreyas se rien

Juego de cañas a 3 y a 6

Juan Gutiérrez de Padilla

131

134

[Coplas]

35

138

les dan pre.sio.sas jo - yas de^al.jo.fa.res y per. las

les dan pre.sio. sas jo. yas de^al.jo.fa.res y per. las

Si al nacer o minino
Gallego a **3** y a 4
con instrumentos

Juan Gutiérrez de Padilla

* Beyond the first seven words in C and first four in ¾, the top part lacks text. Since the rubric "gallego sólo con instrumentos" heads the tenor part, performance of the top part by some such instrument as <u>corneta</u> was doubtless Padilla's intention.

** p in original

Coplas

144

Responsion a 4 ***

*** Copied after the coplas, the Responsion may have been sung after each, or after the sixth and twelfth. A heavy horizontal line separates coplas 1-6 from 7-12

Al dichoso naçer de mi niño
a 4

Juan Hidalgo

* A in MS 3880, Biblioteca Nacional, Madrid

154

Vaya vaya de cantos de amores
A 4 con acompañamiento

José de Loaysa [y Agurto]

qus _ tos va _ ya pas _ to _ res va _ ya pas _ to _

va _ ya va _ ya pas _ to _ res va _ ya pas _ to _

va _ ya va _ ya pas _ to _ res va _ ya pas _ to _

qus _ tos va _ ya pas _ to _ res va _ ya pas _ to _

_ res al sol _____

_ res di _ ui _ no que ra _ ya de mo _ che al sol

_ res al sol _____ di _

_ res di _ ui _ no que ra _ ya de mo _ che al sol di _

. mo - res de gus - tos va - ya pas - to - res pas - to - res.

. mo - res de gus - tos va - ya pas - to - res pas - to - res.

gus - tos pas - to - res va - ya de a - mo - res, de a - mo - res.

gus - tos pas - to - res va - ya de a - mo - res pas - to - res.

[Fine]

1. - Sol   que a Be - len   y - lu - mi - nas   sol   que a Be -
2. - En -   ho - ra bue - na tus lu - ces   en   ho - ra
3. - En -   ho - ra bue - na fe - li - ce   en   ho - ra
4. - y   pues ya ca - mo - ras a - ues   y   pues ya

1. - Sol _____ que a Be - len y - lu - mi - nas
2. - En _____ ho - ra bue - na tus lu - ces
3. - En _____ ho - ra bue - na fe - li - ces
4. - y _____ pues ya ca - mo - ras a -

1. - Sol _____ sol   que a Be -
2. - En _____ en -   ho - ra
3. - En _____ en -   ho - ra
4. - y   y   pues ya

Sol   que a Be - len y - lu - mi -   mas
En -   ho - ra bue - na tus lu -   ces
En -   ho - ra bue - na fe - li -   ce
y   pues ya ca - mo - ras a -   ues

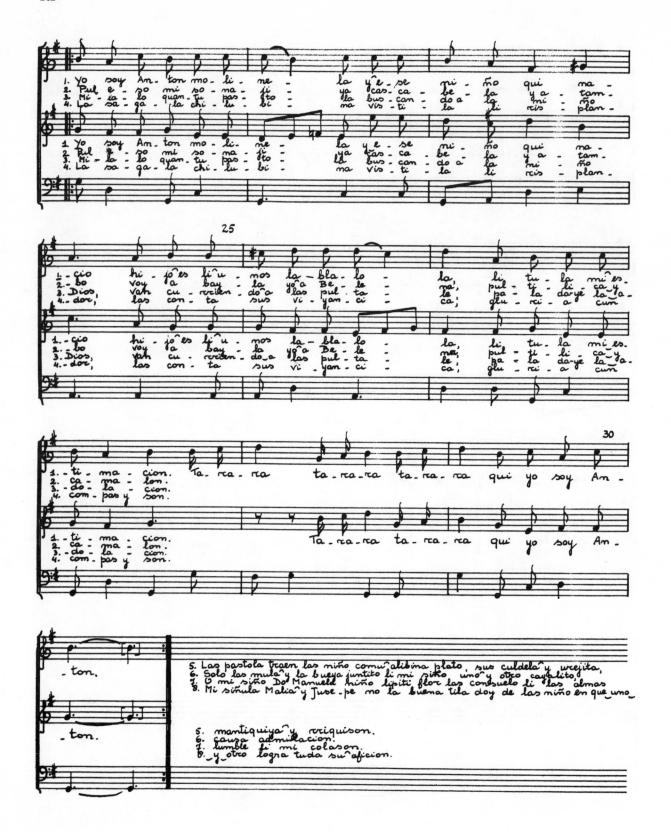

5. Las pastola traen las niño comu̷ alibina plato, sus culdela̷ y ur̷ejita,
6. Solo las mula̷ y la bueya juntito li mi pik̷o uno̷ y otro cay̷alito,
7. O mi siño Do̷ Manuel̷ niño lipiti̷ flor las consuelo li̷ las almas
8. Mi siñula Malia̷ y Juse̷ pe no la buena tila doy de las niño en que̷ uno̷

5. mantiquiya̷ y r̷riquison.
6. cau̷za admilacion!
7. lumble fi̷ mi colason.
8. ̷y otro logra tuda su̷ aficion.

Un ciego que contrabajo canta coplas
A 2 con acompañamiento

Antonio de Salazar

164

Respuesta A las Coplas a duo

[D.C]

Ay como flecha la niña rayos
A 2 con acompañamiento

Francisco de Santiago

Fine

[Coplas]

45

1.- es-ta er-mo-sa ni- ña que Ra- yos del
2.- oi se mos con- fe- de- ra au-ro-ra me-
3.- Des-de cu-ia es-fe- ra que la en- cu-bre
4.- to-da es u-ma gra- çia to-da es un a-

50

1.- sol tan ai-ro-sa tu- bo tan ga-lan ven- çio.
2.- for a cu-ya pu-re do som-bra no fle- gg.
3.- oy al di-siem-bre e-la- ssa en a-bril bol- bio.
4.- mor que pro-me-te ui- da que a fi-gu-ra a Dios.

D.C.

Por selebrar este dia

Negriya a 2 con acompañamiento [1669]

Juan de Vaeza

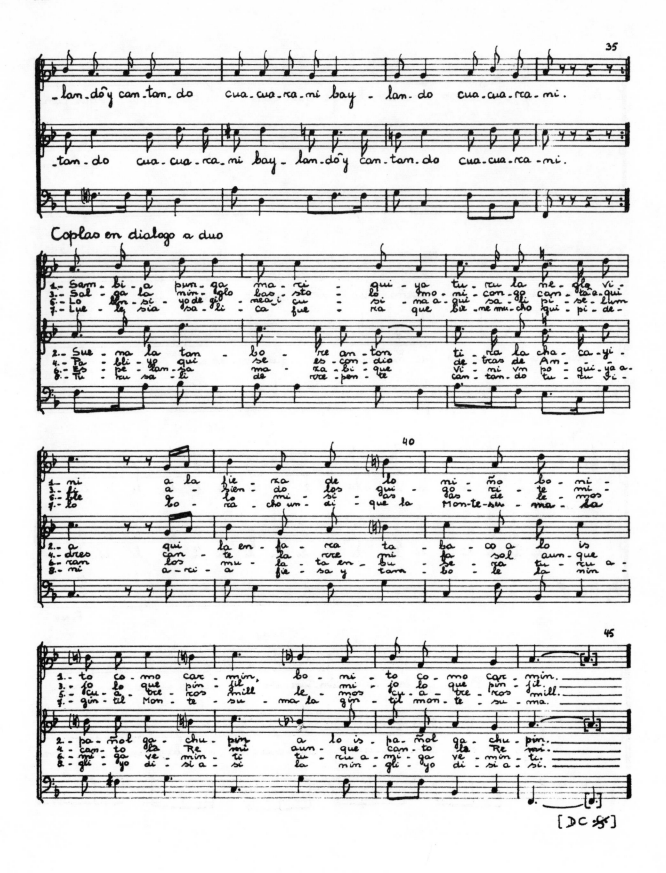

35

Coplas en dialogo a duo

1.- Sam-bi-a pun-ga ma-ri ___ qui-ya tu-ru la me-ßa vi-
3.- Sal-ga la min-glo las-sto lo __ mo-mi con-go can-ta-a-qui
5.- Lo ßon-si-yo de gi-mea i cu ___ si-ma a-qui sa-li pi-se-llum
7.- Lue-le-sia sa-li-ca fue __ ra que bi-me mu-cho qui-pi-de-

2.- Sue-na la tan-bo-re an-ton ti-ra la cha-ca-yi
4.- Pa-bli-yo qui se es-con-dio de tras de Am-
6.- Es-pe-lan-sa ma ra-bi-que Vi-mi vn po-qui-ya a-
8.- Tu-ru sa-li de rre-pen-te can-tan-do tu-ru yi-

40

1.- ni a la ßie-ra de lo mi-ño bo-mi-
3.- ßie a-zien-do los gui go-ri-as de te-mi-
5.- ßte lo mi-si-as cu-a-bre-ros mill
7.- lo to-ra-cho un-di-que la Mon-te-su-ma la

2.- a qui la en-ßa-rra ta-ba-coa lo is
4.- dres can-te la rre-mi-ta sol aun-que
6.- ran los-mu-ßa-ta en-bu-te-ra tu-ru a-
8.- mi a-rri-a ßie-sa y tam-bo-te la min

45

1.- to co-mo car-min, bo-mi-to co-mo car-min. ___
3.- ßo-lo que pin-ßil le mi-jo lo que pin-ßil. ___
5.- cu-a-bre-ros mill le-mos cu-a-bre-ros mill. ___
7.- gin-til Mon-te-su-ma la gin-til mon-te-su-ma. ___

2.- pa-ñol ga-chu-pin a lo is pa-ñol ga-chu-pin. ___
4.- can-to la Re-mi aun-que can-to la Re-mi. ___
6.- mi-ga ve-min-ti tu-ru a-mi-ga ve-min-ti. ___
8.- gli-yo di-si-a-si la min gli-yo di-si-a-si. ___

[DC al §]

Los que fueren de buen gusto
Xacara [con acompañamiento]

Francisco de Vidales

de rui-dos y can.te.mos a las tres; tres a tres y v-

tres a tres y v-

tres a tres y v-

-ma a v-ma va- ya va-ya de xa-ca-ra pues.

-ma a v-ma va- ya va-ya de xa-ca-ra pues.

-ma a v-ma va- ya va-ya de xa-ca-ra pues.

[FINE]

45

En el me- son de la lu- na jun-to a la puer-to del
-se en cu-na de nie- be que no es nue- bo en su a-fi-
per-do-man-do vi- das muy pre-cia- do de Re-

180

Ay ay galeguiños ay que lo veyo
A 5 con acompañamiento

Fabián Ximeno

182

Copla 2a.

Ay fa-ga-mos-le fes-tas q̃en-tre du-ao bes-tas ay que mui-to le

cueo-tas na-çer sen-do mo-bre Ay ay ay na te-rra tan po-bre por os pe-ca-di-ños.

D.C.

Venid venid zagales vereis a un Dios
con acompañamiento

Alonso Xuarces

Coplas

45